words on words

A LANGUAGE READER

words on words

A LANGUAGE READER

Edited by

W·Bruce Finnie   **Thomas L·Erskine**

UNIVERSITY OF DELAWARE

RANDOM HOUSE · NEW YORK

Library of Congress Catalog Card Number: 70–138631

Standard Book Number: 394–31315–1

Manufactured in the United States of America
by The Kingsport Press, Kingsport, Tenn.

Design by Jack Meserole

First Edition

9 8 7 6 5 4 3 2 1

for Nancy and Sue

the plan of this book

The editors feel that no subject could be more appropriate for introductory courses in college English than language itself. Consequently, this book consists of several related, nontechnical language essays written by an especially distinguished group of writers on practical topics of direct concern to the student—topics, indeed, of lifelong concern to the educated man. Through a study of dictionaries and varieties of usage the student will not only be preparing himself for the immediate objectives of writing compositions and communicating effectively in the everyday world, but will be considering as well the exciting issues which such a study raises about attitudes toward language in general and toward questions of authority and social class. The student will be encouraged to question old assumptions and clichés and to investigate both practical and theoretical problems for himself so that he can arrive at his own conclusions with a more informed base of knowledge. Surely this is a major purpose, perhaps *the* major purpose of a college education.

Not only is the study of language important intrinsically and for the practical as well as the generic reasons already mentioned, but it is also relevant to other professional fields, particularly in the social sciences, which are of considerable significance to twentieth-century man. For example, the sociologist needs to know something about the usage as well as the social and regional dialects of the various groups of people whose differences he wants to understand. The close relationship between anthropology and the study of language is now realized to the extent that a new field of study has arisen called "ethnolinguistics," which deals with the mutual influence of language and culture, and one also hears nowadays of "anthropological linguistics." Individual human behavior, in which the psychologist is so interested, is largely expressed through speech, so that the "psycholinguist" is concerned with the use of language in concept formation, learning, abstraction, and so forth. If conceptual thought is possible only by means of language, then the kinds of expression available in a language may be revealing.

The authors and essays have been selected for several reasons. Edward Sapir's essay represents the most lucid writing of an outstanding writer on language earlier in the century, before the age of specialization. Professor Donald F. Lloyd and the late Wilson Follett present especially provocative and entirely differing points of view. The other authors are presently or have been recently engaged in major language projects in this country. The collection is begun by Professor Cassidy, who, at the University of Wisconsin, is editing the *Dictionary of American Regional English*, the first comprehensive dialect dictionary in the United States— a project sponsored by the American Dialect Society and planned for almost a century. Professor Raven I. McDavid of the University of Chicago and Professor Albert H. Marckwardt of Princeton University are helping to prepare materials for the long-awaited *Linguistic Atlas of the United States and Canada*. Professors Thomas Pyles and S. I. Hayakawa are well known for their work in semantics, and Mr. Clarence L. Barnhart for his in lexicography. Mr. Stuart Berg Flexner has coedited the best dictionary of American slang on the market, and Professor Bergen Evans one of the most useful handbooks of usage. Professor Morris Bishop served on the usage panel of the new *American Heritage Dictionary* and wrote a prefatory article on usage for the same dictionary.

The pages that follow include essays of definition and classification-analysis, those meant to inform and those to convince, those written as textbook chapters and those as critical reviews. There are more or less formal pieces as well as decidedly informal ones—the last in the collection being a speech before an audience of newspaper editors. Thus the variety in the kinds and styles of writing allows the essays to be studied not only for their subject matter, but also as examples of differing rhetorical approaches to specific subjects for varying reasons and occasions.

We wish to thank Professor Arthur R. Dunlap for reading portions of the manuscript and for offering useful suggestions.

December 1970

W . B . F .

T . L . E .

CONTENTS

FOREWORD   vii   *The Plan of This Book*

the
nature of
language

INTRODUCTION   3

STUART ROBERTSON
& FREDERIC G. CASSIDY   7   *The Nature and Origin of Language*

EDWARD SAPIR   23   *Language Defined*

THOMAS PYLES   42   *Words and Meanings*

dictionaries

INTRODUCTION   61

S. I. HAYAKAWA   68   *Contexts*

CLARENCE L. BARNHART   81   *Problems in Editing Dictionaries*

MORRIS BISHOP   97   *So to Speak*

WILSON FOLLETT   110   *Sabotage in Springfield*

BERGEN EVANS   123   *But What's a Dictionary For?*

xi

ALBERT H. MARCKWARDT   138   *The New Webster
                                        Dictionary: A Critical
                                        Appraisal*

dialects
and
usage

INTRODUCTION   153

RAVEN I. MCDAVID, JR.   161   *Usage, Dialects, and
                                        Functional Varieties*

DONALD J. LLOYD   171   *Our National Mania for
                                  Correctness*

ALBERT H. MARCKWARDT   179   *Regional and Social
                                        Variations*

STUART BERG FLEXNER   200   *Slang*

BERGEN EVANS   223   *Editor's Choice—
                              You Couldn't Do Woise*

A LANGUAGE READER

the nature of language

Until rather recently it was fashionable for specialists to theorize about the origins of language. It no longer is, not because the subject is unimportant, but because there seems to be no way to discover how language began. The subject is fascinating, of course, for it points us back toward the extremely dim recesses of prehistory; the simple fact is, however, that none of the theories can be either verified or disproved. The theories themselves are ingenious, if often amusing, and the beginning student of language can profit from examining them briefly, if only to learn how complicated a matter language is. A major objection to many of the theories about language origin is that they are too simple to explain such a complex phenomenon. The more we learn about the history of a particular language, the more we realize its complexity. It is significant that the older a language, the more elaborate its inflectional pattern [1] may be, so that any theory which claims language was once simple and has progressively become more complex seems to be entirely wrong. It is true that with the passing of time a language's vocabulary may become larger (although a language always seems to be adequate for the people who speak it), but to know the *words* of a language (its lexicon) is not to know the language, as anyone

---

[1] That is, its morphology—the changes in the sound of a word that cause the word's function in the sentence to change, as when an s sound is added to a noun in English to make the word plural. Modern English retains relatively few morphological signals.

can testify who has tried to pass a German examination by studying only vocabulary.

There are profound implications here, then, if we think of primitive man as a simple creature. How did complex languages originate? How do we reconcile the fact that some culturally primitive tribes in twentieth-century Africa and South America speak languages whose morphological systems are much more intricate than those of sophisticated Europeans?

These are a few of the matters the student might keep in mind as he reads the first essay, "The Nature and Origin of Language." This essay, like the second, is also concerned with the definition of language. Both of them stress the point that language is spoken and that writing is a *representation* of language. Language was spoken long before it was written down, and writing systems were invented to record the spoken language. Anything approaching a complete system for recording language was apparently invented a very few thousand years ago. Man, of course, is much older than that, and, clearly, language is too. Such assertions occasionally seem to offend a few teachers of literature, who, curiously, think that the language expert, in denying the "primacy" of literature (i.e., in denying that literature came first), is denigrating it; actually he is pointing out that literature—the written word in general—has different purposes and uses than the spoken word has. Who, for instance, except on a television quiz game, would think of responding to an oral question by holding up a card in front of himself with the answer on it?

Writing is an attempt to capture language and to preserve it for varying lengths of time for whatever reason. Sometimes, of course, writing is used to produce great works of art, but the point to be stressed is that writing and speech are quite different. It is a simple observation to make, but the layman sometimes believes that the printed letter of the alphabet is a sound, not a symbol which only represents a sound. Just like speaking itself, writing is one of the things man can do that the animals cannot. Among other things, it allows him to study his past. The literary expert should not think that the language scholar is unaware of the importance of writing. For one thing, the ability to represent sounds on paper enormously helps the language specialist study language.

Sapir makes the intriguing semantic observation that what a word does *not* tell us is as essential to its meaning as what it *does* tell us. Thus when we hear the word "house," it is important for purposes of communication that we think only of the features houses have in common and not at all of the incalculable number of differences they may have. The term "house" expresses a concept of "houseness" which includes all houses; otherwise we would have to have a different word for every house. This observation is related to what is probably the most significant feature of language: namely, the fact that it has system and patterning.

Thomas Pyles concludes the section by discussing the meanings of words (semantics). It is important for us to know that in any living language changes of all sorts are going on constantly. A few pedants would have us believe that a word means what it meant hundreds of years ago—or if it is a borrowed word, what it meant in another language before it became English ("the etymological fallacy"); other pedants are likely to insist that a word means today what it meant thirty-five years ago (essentially the same fallacy)— say, when the second edition of *Webster's International Dictionary* was published. Such people sometimes even insist that a word can really have only *one* meaning (usually the one they prefer themselves), regardless of what other speakers use the word to mean. Words frequently have a great variety of meanings, and many if not all of them are in a constant state of change. For some reason English teachers have managed with inordinate success to inculcate in us the absurd notion that everything must be either right or wrong. Professor Pyles' essay helps us see that language and the methods by which language changes are much too complex for such simplistic notions to be valid. Vocabulary is, in fact, probably the least stable feature of a language. We must be prepared to accept new meanings and new pronunciations for old words no less than the new words themselves.

For Further Reading

A good popular introduction to the study of language is Robert A. Hall, Jr., *Linguistics and Your Language* (New York: Doubleday, 1960). Also useful is John P. Hughes, *The Science of Language: An*

Introduction to Linguistics (New York: Random House, 1962). Three excellent collections of essays—and much larger than the present text—are Wallace L. Anderson and Norman C. Stageberg, eds., *Introductory Readings on Language,* 3rd ed. (New York: Holt, Rinehart, & Winston, 1970); Leonard F. Dean and Kenneth G. Wilson, eds., *Essays on Language and Usage,* 2nd ed. (New York: Oxford University Press, 1963); and Harold B. Allen, *Readings in Applied English Linguistics,* 2nd ed. (New York: Appleton-Century-Crofts, 1964). The Anderson-Stageberg collection is, as the title implies, the most introductory, the Allen collection the most sophisticated.

Highly valuable and very readable older books are Otto Jespersen, *Language: Its Nature, Development, and Origin* (New York: Norton, 1949, originally published by Holt, 1924); Edward Sapir, *Language: An Introduction to the Study of Speech* (New York: Harcourt, Brace & World, 1921, reissued 1949 as a Harvest paperback); and Edgar H. Sturtevant, *An Introduction to Linguistic Science* (New Haven: Yale University Press, 1947). Two more recent books of a general nature are Dwight Bolinger, *Aspects of Language* (New York: Harcourt, Brace & World, 1968), and Ronald W. Langacker, *Language and Its Structure: Some Fundamental Linguistic Concepts* (New York: Harcourt, Brace & World, 1967).

STUART ROBERTSON AND

FREDERIC G. CASSIDY

the nature
and origin of
language

Like most words that are often used, the word *language* has
many senses. We will do well to begin our discussion by sorting
out the main ones and seeing how they are related to one another. The English *language,* the *language* of mathematics, deaf-
mutes' *language,* "the subtle *language* of a woman's eyes"—all
these legitimate senses differ so much that some of them, at
least, must represent special uses, extensions, or generalizations
that have grown up in the course of time, presumably from
some basic core of meaning. What is that core? Without indulg-
ing in the etymological fallacy of thinking that the earliest
meaning of a word must necessarily be the "right" one, we may
yet note that *language* is derived from *lingua,* the Latin word for
tongue, which in this case correctly emphasizes speech as the
basic thing in language. For our present purposes we may define as follows: *Language is the vocal and audible medium of
human communication.* And, having stated this definition, we
must next consider each part of it, clarifying where necessary.

To say that language is *vocal and audible* immediately puts
aside everything written—and that is as it should be. For writing is a *record* of language, and is therefore on a different plane
altogether. People spoke long before any means of record was
invented, and the records we make today (in print, or on disks,
wires, tapes, photographic film, and so forth) would have no
meaning if they could not be translated back into speech. True,

Stuart Robertson, Revised by Frederic G. Cassidy, *The Development of
Modern English,* 2nd. Ed., (C) 1954. Reprinted by permission of Prentice-
Hall, Inc., Englewood Cliffs, N.J.

7

they do not always need to be translated so; communication may take place altogether on this second level, as when we correspond with people we have never seen or heard, or when a deaf person learns to read silently the new "visible speech." [1] For to a practiced reader the words on a page need not suggest sounds at all. He has learned to respond directly to what he sees: he has a short cut through the eye that eliminates the ear. This does not change the system, however, which began as a record of speech, and is always potentially retranslatable.

The dots and dashes of the Morse Code are on still a third level, since they are substitutes for the letters with which we spell out our records of speech; and with them are the gestures of the deaf-mute, also substitutes for the letters of a system of writing. In short, our definition recognizes that the basis of language is speech, whatever other structures may be built upon it.

Since gesture has been mentioned, we may ask here whether it is not language. The American Indians had a system of signs once widely used as a kind of diplomatic code by tribes whose dialects were mutually unintelligible. The gestures were conventionalized, and they served for communication, but (unlike deaf-mute gestures) the system bore no relation whatever to vocal sounds. Thus, though it was certainly language in the broader sense, it does not come under our definition. Had vocal communication never been discovered, this kind of sign language might have had to serve for all human communication, though it is hard to imagine how it could have undergone the high degree of elaboration that speech permits of.

Gesture surely preceded speech as a means of human communication and will never be wholly displaced. Some nations and individuals use it more than others, and the gestures themselves differ in meaning from place to place—for example, a nod of the head, which to us means "yes," means "no" in some parts of the East; we clap our hands in applause, but in the Orient this means a summons. However, we all communicate by gesture to some extent. A frown or a shaken fist will every-

---

[1] R. K. Potter, G. A. Kopp, and H. C. Green, *Visible Speech*, New York (Van Nostrand), 1947. A cathode ray tube is used, and sounds are known by the distinctive shapes they make before the eye.

where be recognized as threatening. We indicate the sizes of things with our hands ("about *so* long"), and some shapes and movements are far easier to show than to describe (a spiral staircase, or the playing of a concertina). Gesture, then, though it may serve alone up to a point, is usually no more than an aid to speech, which can be far more detailed and precise, and which can proceed with perfect efficiency (as gesture can not) even when the speakers do not see each other.

Returning to our definition, we find that the use of the word *human* raises a second question: Is it correct to deny the name of language to the sounds made by the "lower animals"? Such sounds are certainly vocal and audible, and many animals appear to be able to communicate a variety of notions to each other by means of sound. Crows and other birds post sentinels to give the cry of alarm when danger threatens, and the barnyard hen makes quite different noises when searching for food for her chicks and when warning them that a hawk is near.[2] But even if there is some likeness in kind, the difference comes in degree, and there it is vast. The language of even the most primitive humans known is enormously more complex than the range of distinctive sounds made by the highest apes.[3] Human speech employs the symbolic process, by which a sound or sound-group is made to "stand for" something with which it may have only a conventional connection—that is, a connection which depends solely upon the tacit agreement, among speakers of the same language, that those particular sounds ("words") will always be interpreted in the same way when used in similar conditions.

Our use of this process is very highly developed; the animals do not appear to use it at all. Their signals seem to refer to broad situations and to concrete things present to their senses; besides, their range of distinctive sounds is too small to permit much elaboration. When (as in the case of bees) they communicate

[2] But note that she does not specify a hawk—merely a source of danger. The significance of the cry is extremely general. It is usually held that "animal language" is instinctive, while human language is learned.

[3] For a list of published "vocabularies" of animal sounds, see G. Révész, *Ursprung und Vorgeschichte der Sprache*, Bern (Francke), 1946, p. 47.

relatively detailed information, this is done by actions, not by speech.[4] Human speech, on the other hand, always has enough distinctive sounds (phonemes) so that their combinations may produce many thousands of "words," which may, in turn, be attached by general agreement to as many things and concepts. It is the possession of this kind of language which separates us widely—one might say essentially—from the rest of the animals.[5]

The third limitation in our definition, that language is a *medium of communication*, will probably raise the largest question, since it is clear that language is not used exclusively for communication. What Madame de Staël has written of the French language surely applies to all others too:

It is not only a means of communicating thoughts, feeling and acts, but an instrument that one loves to play upon, and that stimulates the mental faculties much as music does for some people and strong drink for others.[6]

Children discover very early, and adults never forget, that language may give kinesthetic enjoyment through the mere exercise of the vocal organs, and (what is far deeper) esthetic pleasure by expressing whole complexes of inward sensations.

When we talk at length to animals—as Alice in Wonderland does to her cat Dinah, which is not even present—we do not expect to be understood; like a baby babbling, or like Wordsworth's solitary reaper singing to herself, we often make sounds merely for the enjoyment of utterance. In short, language has an important expressive function, as well as the communicative one. Much of what we say in social intercourse, while ostensibly communicative, is no more than vaguely so and is quite as

[4] Karl von Frisch has shown that the bees perform elaborate dances to indicate to others that they have found nectar. Cf. "The Language of the Bees" in *Smithsonian Institution Annual Report for 1938*, Washington, 1939. Reprinted from *Science Progress*, Vol. 32, No. 125, July 1937.

[5] Physiologically, the capacity for speech depends on the existence of certain centers in the brain. See Sir Arthur Keith, *A New Theory of Human Evolution*, London (Watts), 1948, esp. pages 208–209.

[6] Translated from the French quoted by Jespersen in *Mankind, Nation and Individual*, Oslo (Aschehoug), 1925, p. 7.

much expressive. The words we use in greeting or in being pleasant to people are not to be taken literally; they, and the tone in which they are said, are mostly a means of establishing a friendly atmosphere.

It is probably safe to conjecture that expressive sounds preceded communicative language, since they require a single speaker only, and the noises made are not necessarily conventionalized. As a speaker repeatedly made sounds, however, he might well find them falling into habitual patterns—like the songs of some birds—and another creature, hearing them in connection with particular situations, might interpret them accordingly. Thus the person expressing himself would quite incidentally be communicating. When, for example, he howled with hunger, smaller creatures would keep out of his way. So expression would pass insensibly into communication as the expression became more willful or as one creature's expression brought a reply from another. Cries evoked by pain, fear, anger, love-longing, and such elemental sensations were surely as much the property of primitive man as of modern man and the lower animals. Out of some such crude beginnings must have come the highly developed structure of language—a primarily social thing as we know it, and primarily communicative rather than expressive.

This leads us to ask what theories have been offered of the origin of language, and to glance at some of the better-known ones. The first, now completely discredited, is that which finds the origin of language in a divine fiat. Thus, Plato, in what is perhaps the earliest extant explanation of the beginnings of speech, insists that "names belong to things by nature," and hence "the artisan of words" must be "only he who keeps in view the name which belongs by nature to each particular thing." [7] The implication is that the original perfect language, which humans must rediscover or re-create, is the work of the ruler of the universe, the great "law-giver." Imperfections in human language are thus explained as failures to discover the original "natural" or divine words. Curiously parallel to this is the view

[7] *Cratylus,* New York (Putnam), Loeb ed., p. 31.

of the origin of language that was long the orthodox Hebrew (and Christian) theory, likewise maintaining that language originated in a divine act. It was supposed that God gave to Adam a language fully developed—this was, of course, believed to be Hebrew—and that the confusion of tongues at the building of the Tower of Babel accounted for the variations in human speech. This explanation, it is surely unnecessary to add, has long since been given up, by theologians as by linguists. Language is looked upon today as one of the things achieved by the human creature in the course of his long development—but one so fundamentally human, as we have said, that it is a distinguishing characteristic setting him apart from the lower animals.

Of the more recent theories based on this assumption one encounters two types, resulting from two approaches. The earlier approach sought, by examining the vocabulary of languages as we know them, to isolate the most primitive (least conventionalized) types of words, and to build a theory of origins on these. The more recent approach has been through speculative reconstruction of the broader situation which might have led to the discovery or application of vocal communication. As an example of the first we may look at the echoic (or as it is nicknamed, the "bow-wow") theory. This maintained that primitive language was exclusively onomatopoetic; that is, that its words were directly imitative of the sounds of nature or of animals, all the word-stock being thought to have originated in a way parallel to the child's calling a dog "bow-wow" or a duck "quack-quack." There is undoubtedly some truth in this; but it should be noticed that sheer echoisms are not words; they become words when they are conventionalized in terms of the sound-patterns of the imitator's language. Thus to a German the cock crows "Kikeriki"; to a Frenchman "Cocorico"; to an Englishman "Cock-a-doodle-doo"—not because cocks crow differently in Germany, France, and England, but because these forms are the imitations conventional to each language. Furthermore, once an echoism, duly conventionalized, has entered a language, it is subject to the same kinds of language-change as any other word, and may thus be altered in the course of time until its echoic origin is no longer perceived. The word *cow* is not obviously echoic, because its vowel sounds have changed (with all similar sounds) within the past six hundred years. In Old English, however, its ancestor was *cū*, which more clearly suggests its probable echoic origin.

The obvious objection to the "bow-wow" theory is that it does not explain more than a part, and not the largest part, of language. Not even early or "primitive" languages have been shown to be composed chiefly or altogether of onomatopoetic words. The languages of primitive or savage peoples, indeed, turn out upon examination to be quite as conventional as those of civilized peoples. Thus the "bow-wow" theory, though it contains some truth, claims too much.

Similarly, other discarded theories may contain an element of truth. The principal ones are the so-called "pooh-pooh" (or interjectional) theory, which derives language from instinctive ejaculatory responses to such emotions as pain or joy; and the "ding-dong" theory, which holds that language began with a mystically harmonious response, on the part of man's hitherto slight vocal organs, to a natural stimulus which was fated thus to call forth its perfect expression—"everything that is struck, rings." The obvious criticism of the interjectional theory is the difficulty of bridging the gap between interjections (which on the whole are relatively isolated phenomena in speech) and the main body of language. Indeed, it has been held that this is precisely the chasm that separates animal speech, "exclusively exclamatory," from that of men.[8] It is difficult to see how the theory of interjections accounts for much more than the interjections themselves. The other theory is reminiscent of the ancient Greek belief that words exist by nature, rather than by convention, and that there is a necessary and inherent connection between words and the ideas for which they stand. In its eighteenth- and nineteenth-century phases, this theory (once maintained but later rejected by Max Müller) seems no more acceptable as a complete explanation of the origin of language than it does in its Platonic form.

[8] Cf. Grandgent, C. H., "The Why and How of Speech," *Getting a Laugh,* Cambridge, Mass. (Harvard), 1924, p. 78.

To this account of past theories may be added, in brief summary, the speculations of two twentieth-century students of language. Otto Jespersen's hypothesis [9] based in part on the study of the language of children and of primitive races but chiefly on the history of language, is that emotional songs were the germs of speech. In particular he felt that the emotion of love [10] called forth the earliest songs, that these songs—and others evoked by different emotions (a chant of victory, for example, or a lament for the dead)—were inevitably accompanied by what were at first meaningless syllables and that the circumstance that the same sounds were used on similar occasions brought about the first association of sound and meaning.

Sir Richard Paget, assenting to the general belief that the earliest form of human communication is gesture, has proposed the *oral gesture* theory. This holds that

. . . human speech arose out of a generalized unconscious pantomimic gesture language—made by the limbs and features as a whole (including the tongue and lips)—which became specialized in gestures of the organs of articulation, owing to the human hands (and eyes) becoming continuously occupied with the use of tools. The gestures of the organs of articulation were recognized by the hearer because the hearer unconsciously reproduced in his mind the actual gesture which had produced the sound.[11]

This theory differs from others in considering gesture not as a concomitant of speech, but as the source or at least the articulating factor of speech; it proposes a causal relationship where none had been seen before. There is, of course, no way of either proving or disproving this. Even if we agree that gesture preceded speech as a means of communication, the one need not be accepted as the cause of the other.

The conclusion of the whole matter is that the origin of lan-

[9] *Language,* pp. 412–442.

[10] Professor Arthur E. Hutson reports that his students have dubbed this, by analogy, the "woo-woo" theory.

[11] *Human Speech.* New York: Harcourt, Brace and Company, 1930, p. 174. Quoted by permission. By an interesting coincidence, the same theory was arrived at independently and almost simultaneously in Iceland, by Alexander Jóhannesson; see his *Origin of Language.*

guage is an unsolved and doubtless insoluble enigma.[12] Whatever the origin may have been, it is too remote to admit of more than conjectures about it, of differing degrees of plausibility. Yet the fact that he may never arrive at the truth should not prevent the scientist from making and testing hypotheses. If he gains nothing absolute, at least he dismisses untenable theories and keeps the question alive. As Jespersen has pointed out,[13] "questions which . . . *can* be treated in a scientific spirit, should not be left to the dilettanti." Thus while it is right to reject premature solutions, it is "decidedly wrong to put the question out of court altogether"—as some recent linguists have tended to do.

There is no historical reason or logical necessity, then, to find a single explanation for all types of words. Some were no doubt exclamatory, others imitative; most have changed so entirely from their early form that it cannot be recovered. All we can feel fairly safe about is that at some point the human creature discovered something that the lower animals had not discovered: the symbolic process. His noises could be made to stand for things not present to his senses. Gradually he elaborated this into a system, conventionalizing more and more and combining the symbolic sounds in new ways.

But if the *how* of language can never be known, there can be little doubt as to the *why*. Language must have arisen out of a social necessity—the need for communication between man and man. As soon as human creatures began to live in interdependent groups this need must have been a very powerful stimulus. Perhaps, for a time, communication was achieved by gesture alone. But this would have had serious limitations, through darkness, any obstruction that kept one person from

[12] There are, of course, a great many more theories than have been mentioned here. Sturtevant, for example, argues that "voluntary communication can scarcely have been called upon except to deceive; language must have been invented for the purpose of lying." *An Introduction to Linguistic Science*, New Haven (Yale University), 1947, p. 48. For a brief summary of theories, see Gray, *Foundations of Language*, p. 40. A full, detailed discussion may be found in Révész, *op. cit.*, pp. 30–112, covering biological, anthropological, philosophical, and other theories. (In German.)

[13] *Language*, pp. 96–99.

seeing another, or the occupation of the limbs that did not leave them free for gestures. Sound, on the other hand, was subject to none of these difficulties, and vocal sound was accessible to almost everybody. And once meaningful speech had been discovered it must have proved its worth as a unifying possession of the whole community. Everyone who could use these symbols would be a member of the group; those who could not, or whose speech-symbols were different, were outsiders. Thus language in the abstract becomes concrete, and we can speak of *a* language, or *the* English language, as the possession of a certain "speech-community." Many of the deepest things in our natures become attached to the particular language which, by accident of birth, happens to be our own. And contrariwise, a difference in language prevents us too often from realizing that other men are, in most ways, very much like ourselves.

Writing

Though it must never be forgotten that speech is the real language, and that writing is only a secondary way of recording it, the importance of writing should not be overlooked. History itself depends on the existence of records, and it may safely be said that the discovery and application of means of recording and passing on human knowledge without the necessity of direct contact between man and man has always been the mark of a high level of human society. If speech itself lifted mankind above the beasts, writing has raised him at least one stage further above his primitive forebears. It therefore seems appropriate to say something here about the evolution of writing, of the alphabet which we use, and of the relationship between speech and spelling.

Systems of writing, viewed chronologically, may be divided into the pre-alphabetic (including *ideograms* or *pictographs*, and *hieroglyphics*) and the alphabetic (including *syllable-scripts* and *single-sound scripts*). The first of these, strictly speaking, do not deserve the name of writing at all, for ideograms or pictographs are really drawings. These little pictures do not stand for words or names; if they did, they would have to be interpreted always in the same way, as writing is. They stand rather for ideas; they are symbols that may be put into words in a variety of ways. We do not have real writing until a further stage has been reached, in which the drawing—more and more simplified and conventionalized by repetition—stands for a word, or for part of a word, usually the initial sound or syllable.

Picture-writing, which was apparently developed independently by different peoples in widely separated parts of the world, came eventually into connection with the spoken tongue—though theoretically it might have grown up apart from it, just as the sign language of the American Indians had an existence separate from the spoken dialects. Since it must be assumed, however, that spoken language preceded writing, it seems well-nigh inevitable that sooner or later the two would come into contact with each other. For it would be unthinkable that peoples possessing a well developed set of auditory symbols would continue indefinitely to work out a new set of visual symbols in complete independence of the auditory ones. Drawing became writing when the picture ceased to stand for an idea and came to stand for a combination of sounds. The transition was undoubtedly gradual and came about, probably, "by means of the rebus method . . . by the same sort of process which we apply when we allow a picture of the sun to stand for the first syllable in *sundry*, or let the picture of an eye stand for the pronoun *I*." [14] But of course even after the written symbol came to represent the sounds of some one spoken word by which an idea could be expressed, it also directly signified the idea itself. It was not until the written sign stood only for a sequence of sounds (irrespective of its meaning) that the transition from word-script to sound-script, or from ideogram to *phonogram*, was complete. This was the beginning of the true alphabet. The Egyptian hieroglyphics represent a transitional stage—a mixture—since some of them are ideograms, others phonograms.

[14] Pedersen, *Linguistic Science in the Nineteenth Century*, p. 143. For a very good treatment, with illustrations, see also Sturtevant, *op. cit.*, Chapter III.

The full possibilities of the alphabet were not realized, however, until the clumsy device of using a symbol for a syllable (consisting perhaps of several consonants and a vowel) gave way to the use of a separate symbol for each individual sound. The Semitic alphabet was a syllable script which represented the consonants definitely but left the vowels vague, so that it appears to consist of consonant-characters only. Characters were no longer so numerous as in the older scripts—the Egyptians bequeathed to a Western Semitic people (the Phoenicians) a means of reducing their number—but the alphabet, as we understand the term, was not yet quite evolved. The final contribution was that of the Greeks: the resolution of syllables into their separate vowels and consonants, and the use of individual characters for the sounds thus analyzed. All known alphabets are descended from the Semitic, but only the Greeks revolutionized the alphabet in the way just indicated, by discarding its syllabic nature. Of the Mediterranean peoples who learned the Greek alphabetic system, one nation—the Romans—continued its use from pre-Christian times through the entire Christian era. Because it was inherited by the Romance languages and borrowed by other Indo-European groups, such as the Germanic, the Latin alphabet has long since dominated the modern world.

Of the four stages in the evolution of writing just outlined—the pre-alphabetic word-script, the syllable-script, and the Semitic and the Greek alphabets—Henry Bradley has acutely observed [15] that the third has peculiar interest for the light it throws upon the general relations of spoken and written language. Arabic, he points out, is to this day usually written as a consonant-script, though vowel marks may be added. Yet it is evident that the consonantal outlines can be apprehended, by one familiar with the language, as readily as if the full phonetic indication of the word were given—perhaps more readily, because the practiced eye takes in the simpler symbol more quickly and just as completely. So too the modern stenographer can read the consonantal outline of familiar words without vowel-markings quite as swiftly as the fuller ones. Medieval Latin

[15] *On the Relations between Spoken and Written Language*, p. 6.

manuscripts, Bradley further suggests, were often highly abbreviated, and yet were undoubtedly read with greater rapidity than they would have been if the words had been written in full.

Bradley's point is, of course, that it matters not a jot to the accomplished reader whether his native language is phonetically spelled or not; "what is important is that the group of letters before him shall be that which habit has led him to associate with a certain word." Nor need one limit this to one's *native* language. Certain Latin abbreviations commonly used in English have just as immediate meaning as native ones: thus *e.g.* does not require to be translated into *exempli gratia* and then into *for example,* or *i.e.* into *id est* and then into *that is.* In both instances the eye conveys the meaning without even the suggestion of a phonetic middle stage.

A simple diagram may make this clearer:

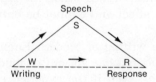

When we speak there is a direct line from the sound-stimulus to its response (S–R). Writing, in its origin at least, substitutes visual characters for sounds, and we have to translate them back into sounds in order to produce the response (W–S–R). But the process is abbreviated when we learn to go directly from the visual stimulus to the response (W–R). Slow readers take the longer route; fast ones take the short-cut.

Just how often the second supersedes the first it is probably impossible to say. Certainly in reading poetry and in reading such prose as that of Milton or Browne, DeQuincey or Coleridge, it may be assumed that the middle stage exists; it would surely be deplorable if it did not. Probably even in the rapid reading of the less poetic types of prose there are some words that call up sound pictures—that is, which the ear responds to as well as the eye. But it seems equally probable that for many words there is no such association; many written or printed words would seem to symbolize their ideas directly.

Bradley's observation should cast doubt upon what is often taken as axiomatic: that the sole function of writing is to represent the *sounds* of language. For, as he argues further,[16] systems of writing that were originally phonetic tend to become at least partly ideographic, as English and other European languages have done—for example, in such matters as the capitalization of proper names, the use of quotation marks, the use of the apostrophe to denote possession, and (most strikingly) the ideographic employment of different spellings to discriminate between words once phonetically distinct but now homophones—such as *rain, rein,* and *reign; or, oar,* and *ore; so, sow,* and *sew.* Even poetry, which normally depends upon sound and therefore necessitates translation from writing to speech, is at times ideographic, as in the use of "eye-rhymes," or in the poems of such writers as E. E. Cummings, in which the typography is deliberately a part of the effect and cannot be entirely rendered into sound.

But even if the writing of Modern English is in some few respects ideographic and has got out of touch with sound to a considerable degree—even if the experienced reader can read directly from eye to brain without involving the ear—the system of spelling is still, in its origin and in actuality, far more dependent on the alphabet than not. And that is altogether as it should be. Alphabetic writing has the enormous advantage over ideographic that it can get on with a very small number of characters: our alphabet has a mere twenty-six letters, while Chinese scholars have been struggling to reduce their picture-writing system to a thousand. The alphabetic system, obviously, is enormously easier to learn and therefore more useful. Universal education becomes a rational ideal only if a system that can be rapidly learned by the mass of people is at hand.

At least one more fact of writing requires attention. In a developed culture, the body of scholarly and artistic writings becomes a repository that can hardly be matched in a culture that

---

[16] *Ibid.,* p. 10.

has no writing, however carefully the memories of the learned may be developed and trained. The world of the written word, therefore, while ultimately based on speech and always referable to it—capable of being translated into sounds—does have a certain undeniable autonomy. It is in this world, the world of literature, that a language is submitted most fully to intellectual and esthetic influences—in short, to cultivation; and in so far as standards of "correctness" or "acceptability" emerge, they come from those members of a community who are not merely literate but who know the language at its more highly developed levels.

If, then, the language of literature, of ideas, of the more complex emotions reflects its influences upon the spoken language, there should be no cause for surprise. Obviously this cannot happen in a simple culture that has no writing or literary tradition. But it does happen in a higher culture, as we shall see in subsequent chapters. Literary purposes, or the adherence to literary ideals—however wrongheaded they may sometimes have been—have continually affected the English vocabulary, idiom, usage, syntax, morphology, and even the sounds of the language. As we come to these successively it will be well to keep in mind the separate but related spheres of speech and writing, the first fundamental to the second, but the second nevertheless having a real existence, without which the first would only be poorer.

Review Questions

1. Why is writing said to be "on a different plane altogether from language"?
2. How does language differ from gesture?
3. How does language differ from the sounds animals make?
4. What is meant by the expressive and communicative functions of language?
5. What theories about the origin of language have been discredited and why?
6. What are the echoic and interjectional theories about the origin of language? What words might they explain?
7. What theories did Jespersen and Paget support?

8. According to the authors, why was language created?
9. Into what two groups do the authors divide the systems of writing?
10. What were the major steps in the development of writing?
11. In Bradley's discussion of reading, what is the difference between reading a poem and reading an editorial?
12. What are the advantages and disadvantages of ideographic and alphabetic writing?

Discussion Questions

1. How do gestures differ from "language" as defined by Robertson and Cassidy? What limitations does gesturing have? What sorts of things are difficult to communicate through gestures?
2. How important is the expressive function of language? How much of our language is expressive? What situations demand expressive language? In conversation do we "express" or "communicate" first? Why?
3. In James Joyce's novel *A Portrait of the Artist as a Young Man*, Stephen Dedalus meditates on the nature of God and concludes that His "real" name is God. Which theory concerning the origin of language development does Stephen's thinking illustrate? Can you think of other similar examples? Is Stephen's assumption related to the common idea that Miss X is an "Elizabeth," not a "Betty"?
4. Review the diagram on page 19. How is the information about fast and slow routes from writing to response related to "speed reading"? When a person reads complex material slowly, is he necessarily converting the visual characters to sounds before responding?

language defined

Speech is so familiar a feature of daily life that we rarely pause to define it. It seems as natural to man as walking, and only less so than breathing. Yet it needs but a moment's reflection to convince us that this naturalness of speech is but an illusory feeling. The process of acquiring speech is, in sober fact, an utterly different sort of thing from the process of learning to walk. In the case of the latter function, culture, in other words, the traditional body of social usage, is not seriously brought into play. The child is individually equipped, by the complex set of factors that we term biological heredity, to make all the needed muscular and nervous adjustments that result in walking. Indeed, the very conformation of these muscles and of the appropriate parts of the nervous system may be said to be primarily adapted to the movements made in walking and in similar activities. In a very real sense the normal human being is predestined to walk, not because his elders will assist him to learn the art, but because his organism is prepared from birth, or even from the moment of conception, to take on all those expenditures of nervous energy and all those muscular adaptations that result in walking. To put it concisely, walking is an inherent, biological function of man.

Not so language. It is of course true that in a certain sense the individual is predestined to talk, but that is due entirely to the circumstance that he is born not merely in nature, but in the lap of a society that is certain, reasonably certain, to lead him to its traditions. Eliminate society and there is every reason to believe that he will learn to walk, if, indeed, he survives at all. But it is just as certain that he will never learn to talk, that is, to communicate ideas according to the traditional system of a particular society. Or, again, remove the new-born individual from the social environment into which he has come and transplant him to an utterly alien one. He will develop the art of walking in his new environment very much as he would have developed it in the old. But his speech will be completely at variance with the speech of his native environment. Walking, then, is a general human activity that varies only within circumscribed limits as we pass from individual to individual. Its variability is involuntary and purposeless. Speech is a human activity that varies without assignable limit as we pass from social group to social group, because it is a purely historical heritage of the group, the product of long-continued social usage. It varies as all creative effort varies—not as consciously, perhaps, but none the less as truly as do the religions, the beliefs, the customs, and the arts of different peoples. Walking is an organic, an instinctive, function (not, of course, itself an instinct); speech is a non-instinctive, acquired, "cultural" function.

There is one fact that has frequently tended to prevent the recognition of language as a merely conventional system of sound symbols, that has seduced the popular mind into attributing to it an instinctive basis that it does not really possess. This is the well-known observation that under the stress of emotion, say of a sudden twinge of pain or of unbridled joy, we do involuntarily give utterance to sounds that the hearer interprets as indicative of the emotion itself. But there is all the difference in the world between such involuntary expression of feeling and the normal type of communication of ideas that is speech. The former kind of utterance is indeed instinctive, but it is non-symbolic; in other words, the sound of pain or the sound of joy does not, as such, indicate the emotion, it does not stand aloof, as it were, and announce that such and such an emotion is being felt. What it does is to serve as a more or less automatic overflow of the emotional energy; in a sense, it is part and parcel of the emotion itself. Moreover, such instinctive cries hardly constitute communication in any strict sense. They are not addressed to any one, they are merely overheard, if heard at all, as the bark of a dog, the sound of approaching footsteps, or the rustling of the wind is heard. If they convey certain ideas to the hearer, it is only in the very general sense in which any and every sound or even any phenomenon in our environment may be said to convey an idea to the perceiving mind. If the involuntary cry of pain which is conventionally represented by "Oh!" be looked upon as a true speech symbol equivalent to some such idea as "I am in great pain," it is just as allowable to interpret the appearance of clouds as an equivalent symbol that carries the definite message "It is likely to rain." A definition of language, however, that is so extended as to cover every type of inference becomes utterly meaningless.

The mistake must not be made of identifying our conventional interjections (our oh! and ah! and sh!) with the instinctive cries themselves. These interjections are merely conventional fixations of the natural sounds. They therefore differ widely in various languages in accordance with the specific phonetic genius of each of these. As such they may be considered an integral portion of speech, in the properly cultural sense of the term, being no more identical with the instinctive cries themselves than such words as "cuckoo" and "killdeer" are identical with the cries of the birds they denote or than Rossini's treatment of a storm in the overture to "William Tell" is in fact a storm. In other words, the interjections and sound-imitative words of normal speech are related to their natural prototypes as is art, a purely social or cultural thing, to nature. It may be objected that, though the interjections differ somewhat as we pass from language to language, they do nevertheless offer striking family resemblances and may therefore be looked upon as having grown up out of a common instinctive base. But their case is nowise different from that, say, of the varying national modes of pictorial representation. A Japanese picture of a hill both differs from and resembles a typical modern European painting of the same kind of hill. Both are suggested by and both "imitate" the same natural feature. Neither the one nor the other is the same thing as, or, in any intelligible sense, a direct outgrowth of, this natural feature. The two modes of representation are not identical because they proceed from differing historical traditions, are executed with differing pictorial techniques. The interjections of Japanese and English are, just so, suggested by a common natural prototype, the instinctive cries, and are thus unavoidably suggestive of each other. They differ, now greatly, now but little, because they are builded out of historically diverse materials or techniques, the respective linguistic traditions, phonetic systems, speech habits of the two peoples. Yet the instinctive cries as such are practically identical for all humanity, just as the human skeleton or nervous system is to all intents and purposes a "fixed," that is, an only slightly and "accidentally" variable, feature of man's organism.

Interjections are among the least important of speech elements. Their discussion is valuable mainly because it can be shown that even they, avowedly the nearest of all language sounds to instinctive utterance, are only superficially of an instinctive nature. Were it therefore possible to demonstrate that the whole of language is traceable, in its ultimate historical and psychological foundations, to the interjections, it would still not follow that language is an instinctive activity. But, as a matter of fact, all attempts so to explain the origin of speech have been fruitless. There is no tangible evidence, historical or otherwise, tending to show that the mass of speech elements and speech processes has evolved out of the interjections. These are a very small and functionally insignificant proportion of the vocabulary of language; at no time and in no linguistic province that we have record of do we see a noticeable tendency towards their elaboration into the primary warp and woof of language. They are never more, at best, than a decorative edging to the ample, complex fabric.

What applies to the interjections applies with even greater force to the sound-imitative words. Such words as "whippoorwill," "to mew," "to caw" are in no sense natural sounds that man has instinctively or automatically reproduced. They are just as truly creations of the human mind, flights of the human fancy, as anything else in language. They do not directly grow out of nature, they are suggested by it and play with it. Hence the onomatopoetic theory of the origin of speech, the theory that would explain all speech as a gradual evolution from sounds of an imitative character, really brings us no nearer to the instinctive level than is language as we know it to-day. As to the theory itself, it is scarcely more credible than its interjectional counter-part. It is true that a number of words which we do not now feel to have a sound-imitative value can be shown to have once had a phonetic form that strongly suggests their origin as imitations of natural sounds. Such is the English word "to laugh." For all that, it is quite impossible to show, nor does it seem intrinsically reasonable to suppose, that more than a negligible proportion of the elements of speech or anything at all of its formal apparatus is derivable from an onomatopoetic source. However much we may be disposed on general principles to assign a fundamental importance in the languages of primitive peoples to the imitation of natural sounds, the actual fact of the matter is that these languages show no particular preference for imitative words. Among the most primitive peoples of aboriginal America, the Athabaskan tribes of the Mackenzie River speak languages in which such words seem to be nearly or entirely absent, while they are used freely enough in languages as sophisticated as English and German. Such an instance shows how little the essential nature of speech is concerned with the mere imitation of things.

The way is now cleared for a serviceable definition of language. Language is a purely human and non-instinctive method of communicating ideas, emotions, and desires by means of a system of voluntarily produced symbols. These symbols are, in the first instance, auditory and they are produced by the so-called "organs of speech." There is no discernible instinctive basis in human speech as such, however much instinctive expressions and the natural environment may serve as a stimulus for the development of certain elements of speech, however much instinctive tendencies, motor and other, may give a predetermined range or mold to linguistic expression. Such human or animal communication, if "communication" it may be called, as is brought about by involuntary, instinctive cries is not, in our sense, language at all.

I have just referred to the "organs of speech," and it would seem at first blush that this is tantamount to an admission that speech itself is an instinctive, biologically predetermined activ-

ity. We must not be misled by the mere term. There are, properly speaking, no organs of speech; there are only organs that
are incidentally useful in the production of speech sounds. The
lungs, the larynx, the palate, the nose, the tongue, the teeth, and
the lips, are all so utilized, but they are no more to be thought
of as primary organs of speech than are the fingers to be considered as essentially organs of piano-playing or the knees as
organs of prayer. Speech is not a simple activity that is carried
on by one or more organs biologically adapted to the purpose. It
is an extremely complex and ever-shifting network of adjustments—in the brain, in the nervous system, and in the articulating and auditory organs—tending towards the desired end of
communication. The lungs developed, roughly speaking, in connection with the necessary biological function known as breathing; the nose, as an organ of smell; the teeth, as organs useful
in breaking up food before it was ready for digestion. If, then,
these and other organs are being constantly utilized in speech,
it is only because any organ, once existent and in so far as it is
subject to voluntary control, can be utilized by man for secondary purposes. Physiologically, speech is an overlaid function, or,
to be more precise, a group of overlaid functions. It gets what
service it can out of organs and functions, nervous and muscular, that have come into being and are maintained for very
different ends than its own.

It is true that physiological psychologists speak of the localization of speech in the brain. This can only mean that the
sounds of speech are localized in the auditory tract of the brain,
or in some circumscribed portion of it, precisely as other classes
of sounds are localized; and that the motor processes involved in
speech (such as the movements of the glottal cords in the
larynx, the movements of the tongue required to pronounce the
vowels, lip movements required to articulate certain consonants,
and numerous others) are localized in the motor tract precisely
as are all other impulses to special motor activities. In the same
way control is lodged in the visual tract of the brain over all
those processes of visual recognition involved in reading. Naturally the particular points or clusters of points of localization in
the several tracts that refer to any element of language are con-

nected in the brain by paths of association, so that the outward, or psycho-physical, aspect of language is of a vast network of associated localizations in the brain and lower nervous tracts, the auditory localizations being without doubt the most fundamental of all for speech. However, a speech-sound localized in the brain, even when associated with the particular movements of the "speech organs" that are required to produce it, is very far from being an element of language. It must be further associated with some element or group of elements of experience, say a visual image or a class of visual images or a feeling of relation, before it has even rudimentary linguistic significance. This "element" of experience is the content or "meaning" of the linguistic unit; the associated auditory, motor, and other cerebral processes that lie immediately back of the act of speaking and the act of hearing speech are merely a complicated symbol of or signal for these "meanings," of which more anon. We see therefore at once that language as such is not and cannot be definitely localized, for it consists of a peculiar symbolic relation— physiologically an arbitrary one—between all possible elements of consciousness on the one hand and certain selected elements localized in the auditory, motor, and other cerebral and nervous tracts on the other. If language can be said to be definitely "localized" in the brain, it is only in that general and rather useless sense in which all aspects of consciousness, all human interest and activity, may be said to be "in the brain." Hence, we have no recourse but to accept language as a fully formed functional system within man's psychic or "spiritual" constitution. We cannot define it as an entity in psycho-physical terms alone, however much the psycho-physical basis is essential to its functioning in the individual.

From the physiologist's or psychologist's point of view we may seem to be making an unwarrantable abstraction in desiring to handle the subject of speech without constant and explicit reference to that basis. However, such an abstraction is justifiable. We can profitably discuss the intention, the form, and the history of speech, precisely as we discuss the nature of any other phase of human culture—say art or religion—as an institutional or cultural entity, leaving the organic and psychological mechanisms back of it as something to be taken for granted. Accordingly, it must be clearly understood that this introduction to the study of speech is not concerned with those aspects of physiology and of physiological psychology that underlie speech. Our study of language is not to be one of the genesis and operation of a concrete mechanism; it is, rather, to be an inquiry into the function and form of the arbitrary systems of symbolism that we term languages.

I have already pointed out that the essence of language consists in the assigning of conventional, voluntarily articulated, sounds, or of their equivalents, to the diverse elements of experience. The word "house" is not a linguistic fact if by it is meant merely the acoustic effect produced on the ear by its constituent consonants and vowels, pronounced in a certain order; nor the motor processes and tactile feelings which make up the articulation of the word; nor the visual perception on the part of the hearer of this articulation; nor the visual perception of the word "house" on the written or printed page; nor the motor processes and tactile feelings which enter into the writing of the word; nor the memory of any or all of these experiences. It is only when these, and possibly still other, associated experiences are automatically associated with the image of a house that they begin to take on the nature of a symbol, a word, an element of language. But the mere fact of such an association is not enough. One might have heard a particular word spoken in an individual house under such impressive circumstances that neither the word nor the image of the house ever recur in consciousness without the other becoming present at the same time. This type of association does not constitute speech. The association must be a purely symbolic one; in other words, the word must denote, tag off, the image, must have no other significance than to serve as a counter to refer to it whenever it is necessary or convenient to do so. Such an association, voluntary and, in a sense, arbitrary as it is, demands a considerable exercise of self-conscious attention. At least to begin with, for habit soon makes the association nearly as automatic as any and more rapid than most.

But we have traveled a little too fast. Were the symbol

"house"—whether an auditory, motor, or visual experience or image—attached but to the single image of a particular house once seen, it might perhaps, by an indulgent criticism, be termed an element of speech, yet it is obvious at the outset that speech so constituted would have little or no value for purposes of communication. The world of our experiences must be enormously simplified and generalized before it is possible to make a symbolic inventory of all our experiences of things and relations and this inventory is imperative before we can convey ideas. The elements of language, the symbols that ticket off experience, must therefore be associated with whole groups, delimited classes, of experience rather than with the single experiences themselves. Only so is communication possible, for the single experience lodges in an individual consciousness and is, strictly speaking, incommunicable. To be communicated it needs to be referred to a class which is tacitly accepted by the community as an identity. Thus, the single impression which I have had of a particular house must be identified with all my other impressions of it. Further, my generalized memory or my "notion" of this house must be merged with the notions that all other individuals who have seen the house have formed of it. The particular experience that we started with has now been widened so as to embrace all possible impressions or images that sentient beings have formed or may form of the house in question. This first simplification of experience is at the bottom of a large number of elements of speech, the so-called proper nouns or names of single individuals or objects. It is, essentially, the type of simplification which underlies, or forms the crude subject of, history and art. But we cannot be content with this measure of reduction of the infinity of experience. We must cut to the bone of things, we must more or less arbitrarily throw whole masses of experience together as similar enough to warrant their being looked upon—mistakenly, but conveniently—as identical. This house and that house and thousands of other phenomena of like character are thought of as having enough in common, in spite of great and obvious differences of detail, to be classed under the same heading. In other words, the speech element "house" is the symbol, first and foremost, not of a single perception, nor even of the notion of a particular object, but of a "concept," in other words, of a convenient capsule of thought that embraces thousands of distinct experiences and that is ready to take in thousands more. If the single significant elements of speech are the symbols of concepts, the actual flow of speech may be interpreted as a record of the setting of these concepts into mutual relations.

The question has often been raised whether thought is possible without speech; further, if speech and thought be not but two facets of the same psychic process. The question is all the more difficult because it has been hedged about by misunderstandings. In the first place, it is well to observe that whether or not thought necessitates symbolism, that is speech, the flow of language itself is not always indicative of thought. We have seen that the typical linguistic element labels a concept. It does not follow from this that the use to which language is put is always or even mainly conceptual. We are not in ordinary life so much concerned with concepts as such as with concrete particularities and specific relations. When I say, for instance, "I had a good breakfast this morning," it is clear that I am not in the throes of laborious thought, that what I have to transmit is hardly more than a pleasurable memory symbolically rendered in the grooves of habitual expression. Each element in the sentence defines a separate concept or conceptual relation or both combined, but the sentence as a whole has no conceptual significance whatever. It is somewhat as though a dynamo capable of generating enough power to run an elevator were operated almost exclusively to feed an electric doorbell. The parallel is more suggestive than at first sight appears. Language may be looked upon as an instrument capable of running a gamut of psychic uses. Its flow not only parallels that of the inner content of consciousness, but parallels it on different levels, ranging from the state of mind that is dominated by particular images to that in which abstract concepts and their relations are alone at the focus of attention and which is ordinarily termed reasoning. Thus the outward form only of language is constant; its inner meaning, its psychic value or intensity, varies freely with attention or the selective interest of the mind, also, needless to

say, with the mind's general development. From the point of
view of language, thought may be defined as the highest latent
or potential content of speech, the content that is obtained by
interpreting each of the elements in the flow of language as possessed of its very fullest conceptual value. From this it follows
at once that language and thought are not strictly coterminous.
At best language can but be the outward facet of thought on the
highest, most generalized, level of symbolic expression. To put
our viewpoint somewhat differently, language is primarily a pre-
rational function. It humbly works up to the thought that is
latent in, that may eventually be read into, its classifications and
its forms; it is not, as is generally but naïvely assumed, the final
label put upon the finished thought.

Most people, asked if they can think without speech, would
probably answer, "Yes, but it is not easy for me to do so. Still
I know it can be done." Language is but a garment! But what if
language is not so much a garment as a prepared road or
groove? It is, indeed, in the highest degree likely that language
is an instrument originally put to uses lower than the conceptual
plane and that thought arises as a refined interpretation of its
content. The product grows, in other words, with the instrument, and thought may be no more conceivable, in its genesis
and daily practice, without speech than is mathematical reasoning practicable without the lever of an appropriate mathematical symbolism. No one believes that even the most difficult
mathematical proposition is inherently dependent on an arbitrary set of symbols, but it is impossible to suppose that the human mind is capable of arriving at or holding such a proposition
without the symbolism. The writer, for one, is strongly of the
opinion that the feeling entertained by so many that they can
think, or even reason, without language is an illusion. The illusion seems to be due to a number of factors. The simplest of
these is the failure to distinguish between imagery and thought.
As a matter of fact, no sooner do we try to put an image into
conscious relation with another than we find ourselves slipping
into a silent flow of words. Thought may be a natural domain
apart from the artificial one of speech, but speech would seem
to be the only road we know of that leads to it. A still more fruit-

ful source of the illusive feeling that language may be dispensed with in thought is the common failure to realize that language is not identical with its auditory symbolism. The auditory symbolism may be replaced, point for point, by a motor or by a visual symbolism (many people can read, for instance, in a purely visual sense, that is, without the intermediating link of an inner flow of the auditory images that correspond to the printed or written words) or by still other, more subtle and elusive, types of transfer that are not so easy to define. Hence the contention that one thinks without language merely because he is not aware of a coexisting auditory imagery is very far indeed from being a valid one. One may go so far as to suspect that the symbolic expression of thought may in some cases run along outside the fringe of the conscious mind, so that the feeling of a free, non-linguistic stream of thought is for minds of a certain type a relatively, but only a relatively, justified one. Psycho-physically, this would mean that the auditory or equivalent visual or motor centers in the brain, together with the appropriate paths of association, that are the cerebral equivalent of speech, are touched off so lightly during the process of thought as not to rise into consciousness at all. This would be a limiting case—thought riding lightly on the submerged crests of speech, instead of jogging along with it, hand in hand. The modern psychology has shown us how powerfully symbolism is at work in the unconscious mind. It is therefore easier to understand at the present time than it would have been twenty years ago that the most rarefied thought may be but the conscious counterpart of an unconscious linguistic symbolism.

One word more as to the relation between language and thought. The point of view that we have developed does not by any means preclude the possibility of the growth of speech being in a high degree dependent on the development of thought. We may assume that language arose pre-rationally—just how and on what precise level of mental activity we do not know— but we must not imagine that a highly developed system of speech symbols worked itself out before the genesis of distinct concepts and of thinking, the handling of concepts. We must rather imagine that thought processes set in, as a kind of psychic overflow, almost at the beginning of linguistic expression; further, that the concept, once defined, necessarily reacted on the life of its linguistic symbol, encouraging further linguistic growth. We see this complex process of the interaction of language and thought actually taking place under our eyes. The instrument makes possible the product, the product refines the instrument. The birth of a new concept is invariably foreshadowed by a more or less strained or extended use of old linguistic material; the concept does not attain to individual and independent life until it has found a distinctive linguistic embodiment. In most cases the new symbol is but a thing wrought from linguistic material already in existence in ways mapped out by crushingly despotic precedents. As soon as the word is at hand, we instinctively feel, with something of a sigh of relief, that the concept is ours for the handling. Not until we own the symbol do we feel that we hold a key to the immediate knowledge or understanding of the concept. Would we be so ready to die for "liberty," to struggle for "ideals," if the words themselves were not ringing within us? And the word, as we know, is not only a key; it may also be a fetter.

Language is primarily an auditory system of symbols. In so far as it is articulated it is also a motor system, but the motor aspect of speech is clearly secondary to the auditory. In normal individuals the impulse to speech first takes effect in the sphere of auditory imagery and is then transmitted to the motor nerves that control the organs of speech. The motor processes and the accompanying motor feelings are not, however, the end, the final resting point. They are merely a means and a control leading to auditory perception in both speaker and hearer. Communication, which is the very object of speech, is successfully effected only when the hearer's auditory perceptions are translated into the appropriate and intended flow of imagery or thought or both combined. Hence the cycle of speech, in so far as we may look upon it as a purely external instrument, begins and ends in the realm of sounds. The concordance between the initial auditory imagery and the final auditory perceptions is the social seal or warrant of the successful issue of the process. As we have already seen, the typical course of this process may undergo endless modifications or transfers into equivalent systems without thereby losing its essential formal characteristics.

The most important of these modifications is the abbreviation of the speech process involved in thinking. This has doubtless many forms, according to the structural or functional peculiarities of the individual mind. The least modified form is that known as "talking to one's self" or "thinking aloud." Here the speaker and the hearer are identified in a single person, who may be said to communicate with himself. More significant is the still further abbreviated form in which the sounds of speech are not articulated at all. To this belong all the varieties of silent speech and of normal thinking. The auditory centers alone may be excited; or the impulse to linguistic expression may be communicated as well to the motor nerves that communicate with the organs of speech but be inhibited either in the muscles of these organs or at some point in the motor nerves themselves; or, possibly, the auditory centers may be only slightly, if at all, affected, the speech process manifesting itself directly in the motor sphere. There must be still other types of abbreviation. How common is the excitation of the motor nerves in silent speech, in which no audible or visible articulations result, is shown by the frequent experience of fatigue in the speech organs, particularly in the larynx, after unusually stimulating reading or intensive thinking.

All the modifications so far considered are directly patterned on the typical process of normal speech. Of very great interest and importance is the possibility of transferring the whole system of speech symbolism into other terms than those that are involved in the typical process. This process, as we have seen, is a matter of sounds and of movements intended to produce these sounds. The sense of vision is not brought into play. But let us suppose that one not only hears the articulated sounds but sees the articulations themselves as they are being executed by the speaker. Clearly, if one can only gain a sufficiently high degree of adroitness in perceiving these movements of the speech organs, the way is opened for a new type of speech symbolism—that in which the sound is replaced by the visual image of the articulations that correspond to the sound. This

sort of system has no great value for most of us because we are
already possessed of the auditory-motor system of which it is
at best but an imperfect translation, not all the articulations
being visible to the eye. However, it is well known what excellent
use deaf-mutes can make of "reading from the lips" as a sub-
sidiary method of apprehending speech. The most important of
all visual speech symbolisms is, of course, that of the written or
printed word, to which, on the motor side, corresponds the system of delicately adjusted movements which result in the writing or typewriting or other graphic method of recording speech.
The significant feature for our recognition in these new types of
symbolism, apart from the fact that they are no longer a by-
product of normal speech itself, is that each element (letter or
written word) in the system corresponds to a specific element
(sound or sound-group or spoken word) in the primary system.
Written language is thus a point-to-point equivalence, to borrow
a mathematical phrase, to its spoken counterpart. The written
forms are secondary symbols of the spoken ones—symbols of
symbols—yet so close is the correspondence that they may, not
only in theory but in the actual practice of certain eye-readers
and, possibly, in certain types of thinking, be entirely substituted
for the spoken ones. Yet the auditory-motor associations are
probably always latent at the least, that is, they are unconsciously brought into play. Even those who read and think without the slightest use of sound imagery are, at last analysis, dependent on it. They are merely handling the circulating medium,
the money, of visual symbols as a convenient substitute for the
economic goods and services of the fundamental auditory
symbols.

The possibilities of linguistic transfer are practically un-
limited. A familiar example is the Morse telegraph code, in
which the letters of written speech are represented by a conventionally fixed sequence of longer or shorter ticks. Here the
transfer takes place from the written word rather than directly
from the sounds of spoken speech. The letter of the telegraph
code is thus a symbol of a symbol of a symbol. It does not, of
course, in the least follow that the skilled operator, in order to
arrive at an understanding of a telegraphic message, needs to

transpose the individual sequence of ticks into a visual image of the word before he experiences its normal auditory image. The precise method of reading off speech from the telegraphic communication undoubtedly varies widely with the individual. It is even conceivable, if not exactly likely, that certain operators may have learned to think directly, so far as the purely conscious part of the process of thought is concerned, in terms of the tick-auditory symbolism or, if they happen to have a strong natural bent toward motor symbolism, in terms of the correlated tactile-motor symbolism developed in the sending of telegraphic messages.

Still another interesting group of transfers are the different gesture languages, developed for the use of deaf-mutes, of Trappist monks vowed to perpetual silence, or of communicating parties that are within seeing distance of each other but are out of earshot. Some of these systems are one-to-one equivalents of the normal system of speech; others, like military gesture-symbolism or the gesture language of the Plains Indians of North America (understood by tribes of mutually unintelligible forms of speech) are imperfect transfers, limiting themselves to the rendering of such grosser speech elements as are an imperative minimum under difficult circumstances. In these latter systems, as in such still more imperfect symbolisms as those used at sea or in the woods, it may be contended that language no longer properly plays a part but that the ideas are directly conveyed by an utterly unrelated symbolic process or by a quasi-instinctive imitativeness. Such an interpretation would be erroneous. The intelligibility of these vaguer symbolisms can hardly be due to anything but their automatic and silent translation into the terms of a fuller flow of speech.

We shall no doubt conclude that all voluntary communication of ideas, aside from normal speech, is either a transfer, direct or indirect, from the typical symbolism of language as spoken and heard or, at the least, involves the intermediary of truly linguistic symbolism. This is a fact of the highest importance. Auditory imagery and the correlated motor imagery leading to articulation are, by whatever devious ways we follow the

process, the historic fountain-head of all speech and of all
thinking. One other point is of still greater importance. The
ease with which speech symbolism can be transferred from one
sense to another, from technique to technique, itself indicates
that the mere sounds of speech are not the essential fact of
language, which lies rather in the classification, in the formal
patterning, and in the relating of concepts. Once more, language, as a structure, is on its inner face the mold of thought. It
is this abstracted language, rather more than the physical facts
of speech, that is to concern us in our inquiry.

There is no more striking general fact about language than
its universality. One may argue as to whether a particular tribe
engages in activities that are worthy of the name of religion or
of art, but we know of no people that is not possessed of a fully
developed language. The lowliest South African Bushman
speaks in the forms of a rich symbolic system that is in essence
perfectly comparable to the speech of the cultivated Frenchman.
It goes without saying that the more abstract concepts are not
nearly so plentifully represented in the language of the savage,
nor is there the rich terminology and the finer definition of
nuances that reflect the higher culture. Yet the sort of linguistic
development that parallels the historic growth of culture and
which, in its later stages, we associate with literature is, at best,
but a superficial thing. The fundamental groundwork of language—the development of a clear-cut phonetic system, the
specific association of speech elements with concepts, and the
delicate provision for the formal expression of all manner of
relations—all this meets us rigidly perfected and systematized
in every language known to us. Many primitive languages have
a formal richness, a latent luxuriance of expression, that
eclipses anything known to the languages of modern civiliza-
tion. Even in the mere matter of the inventory of speech the layman must be prepared for strange surprises. Popular statements
as to the extreme poverty of expression to which primitive languages are doomed are simply myths. Scarcely less impressive
than the universality of speech is its almost incredible diversity.
Those of us that have studied French or German, or, better yet,

Latin or Greek, know in what varied forms a thought may run. The formal divergences between the English plan and the Latin plan, however, are comparatively slight in the perspective of what we know of more exotic linguistic patterns. The universality and the diversity of speech lead to a significant inference. We are forced to believe that language is an immensely ancient heritage of the human race, whether or not all forms of speech are the historical outgrowth of a single pristine form. It is doubtful if any other cultural asset of man, be it the art of drilling for fire or of chipping stone, may lay claim to a greater age. I am inclined to believe that it antedated even the lowliest developments of material culture, that these developments, in fact, were not strictly possible until language, the tool of significant expression, had itself taken shape.

Review Questions

1. What, according to Sapir, is the essential difference between walking and talking?
2. Why does Sapir not include involuntary cries in his definition of language?
3. How do conventional interjections differ from involuntary cries?
4. How does Sapir evaluate the interjectional and echoic theories of language development?
5. How does Sapir define "language"? Be able to discuss the component parts of the definition.
6. What does Sapir mean when he states, "Physiologically, speech is an overlaid function, or, to be more precise, a group of overlaid functions"?
7. Why does Sapir claim that language cannot be "localized"?
8. What is the relation between abstraction and communication?
9. How do language and thought interact?
10. What is the most important modification of the speech process involved in thinking?
11. What is the relation between the written language and its spoken counterpart? What does Sapir mean by "linguistic transfer"?
12. What inference does Sapir draw from the facts about the universality and diversity of speech?

Discussion Questions

1. Pierre Vashon is the son of French parents, but after his birth in Paris he was adopted by an English couple, who took him to their home in London, where he has lived for eighteen years. He is currently beginning to study French. Will French be an easier language for Pierre to learn than it will be for his native-born classmates of equal intelligence? Why?

2. Review Sapir's discussion of speech and language. How does it explain the old expression, "I've got it on the tip of my tongue, but I can't express it"? People have claimed, "You can only write as well as you can think." Can you find evidence in Sapir's essay to support the claim?

3. In *Gulliver's Travels* Gulliver describes an attempt by the Grand Academy of Lagado to abolish words: "Since Words are only Names for *Things*, it would be more convenient for all Men to carry about with them, such *Things* as were necessary to express the particular Business they are to discourse on." One of the advantages of the scheme, according to its creators, was its potential as "an universal Language to be understood in all civilized Nations, whose Goods and Utensils are generally of the same Kind, or nearly resembling, so that their Uses might easily be comprehended." In Sapir's terms, does language involve the use of objects? What would be the advantages and disadvantages of using objects instead of words in order to communicate?

4. Does the word "house" refer to a particular structure? Explain fully the implications of the question; for example, what would happen to the vocabulary of the language if every object, unique as it is, had a separate word to describe it? Would the result be any better than the proposal of the Grand Academy of Lagado? What fundamental principle about language emerges from this consideration?

5. Review Sapir's discussion of the process by which one moves from writing to response and compare it with Robertson and Cassidy's discussion of that subject. What similarities and differences do you find in the two treatments?

6. Does Sapir claim that the very existence of society is possible only because of language? Explain.

words and
meanings

Devices for Signaling Meaning

The educated man or woman is by long tradition expected to possess what is frequently referred to as "a good command of language." Actually, as has been pointed out in our introductory chapter, a child of five or so already has a "good command," in the sense that he uses without effort practically all the devices by which meaning is signaled vocally, sometimes with the aid of gestures. No normal child of even tenderer years would fail to understand, and to make an appropriate response to, such an utterance as "Is your mother busy?" or to distinguish it from the utterances "Your mother is busy" and "Your mother is busy?" It will be noted that the words in these utterances are identical in form and in meaning. What, then, are the linguistic devices by which the child distinguishes any one of these utterances from the others? Word order and intonation do the trick; in "Your mother is busy?" intonation alone (the rising tone beginning on the first syllable of *busy*) does it.

After we have mastered the use of such devices—we did so more or less unconsciously, of course, long before we could make any analysis of what we do or how we do it—about all that we acquire, except for a few more or less sophisticated "literary" constructions, are vocabulary items. Though we should as educated persons be able to analyze the linguistic devices by which we communicate with one another, we actually acquire these devices without formal instruction. But in the process we ac-

From *The Origins and Development of the English Language* by Thomas Pyles, © 1964 by Harcourt, Brace & World, Inc. and reprinted with their permission.

quire only the most useful, everyday words—usually words which have been a part of the English language from the earliest times (*mother, moon, busy, ready, good, run, have, to, and*), along with some words of foreign origin which have been a part of it for a very long time (*giant, chase, catch*) or which for some other reason have been thoroughly naturalized—more or less homely words which continue for all our lives to provide our basic word hoard. But such equipment, common to all speakers of a language, does not comprise what is meant by "a good command of language."

Why Study Words?

The fact is that, if we are going to be able to talk about anything very far beyond our day-to-day, bread-and-butter living, if we are going to associate in an easy manner with cultivated people, if we are going to read books which such people have found to be important and significant, then we must have at our command a great many words that the man in the street and the man with the hoe neither know nor use. This is not to imply that there is anything wrong in being a common man; his name is Legion, he is the salt of the earth and "a man for a' that." But it is assumed that most people, even though they may have no real intellectual aspirations, want to be—or at least to pass for—something more than, or at least different from, common men and women.

To begin the study of language with an examination of its word stock is, however, to put the cart before the horse, for words come later to us in our linguistic development than sentences—even the child's first meaningful utterances are sentences, though many of them may consist of only a single word each. But the fact remains that most people find the study of words and their meanings interesting and colorful. Witness in newspapers and magazines the number of "letters to the editor," usually sadly misinformed, which are devoted to the uses and misues of words. These are frequently etymological in nature, like the old and oft recurring wheeze that sirloin is so called because King Henry VIII (or James I or Charles II) liked a loin of beef so well that he knighted one, saying "Arise, Sir Loin" at the conferring of the accolade.

Why Meaning Varies

The attribution of some sort of meaning to combinations of distinctive speech sounds and in a few instances to single sounds is a matter of social custom, and like other customs may vary in time, place, and situation: thus *tonic* may mean 'soft drink made with charged water' in parts of eastern New England, though elsewhere it usually means 'liquid medicinal preparation to invigorate the system' or in the phrase *gin and tonic,* 'quinine water'; in the usage of musicians the same word may also mean the first tone of a musical scale. It is also true that many words in frequent use, like *nice, God,* and *democracy,* have among speakers and writers of the same intellectual and social level meanings which are more or less subjective, and hence loose. All meanings of what is thought of as the same word have, however, certain elements in common—elements which may be said to operate within a certain field of meaning. If this were not true, there would be no communication.[1] But this is quite different from assuming the existence of "fixed," or "real," meanings.

Even though words do not have such inflexible meanings as we might prefer them to have, but only a field of meaning in which they operate and which may be extended in any direction or narrowed likewise, it is possible to be irritated at what we may consider a too-loose use of words. For instance, after relating that he had seen a well-dressed man take the arm of a blind and ragged beggar and escort him across a crowded thoroughfare, a rather sentimental man remarked, "That was true democracy." It was, of course, only ordinary human decency, as likely to occur in a monarchy as in a democracy, and by no

[1] It is neither appropriate nor necessary here to go into the vexed philosophical question of what constitutes meaning—the "meaning" of *meaning*—which belongs in the realm of general semantics.

means impossible under a totalitarian form of government like, say, that of Oliver Cromwell or Adolf Hitler. The semantic element of the word *democracy* which was in the speaker's mind was kindness to those less fortunate than oneself. He approved of such kindness, as indeed we all do; it was "good," and "democracy" was also "good." Hence, as soft-minded people are quite prone to do, he equated "democracy" with goodness.

We are defeating the purpose of accurate communication when we use words thus loosely. It is true that some words are by general consent used with a very loose meaning, and it is very likely that we could not get along without a certain number of such words—*nice*, for instance, as in "She's a nice girl" (meaning that she has been well brought up, is kind, gracious, and generally well-mannered, or, with the word stressed, merely that she is chaste), in contrast to "That's a nice state of affairs" (meaning that it is a perfectly awful state of affairs). There is certainly nothing wrong with expressing pleasure and appreciation to a hostess by a heartfelt "I've had a very nice time," or even "I've had an awfully nice time." To seek for a more "accurate" word, one of more limited meaning, would be self-conscious and affected.

A large number of educated speakers and writers, for whatever reason, refuse to use *disinterested* in the sense 'uninterested,' a sense which it previously had and lost for a while, and reserve the word for the meaning 'impartial, unprejudiced.' The meaning 'uninterested' has gained ground at a terrific rate, and it is possible that before long it will completely drive out the other one. There will have been no great loss to language *qua* communication. We shall merely have lost a synonym for *impartial* and acquired on all levels another way of saying 'uninterested.' Educated readers of the future will be no more annoyed by the change than they are by similar changes that have given some of the words used in, say, the plays of Shakespeare and in the King James Bible different meanings for us from those which they had in early Modern English. Uneducated readers will be baffled and misled, to be sure; but simple people today frequently misinterpret the King James Bible (the only literature in early Modern English which they are likely ever to read) with complete satisfaction to themselves. It is hardly feasible to expect language to stand still for the sake of ignorant people, who as a matter of fact manage quite well enough, as do the rest of us so long as our less informed fellows are restrained from forcibly imposing their interpretations of what they read, whether sacred or profane, upon us. How long they can be so restrained in a democracy, where numbers are all-important, is a very important question, but it is outside the scope of the present discussion.

Etymology and Meaning

There is a widespread belief, held even by some quite learned people, that the way to find out what a word means is to find out what it previously meant—or, preferably, if it were possible to do so, what it originally meant—a notion similar to the Greek belief in the etymon. Such is the frequent method of dealing with borrowed words, the mistaken idea being that the meaning of the word in current English and the meaning of the non-English word from which the English word is derived must be, or at any rate ought to be, one and the same. As a matter of fact, such an appeal to etymology to determine present meaning is as unreliable as would be an appeal to spelling to determine modern pronunciation. Change of meaning—semantic change, as it is called—may, and frequently does, alter the so-called etymological sense (that is to say, the earliest sense we can *discover*, which is not necessarily the very earliest sense), which may have become altogether obsolete. The study of etymologies is of course richly rewarding. It may, for instance, throw a great deal of light on present meanings, and it frequently tells us something of the workings of the human mind in dealing with the phenomenon of meaning, but it is of very limited help in determining for us what a word "actually" means.

Certain popular writers, overeager to display their learning, have asserted that words are misused when they depart from their etymological meanings. Thus Ambrose Bierce once declared that *dilapidated*, because of its ultimate derivation from

Latin *lapis* 'stone,' could appropriately be used only of a stone structure.[2] Such a notion if true would commit us to the parallel assertion that only what actually had roots could properly be eradicated, since *eradicate* is ultimately derived from Latin *rādix* 'root,' that *calculation* be restricted to counting pebbles (Lat. *calx* 'stone'), that *sinister* be applied only to leftists, and *dexterous* to rightists. By the same token we should have to insist that we could *admire* only what we could 'wonder at,' inasmuch as the English word comes from Latin *ad* 'at' plus *mīrāri* 'to wonder,'[3] or that *giddy* persons must be divinely inspired, inasmuch as *gid* is a derivative of *god*.[4] Or that only men may be virtuous, because *virtue* is derived from Latin *virtus* 'manliness,' itself a derivative of *vir* 'man.' Now, alas for the wicked times in which we live, *virtue* is applied exclusively to women. *Virile*, also a derivative of *vir*, has retained all of its earlier meaning, and has even added to it.

From these few examples, it must be obvious that we cannot ascribe anything like "fixed" meanings to words. What we actually encounter much of the time are meanings that are variable, and that may have wandered from what their etymologies suggest. To suppose that invariable meanings exist, quite apart from context, is to be guilty of a type of naïveté which may vitiate all our thinking.

.   .   .   .   .

Generalization and Specialization

An obvious classification of meaning is that based on scope. This is to say, meaning may be generalized (extended, widened) or it may be specialized (restricted, narrowed). When we in-

[2] In his *Write It Right* (New York, 1928), cited in Stuart Robertson, *The Development of Modern English*, 2nd ed., rev. Frederic G. Cassidy (New York, 1954), p. 234.

[3] Compare Hamlet's use of *admiration* in the sense 'wonderment, amazement' in "Season your admiration for a while/With an attent eare" (I.ii. 192–93).

[4] Compare *dizzy*, which may in very early times have had the same meaning. See Henry Bradley, *The Making of English* (New York, 1904), pp. 198–200. *Enthusiastic*, from the Greek, also had this meaning.

crease the scope of a word, we reduce the elements of its contents. For instance, *tail* (from OE *tægl*) in earlier times seems to have meant 'hairy caudal appendage, as of a horse.' When we eliminated the hairiness (or the horsiness) from the meaning, we increased its scope, so that in modern English the word means simply 'caudal appendage.' The same thing has happened to Danish *hale*, earlier 'tail of a cow.' In course of time the cow was eliminated, and in present-day Danish the word means simply 'tail,' having undergone a semantic generalization precisely like that of the English word cited; the closely related Icelandic *hali* still keeps the cow in the picture. Similarly, a *mill* was earlier a place for making things by the process of grinding, that is, for making meal. The words *meal* and *mill* are themselves related, as one might guess from their similarity. A mill is now simply a place for making things: the grinding has been eliminated, so that we may speak of a woolen mill, a steel mill, or even a gin mill. The word *corn* earlier meant 'grain' and is in fact related to the word *grain*. It is still used in this general sense in England, as in the "Corn Laws," but specifically it may mean either oats (for animals) or wheat (for human beings). In American usage *corn* denotes maize, which is of course not at all what Keats meant in his "Ode to a Nightingale" when he described Ruth as standing "in tears amid the alien corn." The building in which corn, regardless of its meaning, is stored is called a barn. *Barn* earlier denoted a storehouse for barley; the word is in fact a compound of two Old English words, *bere* 'barley' and *ærn* 'house.' By elimination of a part of its earlier content, the scope of this word has been extended to mean a storehouse for any kind of grain. American English has still further generalized by eliminating the grain, so that *barn* may mean also a place for housing livestock.

The opposite of generalization is specialization, a process in which, by adding to the elements of meaning, the semantic content of a word is reduced. *Deer*, for instance, used to mean simply 'animal' (OE *dēor*) as its German cognate *Tier* still does. Shakespeare writes of "Mice, and Rats, and such small Deare" (*King Lear* III.iv.144). By adding something particular (the family *Cervidae*) to the content, the scope of the word has been reduced, and it has come to mean a specific kind of animal. Similarly *hound* used to mean 'dog,' as does its German cognate *Hund.* To this earlier meaning we have in the course of time added the idea of hunting, and thereby restricted the scope of the word, which to us means a special sort of dog, a hunting dog. To the earlier content of *liquor* 'fluid' (compare *liquid*) we have added 'alcoholic.' But generalization, the opposite tendency, has occurred in the case of the word *rum,* the name of a specific alcoholic drink, which in the usage of those who disapprove of all alcoholic beverages long ago came to mean strong drink in general, even though other liquors are much more copiously imbibed today. The word has even been personified in *Demon Rum.*

Meat once meant simply 'food,' a meaning which it retains in *sweetmeat* and throughout the King James Bible ("meat for the belly," "meat and drink"), though it acquired the meaning 'flesh' much earlier and had for a while both the general and the specialized meaning. *Starve* (OE *steorfan*) used to mean simply 'to die,' as its German cognate *sterben* still does.[5] Chaucer writes, for instance, "But as hire man I wol ay lyve and sterve" (*Troilus and Criseyde* I.427). A specific way of dying had to be expressed by a following phrase, for example "of hunger, for cold." The *OED* cites "starving with the cold," presumably dialectal, as late as 1867. The word came somehow to be primarily associated with death by hunger, and for a while there existed a compound verb *hunger-starve.* Usually nowadays we put the stress altogether on the added idea of hunger and lose the older meaning altogether. Although the usual meaning of *to starve* now is 'to die of hunger,' we also use the phrase "starve to death," which in earlier times would have been tautological. An additional, toned-down meaning grows out of hyperbole, so that "I'm starving" may mean only 'I'm very hungry.' The word is of course used figuratively, as in "starving for love," which, as we have seen, once meant 'dying for love.' This word furnishes a striking example of specialization and proliferation of meaning.

[5] An even earlier meaning may have been 'to grow stiff.'

Pejoration and Amelioration

Change in meaning is frequently due to ethical, or moral, considerations. A word may, as it were, go downhill, or it may rise in the world; there is no way of predicting what its career may be. *Politician* has had a downhill development in American English; in British English it is still not entirely without honor. *Knave* (OE *cnafa*), which used to mean simply 'boy'—it is cognate with German *Knabe,* which retains the earlier meaning —is another example of pejorative (from Lat. *pējor* 'worse') development; it came to mean successively 'serving boy' [6] (specialization), like that well-known knave of hearts [7] who was given to stealing tarts, and ultimately 'bad human being,' so that we may now speak of an old knave, or conceivably even a knavish woman. On its journey downhill this word has thus undergone both specialization and generalization. *Boor,* once meaning 'peasant,' [8] has had a similar pejorative development, as has *lewd,* earlier 'lay, as opposed to clerical,' and thereafter 'ignorant,' 'base,' and finally 'obscene,' which is the only meaning to survive. [9] The same fate has befallen the Latin loan-word *vulgar,* ultimately from *vulgus* 'the common people'; the earlier meaning is retained in *Vulgar Latin,* the Latin which was spoken by the people up to the time of the early Middle Ages and was to develop into the various Romance languages. *Censure* earlier meant 'opinion.' In the course of time it has come to mean 'bad opinion'; *criticism* is well on its way to the same pejorative goal,

[6] Cf. French *garçon* 'boy,' which in a similarly specialized use means 'waiter.'

[7] Actually a further specialization: the jacks in card games are called the knaves in upper-class British usage.

[8] Its cognate *Bauer* is the usual equivalent of *jack* or *knave* in German card-playing, whence English *bower* (as in *right bower* and *left bower*) in certain card games such as euchre and five hundred.

[9] The development of *nice,* going back to Latin *nescius* 'ignorant,' has been just the opposite. The Old French form used in English meant 'simple,' a meaning retained in Modern French *niais.* In the course of its career in English it has had the meanings 'foolishly particular' and then merely 'particular' (as in *a nice distinction*), among others.

ordinarily meaning nowadays 'adverse judgment.' The verbs *to censure* and *to criticize* have undergone a similar development. *Deserts* (as in *just deserts*) likewise started out indifferently to mean simply what one deserved, whether good or bad, but has come to mean 'punishment.' A few more examples of this tendency must suffice. *Silly* (OE *sǣlig*), earlier 'timely,' came to mean 'happy, blessed,' and subsequently 'innocent, simple'; then the simplicity, a desirable quality under most circumstances, was misunderstood (note the present ambiguity of *a simple man*), and the word took on its present meaning. Its German cognate *selig* progressed only to the second stage, though the word may be used facetiously to mean 'tipsy.'

Like *censure* and *criticize, praise* started out indifferently; it is simply *appraise* 'put a value on' with loss of its initial unstressed syllable (aphesis). But *praise* has come to mean 'value highly.' Here what has been added has ameliorated, or elevated, the semantic content of the word. Amelioration, the opposite of pejoration, is well illustrated by *knight*, which used to mean 'servant,' as its German relative *Knecht* still does.[10] This particular word has obviously moved far from its earlier meaning, denoting as it usually now does a very special and exalted man who has been signally honored by his sovereign and who is entitled to prefix *Sir* to his name. *Earl* (OE *eorl*) once meant simply 'man,' though in ancient Germanic times it was specially applied to a warrior, who was almost invariably a man of good birth, in contrast to a *ceorl* (*churl*), or ordinary freeman. When under the Norman kings French titles were adopted in England, *earl* failed to be displaced, but remained as the equivalent of the Continental *count*.

.   .   .   .   .

[10] It must not be supposed that, because German cognates have frequently been cited as still having meanings which have become archaic in English, German words are necessarily less susceptible to semantic change than English ones. With different choices of examples it is possible that a contrary impression might be given.

Taboo and Euphemism

It will by now be apparent that many factors must be taken into account in any discussion of change in meaning. It is not surprising that superstition should play a part, as when *sinister*, the Latin word for 'left' (the unlucky side) acquired its present baleful significance. The verb *die*, of Germanic origin, is not once recorded in Old English. This does not necessarily mean that it was not a part of the Old English word stock; however, in the writings that have come down to us, roundabout, toning-down expressions such as "go on a journey" are used instead, perhaps because of superstitions connected with the word itself —superstitions which survive into our own day, when people (at least those whom we know personally) "pass away," "go to sleep," or "go to their Great Reward." Louise Pound collected an imposing and—to the irreverent—amusing list of words and phrases used in referring to death in her article "American Euphemisms for Dying, Death, and Burial." [11] Miss Pound concludes that "one of mankind's gravest problems is to avoid a straightforward mention of dying or burial."

Name-shifting is especially frequent, and probably always has been, when we must come face to face with the less happy facts of our existence, for life holds even for the most fortunate of men experiences which are inartistic, violent, and hence shocking to contemplate in the full light of day—for instance, the first and last facts of human existence, birth and death, despite the sentimentality with which we have surrounded them. And it is certainly true that the sting of the latter is somewhat alleviated—for the survivors, anyway—by calling it by some other name, such as "the Great Adventure," "the flight to glory," and "the final sleep," which are among the many terms cited by Miss Pound in the article just alluded to. *Mortician* is a much flossier word than *undertaker* (which is itself a euphemism with the earlier meanings 'helper,' 'contractor,' 'publisher,' and 'bap-

[11] *American Speech*, XI (1936), 195–202. Reprinted in *Selected Writings of Louise Pound* (Lincoln, Nebr., 1949), pp. 139–47.

tismal sponsor,' among others), but the *loved one* whom he prepares for public view and subsequent interment in a *casket*
(earlier a jewel-box, as in *The Merchant of Venice*) is just as
dead as a *corpse* in a *coffin*. But such verbal subterfuges are apparently thought to rob the grave of some of its victory; the
notion of death is made more tolerable to the human consciousness than it would otherwise be. Birth is much more plainly alluded to nowadays than it used to be, particularly by young
married people, who seem to be strangely fascinated by the un-
pleasant clinical details attendant upon it. The free use of
pregnant is not much older than World War II. A woman *with
child, going to have a baby,* or *enceinte* used to terminate her
condition by her *confinement,* or, if one wanted to be really
fancy about it, her *accouchement.*

Ideas of decency likewise profoundly affect language. All
during the Victorian era, ladies and gentlemen were very sensitive about using the word *leg, limb* being almost invariably
substituted, sometimes even if only the legs of a piano were being referred to. In the very year which marks the beginning of
Queen Victoria's long reign, Captain Frederick Marryat noted in
his *Diary in America* (1837) the American taboo on this word,
when, having asked a young American lady who had taken a
spill whether she had hurt her leg, she turned from him, "evidently much shocked, or much offended," later explaining to
him that in America the word *leg* was never used in the presence
of ladies. Later, the captain visited a school for young ladies
where he saw, according to his own testimony, "a square
pianoforte with four limbs," all dressed in little frilled panta-
lettes. For reasons which it would be difficult to analyze, a similar taboo was placed upon *belly, stomach* being usually substituted for it, along with such nursery terms as *tummy* and
breadbasket and the advertising copy writer's *midriff. Toilet,* a
diminutive of French *toile* 'cloth,' in its earliest English uses
meant a piece of cloth in which to wrap clothes, subsequently
coming to be used for a cloth cover for a dressing table, and then
the table itself, as when Lydia Languish in Sheridan's *The Rivals*
says, "Here, my dear Lucy, hide these books. Quick, quick! Fling
Peregrine Pickle under the toilet—throw *Roderick Random* into

the closet . . . ." [12] There are other related meanings. The word came to be used in America as a euphemism for *privy*—itself in turn a euphemism, as are *latrine* (ultimately derived from Lat. *lavāre* 'to wash') and *lavatory* (note the euphemistic phrase "to wash one's hands"). But *toilet* is now frequently replaced by *rest room, comfort station, powder room,* or the intolerably coy *little boys'* (or *girls'*) *room.* It is safe to predict that these evasions will in their turn come to be regarded as indecorous, and other expressions substituted for them.

Euphemism is likewise resorted to in reference to certain diseases. Like that which attempt to prettify, or at least to mollify birth, death, and excretion, this type of verbal subterfuge is doubtless deeply rooted in fear and superstition. An ailment of almost any sort, for instance, is nowadays often referred to as a *condition* (*heart condition, kidney condition, malignant condition,* and so forth), so that *condition,* hitherto a more or less neutral word, has thus had a pejorative development, coming to mean 'bad condition.' [13] *Leprosy* is no longer used by the American Medical Association because of its repulsive connotations; it is nowadays replaced by the colorless *Hansen's Disease. Cancer* may be openly referred to, though it is notable that in the syndicated horoscopes of Carroll Righter, a well-known Hollywood astrologer, the term is no longer used as a sign of the zodiac; those born under Cancer are now designated "Moon Children." The taboo has been removed from reference to the various specific venereal diseases, formerly *blood diseases* or *social diseases.*

Old age and its attendant decay have probably been made more bearable for many elderly and decrepit people by calling them *senior citizens.* A similar verbal humanitarianism is responsible for *under-privileged* 'poor,' the previously mentioned

[12] It should be pointed out that about fifty years ago the direction for the disposal of *Roderick Random* would have been as risible as that for *Peregrine Pickle,* when *closet* was frequently used for *water closet,* now practically obsolete in American English.

[13] Note that, although *to have a condition* means 'to be in bad health,' *to be in condition* continues, confusingly enough, to mean 'to be in good health.'

sick 'insane,' *social justice* 'charity,' *exceptional child* 'a pupil of subnormal mentality,' [14] and a good many other voguish euphemisms, some of which have been cited in another connection. In the last cited example, pejoration has also operated—unless it can be conceived generally that being below par intellectually is a desirable thing, as the schools would seem to have supposed. One wonders whether to the next generation an "exceptional man" will be thought of as a dull and stupid man, that is, an exceptional child grown to maturity, and whether the "exceptional bargains" offered by the stores had not better be passed up in favor of merely average ones. Sentimental equalitarianism has led us to attempt to dignify humble occupations by giving them high-sounding titles: thus a *janitor* (originally a doorkeeper, from *Janus*, the doorkeeper of heaven in Roman mythology) has in many parts of America become a *custodian* and there are many engineers who would not know the difference between a slide rule and a cantilever. H. L. Mencken cites, among a good many others, *demolition engineer* 'housewrecker,' *sanitary engineer* 'garbage man,' and *extermination engineer* 'rat-catcher.' [15] The meaning of *profession* has been generalized to such an extent that it may include practically any trade or vocation. The writer of a letter to the editor of *Life* comments as follows on the publication of a picture of a plumber in a previous issue: "I think you have done an injustice to the plumbing profession" (August 6, 1951); and a regional chairman of the Wage Stabilization Board informed a waitress who complained of the smallness of her tips, according to an Associated Press item of June 19, 1952, that "if tipping were viewed by your profession as a true incentive for better, faster and more agreeable service, this might go a long way toward relieving the situation." Long ago James Fenimore Cooper in *The American Democrat* (1838) denounced such democratic subterfuges as *boss* for *master* and *help* for *servant*, but these seem very mild nowadays. One of the great concerns of the demo-

[14] Note that the child who exceeds expectations has been stigmatized by the schools as an *over-achiever*.

[15] *The American Language*, 4th ed. (New York, 1936), pp. 289–91.

cratic and progressive age in which we live would seem to be to ensure that nobody's feelings shall ever be hurt—at least, not by words.

It is characteristic of the human mind, in varying degrees of course, to identify words with objects, persons, and ideas—to think much of the time not in terms of the actual situations of flesh-and-blood life, but in relation to words, like that oft quoted little girl who, upon first seeing a pig, remarked that it was certainly rightly named, for it was a very dirty animal. But a pig by any other name—even if it were called a rose—would smell as bad. What one happens to call it—*Schwein, lechón, porco,* or *pig*—makes no difference in the nature of the creature, nor is one name any more appropriate than another. To suppose that our term is superior—that a pig really *is* a pig and hence that we who speak English are more perceptive than foreigners in calling it by its "right" name—is so naïve that no one would own to such a belief. Yet it is certainly true that in their everyday lives people frequently act as though they thought words were identical with what they designate.

During World War II the name of a widely known and highly satisfactory pencil was changed from Mikado to Mirado —a hardly noticeable change, involving a single letter. Yet it is doubtful that the manufacturer would have gone to such trouble and expense as must have been involved in making that little change had he not been convinced that, with Japan as our enemy, many patriots would refuse to buy a pencil named for its emperor, although no one in his right mind could imagine that the pencil was a whit superior because of the change of name.

The Fate of Intensifying Words

Intensifiers constantly stand in need of replacement, being so frequently used that their intensifying force is worn down. As an adverb of degree, *very* has only an intensifying function; it has altogether lost its independent meaning 'truly,' though as an adjective it survives with older meanings in such phrases as "the very man for the job" and "this very afternoon." Chaucer does not use *very* as an intensive adverb; the usage was doubtless beginning to be current in his day, though the *OED* has no contemporary citations. As everyone must be aware, the *verray* in the well-known line "He was a verray, parfit gentil knyght" is an adjective modifying *knyght:* the meaning is approximately 'He was a fully accomplished gentle knight in the widest sense of the term.'

For Chaucer and his contemporaries *full* seems to have been the usual intensive adverb, though Old English *swīðe* (the adverbial form of *swīð* 'strong') retained its intensifying function until the middle of the fifteenth century, with independent meanings 'rapidly' and 'instantly' surviving much longer. *Right* was also widely used as an intensive in Middle English times, as in Chaucer's description of the Clerk of Oxenford: "he nas [that is,*ne was*] nat right fat," which is to say 'He wasn't very fat.' This usage survives formally in *Right Reverend*, the title of a bishop,[16] in *Right Honourable*, that of members of the Privy Council and a few other dignitaries; and in *Right Worshipful*, that of most lord mayors, as also in the more or less informal usages *right smart, right well, right away, right there*, and the like.

Sore, as in *sore afraid*, was similarly long used as an intensive modifier of adjectives and adverbs; its use to modify verbs is ever older. Its cognate *sehr* is still the usual intensive in German, in which language it has completely lost its independent use.

In view of the very understandable tendency of such intensifying words to become dulled, it is not surprising that we should cast about for other words to replace them when we really want to be emphatic. "It's been a very pleasant evening" seems quite inadequate under certain circumstances, and we may instead say, "It's been an *awfully* pleasant evening"; *very nice* may likewise become "*terribly* nice." In negative utterances, *too* is coming to be widely used as an intensive: "New-

---

[16] The dean's title *Very Reverend* has exactly the same meaning, but is, naturally, less exalted in its connotations.

berry's not too far from here"; "Juvenile-court law practice is not too lucrative."

Prodigiously was for a while a voguish substitute for *very*, so that a Regency "blood" like Thackeray's Jos Sedley might speak admiringly of a shapely woman as "a prodigiously fine gel" or even a "monstrous fine" one. The first of these now-forgotten intensifiers dates approximately from the second half of the seventeenth century; the second is about a century earlier. An anonymous contributor to the periodical *The World* in 1756 deplored the "pomp of utterance of our present women of fashion; which, though it may tend to spoil many a pretty mouth, can never recommend an indifferent one," citing in support of his statement the feminine overuse of *vastly, horridly, abominably, immensely,* and *excessively* as intensifiers.[17]

Semantic Change is Inevitable

It is a great pity that language cannot be the exact, finely attuned instrument that deep thinkers wish it to be. But the facts are, as we have seen, that the meaning of practically any word is susceptible to change of one sort or another, and some words have so many individual meanings that we cannot really hope to be absolutely certain of the sum of these meanings. But it is probably quite safe to predict that the members of the human race, *homines sapientes* more or less, will go on making absurd noises with their mouths at one another in what idealists among them will go on considering a deplorably sloppy and inadequate manner, and yet manage to understand one another well enough for their own purposes.

The idealists may, if they wish, settle upon Esperanto, Ido, Ro, Volapük, or any other of the excellent scientific languages which have been laboriously constructed. The game of constructing such languages is still going on; it is assumed that these will not be susceptible to the kind of change which we

[17] Reprinted in Susie I. Tucker's useful little collection, *English Examined: Two Centuries of Comment on the Mother Tongue* (Cambridge, Eng., 1961), p. 96.

have been considering here, any more than to changes in structure such as have been undergone by those languages which
have evolved over the eons. But most of the manifold phenomena of life—disease, famine, birth, death, sex, war, atoms,
isms, and people, to name only a few—will doubtless remain as
messy and hence as unsatisfactory to those unwilling to accept
them as they have always been, no matter what form of speech
we employ when we have to deal with them verbally.

Review Questions

1. What devices do people use to distinguish between utterances
   which contain the same words? In other words, what devices do
   we use to signal meaning?
2. What are two main reasons why people study words?
3. To what extent do words have "fixed" meanings?
4. What is the effect of the "too-loose" use of words? Are we ever
   justified in using words in a loose way?
5. Why is the etymology of a word an unreliable guide to its
   meaning?
6. Define "generalization" and "specialization" as they apply to
   language study.
7. Define "pejoration" and "amelioration" as they apply to language
   study.
8. Define "euphemism." Why are euphemisms used, and what "less
   happy facts" of human existence are they used to describe?
9. Why has "sentimental equalitarianism" led to the use of euphemisms in education and in occupations? Give some examples of
   euphemisms which support your answer.
10. What attitude toward words and objects is illustrated by a
    person who faints when someone mentions a snake?
11. What is the fate of intensifying words?
12. Does Pyles believe that the substitution of a scientific language
    for English would prevent semantic change?

Discussion Questions

1. What factors contribute to pejoration and amelioration? How do
   you explain the change in meaning of "appeasement," for example? From Pyles' discussion do you think that pejoration or

amelioration is more common? Why? How have the following words changed: "genteel," "demure," "egregious," "sophistication," and "sanctimonious"?

2. Pyles discusses the use of euphemisms in some professions. Can you add any examples to his list? How do you explain the creation of euphemisms for certain jobs? How is this use of euphemisms related to social, political, and economic factors?

3. Pyles mentions the euphemism "exceptional child" used by educators, who recently have increased their use of euphemisms. How might a teacher comment euphemistically about children who are lazy, stupid, selfish bullies? Why would he euphemize? Are there valid reasons for euphemisms in education?

4. Why do some people write "G-d" and newspapers use "a four-letter word for intercourse" when describing someone's "obscene" remark? What is accomplished through such devices, which rely on a reader's knowledge of what is omitted or meant? The force of "darn" and "heck" in conversation depends on the fact that both speaker and audience know "damn" and "hell" are meant. Can you think of other examples? What does our use of such euphemisms and our avoidance of taboo words indicate about our attitudes toward language? Are our attitudes toward words colored by our attitudes about the things the words refer to?

5. Are certain kinds of words more likely to change meanings than others? Would you expect common words or rarely used words to change most? technical words or nontechnical words? Why do you suppose vocabulary is so unstable in English, as compared, say, with grammatical features?

6. Viewing the immediately preceding questions in a slightly different way, why do you suppose that with the passage of time the inflectional patterns of a language often simplify markedly, while concurrently the vocabulary vastly increases?

7. Does language "degenerate" or become "corrupt," as some people insist? Explore a few of the implications of such an assumption.

dictionaries

The 1960s was a decade of great lexicographical activity. By far the most significant event was the publication in 1961 of *Webster's Third New International Dictionary* by the G. and C. Merriam Company. The publication of this dictionary, together with the critical and public response to it, set the tone for the lexicographical work of the rest of the decade. The last three essays in this section of the book reflect some of the most provocative commentary which resulted. Focusing largely upon one dictionary, the essays will allow the student to learn more about *Webster's Third*—the most important dictionary to appear since *Webster's Second* in 1934— and at the same time will give him an idea about the nature of dictionaries in general. The essays will necessarily require the student to examine his preconceptions about these matters and to reexamine his attitudes about the language he speaks. The first two essays are general discussions and will help prepare the student to deal with some of the problems raised by the other essays.

Before going on, it may be helpful to consider briefly the function of a dictionary. Nothing is more revealing about a person's attitudes toward language than what he thinks a dictionary to be. There has always been a great discrepancy in the United States between what the general public (including a fair number of Ph.D.'s in English literature and many secondary and elementary teachers) thinks a dictionary contains and what the lexicographers themselves, who ought to know, insist it contains. The former all too often think that a dictionary prescribes what the language ought to be, while the latter assert that it describes the language as it is.

What are the reasons for this discrepancy? One may be that many older people think a dictionary should reflect the language of their own school years or much earlier. They apparently feel that the pronunciation or the meaning of a word they were obliged to learn is that which will always be used, and that having once mastered a given point about language, they can rest assured that the point will never have to be modified. Language, as we noted earlier, changes in a variety of ways, and a dictionary must reflect these changes. Ever since the days of Samuel Johnson, the main trend in lexicography has been for dictionary entries to be based on citation slips with quotations reflecting firsthand evidence of the state of the language. (See S. I. Hayakawa's essay.) Dictionaries record and describe usage; they do not prescribe it.

Dr. Johnson originally thought his duty was to "fix" the language, to establish unalterable meanings of words, but it is sometimes forgotten that even he soon despaired of the naïve attitude toward language which this wish belied and resigned himself to the less divine task of merely recording. The editors of the multivolumed *Oxford English Dictionary* and of the Merriam-Webster dictionaries, including not only the third unabridged edition, but the first and second as well, have been quite clear about this matter and have even disclaimed any pretentions about prescribing and giving editorial opinions—a disclaimer not clarified, unfortunately, by the people sometimes in charge of advertising the dictionaries, especially on dust jackets, who insist upon calling attention to the "authority" of the work. Dictionary makers, more than anyone else perhaps, know that language changes, and they are guided accordingly. Dictionary users who do sense that dictionary entries are based, and should be based, on recorded usage often want only archaic or older usage reflected in their dictionaries, not the current, the contemporary. They want a "descriptive" dictionary, to be sure, but one not brought up to date. They seem to find security in the past. Indeed, some people even refuse to buy recent dictionaries, and some teachers refuse to recommend them, preferring instead to be guided by those of a generation ago.

Most of the public's attitudes are understandable, since few people bother to read the prefatory matter in a dictionary, least of all the editor's special instructions about how to use the book. People seem to regard as intuitive their knowledge about the proper use of a dictionary, partly because they expect an oversimplification in language matters. Even if they realize that somehow language changes, they are often unwilling to accept the implications of these changes and simply want a dictionary to tell them what is right and wrong. They seem to feel that the dictionary came first and that the language, based on it, came later. The desire for oversimplification in large measure explains the public's mixed reception of *Webster's Third*. Great comfort may be derived from the assurance afforded by such a right-or-wrong philosophy, but language and its use are often much more complex than such a simple approach to it admits.

Not realizing the enormity of the dictionary maker's task, then, dictionary users may want not only the usual information about spelling, pronunciation, and meaning, but encyclopedic and reference material as well, the sort found in biographies, gazetteers, tables of weights, and so on. If the lexicographer tries to include all of this information, he must consider how to save space elsewhere. Should he cut back on the number of word entries? on the variety of meanings? If he objects to diluting the purely lexicographic content, he may decide to omit the reference information readily available elsewhere. As Professors Evans and Marckwardt explain, the editors of *Webster's Third* have chosen the last course of action.

Wanting quick assurances about proper social conduct, the public has come to expect a dictionary to supply information about disputed usages. No reasonably comprehensive dictionary of the English language can ever include really adequate usage notes if sufficient space is to be devoted to matters like pronunciation, etymology, and definitions. This need is probably best fulfilled by separate usage handbooks—a subject discussed in the introduction to the final section of this book—in which the compilers have the space to document and analyze the usages about which the speakers and writers of the language fail to agree or about which they show divergent practice. Great diversity indeed can be expected when the language is used by extremely large numbers of people who are spread out over a large geographical area and who are grouped into many social strata. *Webster's Third* does manage to include a great many comments on usage, but these are by no means exhaustive.

Webster's Third has been criticized for its sparing use of status labels. A dictionary must in some way indicate the appropriateness of words and their uses, but often the most accurate way is not by using one-word labels like "illiterate," "slang," or "colloquial," since what is appropriate usage varies with differing situations, social classes, and geographical areas, and since one-word labels tend to oversimplify the issue and, accordingly, distort it. Because of limited space, the editors of *Webster's Third* can often do no more than give examples of various usages so that the dictionary user can see for himself under what circumstances a word or a particular use of it seems acceptable. It would be preferable to have some analysis of the evidence, but, if this is impractical, the examples themselves provide us with much more information than an unexplained one-word label ever could. It is not, therefore, that the Merriam-Webster lexicographers think status labels are inherently bad; they feel that labels oversimplify and distort. The more the contextual, social, and geographical status of a word can be accurately revealed, the more purely descriptive the dictionary is. To repeat, a dictionary is best used in conjunction with a usage handbook—perhaps a variety of handbooks (as discussed later), in order to be sure a wide sampling of attitudes is available, not just the *ex cathedra* remarks of a single "authority." Dictionaries cannot do everything.

Another problem in lexicography is that the pronunciation a dictionary gives for a word is merely a compromise, an abstract generalization. Words are usually not spoken outside the continuum of speech, as the dictionary, with its simple *listing* of words, might lead us to believe. In the phrase "for Christ's sake," the *t* and all of the *s*'s are rarely pronounced, but a dictionary is not likely to record this fact anywhere. Even when a dictionary does give variant possibilities for the pronunciation of a word, there is not enough space to explain the sorts of circumstances under which variants are likely to occur (cf. the pronunciations of "have" and "of" in stressed and unstressed positions, and the variable stress patterns of "ally," "address," and "fourteenth"). Words sound different in differing contexts.

Unless the student has such things pointed out to him, that is, raised to his level of awareness, he will probably be unaware of their existence. The more he can be made aware of some of the things a dictionary *cannot* do, the more he will discover what a dictionary *can* do and what he should and should not expect of it. He will also learn a great deal about language in the process.

Several dictionaries have appeared since *Webster's Third*. A brief survey of them here may help the student get a more rounded view of American lexicography and of attitudes toward language in the United States. *The Random House Dictionary of the English Language,* published in 1966, is called "unabridged," but is not as comprehensive as *Webster's Third*. It is a solid piece of work, however, and has particularly valuable usage notes; it also contains excellent introductory essays. The encyclopedic collections in the back—precisely because they are *not* lexicographic—make the book useful for general reference. Not its least appealing feature is the price: it retails for almost half the cost of *Webster's Third*.

There are several important desk dictionaries. The chief virtue of the excellent *Webster's Seventh New Collegiate Dictionary* is that it is the offspring of the larger *Webster's Third,* and so has a very large collection of citation slips as evidence for the information given under the individual entries. It does not have any general introductory essays. *The American College Dictionary* has ranked well among desk dictionaries, but is being superseded now by the desk-sized *Random House Dictionary* (1968), which is, of course, based on the larger *Random House Dictionary,* and which has the same excellent introductory essays and contemporary usage notes, although the precise meaning of the usage labels is difficult to determine. *Webster's New World Dictionary,* published by the World Publishing Company, revised its college edition in 1970; it has long been hailed for its excellence in etymology. *Funk and Wagnall's Standard College Dictionary,* published by Harcourt, Brace & World in 1963, has an unusually distinguished staff, and like *Webster's Seventh,* the *Random House Dictionary,* and *Webster's New World Dictionary,* is a very good college dictionary. Like the *Random House Dictionary,* it is particularly valuable for its usage notes and its introductory essays.

The most recent major dictionary to appear, as the present book goes to press, is *The American Heritage Dictionary of the English Language* (the American Heritage Company and Houghton Mifflin,

1969). In one important way it seems more conservative than the other dictionaries, giving as it does the opinions of one hundred "experts" about a variety of usage matters. It claims more attention to usage than other desk dictionaries, but clearly much of this attention involves giving the purely subjective views of what is really a disproportionately small representative body of speakers. The editors of the *American Heritage Dictionary* are interested in what the members of the usage panel *think* about certain traditionally controversial matters of usage. What people think they say and would like others to say may be somewhat removed from the reality of what is actually said. The purpose seems to be not so much to reflect the language as it is currently spoken as to reflect the opinions about what a small group of educated speakers might *like* to hear spoken. Thus the editors are clearly departing from the lexicographical tradition that has been in the making since the days of Dr. Johnson.

When the *American Heritage Dictionary* is viewed in light of the increasing attention which other recent dictionaries have paid to usage problems, it continues what now seems to be a trend toward a kind of book we have not had in the past, and which will be very difficult to produce within the pages of a single book: a dictionary and a usage handbook combined. The more attention a dictionary gives to problems of usage, the less room there is left for word entries and definitions. One may suppose that the logical result of this trend would be a handbook of only several hundred entries focusing on problems in usage. Thus the trend seems ultimately self-defeating, and lexicographers will probably not go much farther in this direction. Dictionaries and usage handbooks tend to be mutually exclusive. Insofar as the *American Heritage Dictionary* serves as a usage handbook, it should be noted that its conservatism, as exemplified by the mere existence of a usage panel, runs counter to the trend not only in other dictionaries, but in usage handbooks as well. (See the introductory comments to the final section of this book.)

In another important way, the *American Heritage Dictionary* is quite liberal. The editors have purposely included many more words spoken very informally by young people than the editors of other dictionaries have ventured to do. Many of these words—

and they are labeled clearly—are slang and even vulgar slang or taboo terms, although there are some puzzling omissions. This is an attempt, then, to present the language as it is actually spoken, for slang is much more often spoken than written. For every slang word included, of course, another word from the general vocabulary must be left out, or, at the very least, less information can be given about it. Some critics (and many schoolteachers) will insist that, however viable and important slang words may be, the bulk of them would be more appropriate to a dictionary of slang, such as the Wentworth-Flexner book considered in the next section. Other critics may think that the inclusion of slang is at odds with the prescriptive tone established by the existence of the usage panel. (Why weren't the panel members consulted about the four-letter words?) The *American Heritage Dictionary* has one strikingly attractive feature, of course: it is the most recent dictionary and therefore reflects, at least theoretically, the most current vocabulary of the English language.

For Further Reading

For a collection of essays on lexicography and on attitudes toward dictionaries, see James Sledd and Wilma R. Ebbitt, eds., *Dictionaries and* That *Dictionary: A Casebook on the Aims of Lexicographers and the Targets of Reviewers* (Chicago: Scott, Foresman & Co., 1962). The essays focus on the publication of *Webster's Third,* but raise important problems which deal with dictionaries in general.

The student can also profitably examine the prefaces and introductions to some of the dictionaries referred to in the preceding introduction, including those of the *Oxford English Dictionary* and its 1933 Supplement. There is also valuable prefatory matter in the *Dictionary of American English* and the *Dictionary of Americanisms.*

contexts

How Dictionaries Are Made

It is widely believed that every word has a correct meaning, that we learn these meanings principally from teachers and grammarians (except that most of the time we don't bother to, so that we ordinarily speak "sloppy English"), and that dictionaries and grammars are the supreme authority in matters of meaning and usage. Few people ask by what authority the writers of dictionaries and grammars say what they say. The writer once got into a dispute with an Englishwoman over the pronunciation of a word and offered to look it up in the dictionary. The Englishwoman said firmly, "What for? I am English. I was born and brought up in England. The way I speak *is* English." Such self-assurance about one's own language is not uncommon among the English. In the United States, however, anyone who is willing to quarrel with the dictionary is regarded as either eccentric or mad.

Let us see how dictionaries are made and how the editors arrive at definitions. What follows applies, incidentally, only to those dictionary offices where first-hand, original research goes on—not those in which editors simply copy existing dictionaries. The task of writing a dictionary begins with reading vast amounts of the literature of the period or subject that the dictionary is to cover. As the editors read, they copy on cards every interesting or rare word, every unusual or peculiar occurrence of a common word, a large number of common words in their

From *Language in Thought and Action*, Second Edition, by S. I. Hayakawa, copyright, 1941, 1949 © 1963, 1964, by Harcourt, Brace & World, Inc. and reprinted with their permission. Also reprinted by permission of Allen & Unwin Ltd.

ordinary uses, and also the sentences in which each of these words appears, thus:

> pail
> The dairy *pails* bring home increase of milk
> Keats, *Endymion*
> I, 44–45

That is to say, the context of each word is collected along with the word itself. For a really big job of dictionary writing, such as the *Oxford English Dictionary* (usually bound in about twenty-five volumes), millions of such cards are collected, and the task of editing occupies decades. As the cards are collected, they are alphabetized and sorted. When the sorting is completed, there will be for each word anywhere from two or three to several hundred illustrative quotations, each on its card.

To define a word, then, the dictionary editor places before him the stack of cards illustrating that word; each of the cards represents an actual use of the word by a writer of some literary or historical importance. He reads the cards carefully, discards some, rereads the rest, and divides up the stack according to what he thinks are the several senses of the word. Finally, he writes his definitions, following the hard-and-fast rule that each definition *must* be based on what the quotations in front of him reveal about the meaning of the word. The editor cannot be influenced by what *he* thinks a given word *ought* to mean. He must work according to the cards or not at all.

The writing of a dictionary, therefore, is not a task of setting up authoritative statements about the "true meanings" of words, but a task of *recording*, to the best of one's ability, what various words *have meant* to authors in the distant or immediate past. *The writer of a dictionary is a historian, not a lawgiver.* If, for example, we had been writing a dictionary in 1890, or even as late as 1919, we could have said that the word "broadcast" means "to scatter" (seed and so on) but we could not have decreed that from 1921 on, the commonest meaning of the word should become "to disseminate audible messages, etc., by radio transmission." To regard the dictionary as an "authority," therefore, is to credit the dictionary writer with gifts of prophecy which neither he nor anyone else possesses. In choosing our words when we speak or write, we can be *guided* by the historical record afforded us by the dictionary, but we cannot be *bound* by it, because new situations, new experiences, new inventions, new feelings, are always compelling us to give new uses to old words. Looking under a "hood," we should ordinarily have found, five hundred years ago, a monk; today, we find a motorcar engine.[1]

VERBAL AND PHYSICAL CONTEXTS

The way in which the dictionary writer arrives at his definitions merely systematizes the way in which we all learn the meanings of words, beginning at infancy, and continuing for the rest of our lives. Let us say that we have never heard the word "oboe" before, and we overhear a conversation in which the following sentences occur:

He used to be the best *oboe* player in town. . . . Whenever they came to that *oboe* part in the third movement, he used to get very excited. . . . I saw him one day at the music shop, buying a new reed for his *oboe*. . . . He never liked to play the clarinet after he started playing the *oboe*. . . . He said it wasn't much fun, because it was too easy.

Although the word may be unfamiliar, its meaning becomes clear to us as we listen. After hearing the first sentence, we know that an "oboe" is "played," so that it must be either a game or a musical instrument. With the second sentence the possibility of its being a game is eliminated. With each succeeding sentence the possibilities as to what an "oboe" may be are nar-

[1] *Webster's Third New International Dictionary* lists the word "hood" also as a shortened form of "hoodlum."

The time that elapsed between *Webster's Second Edition* (1934) and the *Third* (1961) indicates the enormous amount of reading and labor entailed in the preparation of a really thorough dictionary of a language as rapidly changing and as rich in vocabulary as English.

rowed down until we get a fairly clear idea of what is meant. This is how we learn by *verbal context*.

But even independently of this, we learn by physical and social context. Let us say that we are playing golf and that we have hit the ball in a certain way with certain unfortunate results, so that our companion says to us, "That's a bad *slice*." He repeats this remark every time our ball fails to go straight. If we are reasonably bright, we learn in a very short time to say, when it happens again, "That's a bad slice." On one occasion, however, our friend says to us, "That's not a *slice* this time; that's a *hook*." In this case we consider what has happened, and we wonder what is different about the last stroke from those previous. As soon as we make the distinction, we have added still another word to our vocabulary. The result is that after nine holes of golf, we can use both these words accurately—and perhaps several others as well, such as "divot," "number-five iron," "approach shot," *without ever having been told what they mean*. Indeed, we may play golf for years without ever being able to give a dictionary definition of "to slice": "To strike (the ball) so that the face of the club draws inward across the face of the ball, causing it to curve toward the right in flight (with a right-handed player)" (*Webster's New International Dictionary, Second Edition*). But even without being able to give such a definition, we should still be able to use the word accurately whenever the occasion demanded.

We learn the meanings of practically all our words (which are, it will be remembered, merely complicated noises), not from dictionaries, not from definitions, but from hearing these noises as they accompany actual situations in life and then learning to associate certain noises with certain situations. Even as dogs learn to recognize "words," as for example by hearing "biscuit" at the same time as an actual biscuit is held before their noses, so do we all learn to interpret language by being aware of the happenings that accompany the noises people make at us—by being aware, in short, of contexts.

The definitions given by little children in school show clearly how they associate words with situations; they almost always define in terms of physical and social contexts: "Punishment is

when you have been bad and they put you in a closet and don't
let you have any supper." "Newspapers are what the paper boy
brings and you wrap up the garbage with it." These are good
definitions. They cannot be used in dictionaries mainly because
they are too specific; it would be impossible to list the myriads of
situations in which every word has been used. For this reason,
dictionaries give definitions on a high level of abstraction; that
is, with particular references left out for the sake of conciseness.
This is another reason why it is a great mistake to regard a
dictionary definition as telling us all about a word.

EXTENSIONAL AND INTENSIONAL MEANING

Dictionaries deal with the world of intensional meanings,
but there is another world which a dictionary by its very nature
ignores: the world of extensional meanings. *The extensional
meaning of an utterance is that which it points to in the extensional (physical) world.* That is to say, the extensional meaning
cannot be expressed in words, because it is that which words
stand for. An easy way to remember this is *to put your hand
over your mouth and point* whenever you are asked to give an
extensional meaning.

Of course, we cannot always point to the extensional meanings of the words we use. Therefore, so long as we are *discussing* meanings, we shall refer to that which is being talked about
as the *denotation* of an utterance. For example, the denotation
of the word "Winnipeg" is the prairie city of that name in southern Manitoba; the denotation of the word "dog" is a class of
animals which includes dog_1 (Fido), dog_2 (Rex), dog_3 (Rover)
. . . dog_n.

The *intensional meaning* of a word or expression, on the
other hand, is that which is *suggested* (connoted) inside one's
head. Roughly speaking, whenever we express the meaning of
words by uttering more words, we are giving intensional meaning, or connotations. To remember this, put your hand over your
eyes and let the words spin around in your head.

Utterances may have, of course, both extensional and inten-

sional meaning. If they have no intensional meaning at all—
that is, if they start no notions whatever spinning about in our
heads—they are meaningless noises, like foreign languages that
we do not understand. On the other hand, it is possible for utterances to have no extensional meaning at all, in spite of the
fact that they may start many notions spinning about in our
heads. The statement, "Angels watch over my bed at night," is
one that has intensional but no extensional meaning. This does
not mean that there are no angels watching over my bed at
night. When we say that the statement has no extensional
meaning, we are merely saying that we cannot see, touch, photo-
graph, or in any scientific manner detect the presence of angels.
The result is that, if an argument begins on the subject whether
or not angels watch over my bed, *there is no way of ending the
argument to the satisfaction of all disputants,* the Christians
and the non-Christians, the pious and the agnostic, the mystical
and the scientific. Therefore, whether we believe in angels or
not, knowing in advance that any argument on the subject will
be both endless and futile, we can avoid getting into fights
about it.

When, on the other hand, statements have extensional content, as when we say, "This room is fifteen feet long," arguments
can come to a close. No matter how many guesses there are
about the length of the room, all discussion ceases when someone produces a tape measure. This, then, is the important difference between extensional and intensional meanings: namely,
when utterances have extensional meanings, discussion can be
ended and agreement reached; when utterances have intensional meanings only and no extensional meanings, arguments
may, and often do, go on indefinitely. Such arguments can result
only in conflict. Among individuals, they may result in the
breaking up of friendships; in society, they often split organizations into bitterly opposed groups; among nations, they may
aggravate existing tensions so seriously as to become real ob-
stacles to the peaceful settling of disputes.

Arguments of this kind may be termed "non-sense arguments," because they are based on utterances about which no

sense data can be collected. Needless to say, there are occasions when the hyphen may be omitted—that depends on one's feelings toward the particular argument under consideration. The reader is requested to provide his own examples of "non-sense arguments." Even the foregoing example of the angels may give offense to some people, despite the fact that no attempt is made to deny or affirm the existence of angels. Imagine, then, the uproar that might result from giving a number of examples from theology, politics, law, economics, literary criticism, and other fields in which it is not customary to distinguish clearly sense from non-sense.

THE "ONE WORD, ONE MEANING" FALLACY

Everyone, of course, who has ever given any thought to the meanings of words has noticed that they are always shifting and changing in meaning. Usually, people regard this as a misfortune, because it "leads to sloppy thinking" and "mental confusion." To remedy this condition, they are likely to suggest that we should all agree on "one meaning" for each word and use it only with that meaning. Thereupon it will occur to them that we simply cannot make people agree in this way, even if we could set up an ironclad dictatorship under a committee of lexicographers who would place censors in every newspaper office and microphones in every home. The situation, therefore, appears hopeless.

Such an impasse is avoided when we start with a new premise altogether—one of the premises upon which modern linguistic thought is based: namely, that *no word ever has exactly the same meaning twice*. The extent to which this premise fits the facts can be demonstrated in a number of ways. First, if we accept the proposition that the contexts of an utterance determine its meaning, it becomes apparent that since no two contexts are ever *exactly* the same, no two meanings can ever be exactly the same. How can we "fix the meaning" even for so common an expression as "to believe in" when it can be used in such sentences as the following:

I believe in you (I have confidence in you).

I believe in democracy (I accept the principles implied by the term democracy).

I believe in Santa Claus (It is my opinion that Santa Claus exists).

Second, we can take, for example, a word of "simple" meaning, like "kettle." But when John says "kettle," its intensional meanings to him are the common characteristics of all the kettles John remembers. When Peter says "kettle," however, its intensional meanings to him are the common characteristics of all the kettles he remembers. *No matter how small or how negligible the differences may be between John's "kettle" and Peter's "kettle," there is some difference.*

Finally, let us examine utterances in terms of extensional meanings. If John, Peter, Harold, and George each say "my typewriter," we would have to point to four different typewriters to get the extensional meaning in each case: John's new Olivetti, Peter's old Remington, Harold's Smith-Corona portable, and the undenotable intended "typewriter" that George plans some day to buy: "My typewriter, when I buy it, will be an electric." Also, if John says "my typewriter" today, and again "my typewriter" tomorrow, the extensional meaning is different in the two cases, because the typewriter is not exactly the same from one day to the next (nor from one minute to the next): slow processes of wear, change, and decay are going on constantly. Although we can say, then, that the differences in the meanings of a word on one occasion, on another occasion a minute later, and on still another occasion another minute later, are negligible, we cannot say that the meanings are *exactly* the same.

To insist dogmatically that we know what a word means *in advance of its utterance* is nonsense. All we can know in advance is *approximately* what it will mean. After the utterance, we interpret what has been said in the light of both verbal and physical contexts, and act according to our interpretation. An examination of the verbal context of an utterance, as well as the examination of the utterance itself, directs us to the intensional meanings; an examination of the physical context directs us to the extensional meanings. When John says to James, "Bring me that book, will you?" James looks in the direction of John's pointed finger (physical context) and sees a desk with several books on it (physical context); he thinks back over their previous conversation (verbal context) and knows which of those books is being referred to.

Interpretation *must* be based, therefore, on the totality of contexts. If it were otherwise, we should not be able to account for the fact that even if we fail to use the right (customary) words in some situations, people can very frequently understand us. For example:

> A: Gosh, look at that second baseman go!
> B [*looking*]: You mean the shortstop?
> A: Yes, that's what I mean.

> A: There must be something wrong with the oil line; the engine has started to balk.
> B: Don't you mean "gas line"?
> A: Yes—didn't I say "gas line"?

Contexts often indicate our meaning so clearly that we do not even have to say what we mean in order to be understood.

IGNORING CONTEXTS

It is clear, then, that the ignoring of contexts in any act of interpretation is at best a stupid practice. At its worst, it can be a vicious practice. A common example is the sensational newspaper story in which a few words by a public personage are torn out of their context and made the basis of a completely misleading account. There is the incident of a Veterans Day speaker, a university teacher, who declared before a high-school assembly that the Gettysburg Address was "a powerful piece of propaganda." The context clearly revealed that "propaganda" was being used, not according to its popular meaning, but rather, as the speaker himself stated, to mean "explaining the moral purposes of a war." The context also revealed that the speaker was a very great admirer of Lincoln. However, the local newspaper, ignoring the context, presented the account in such a way as to suggest that the speaker had called Lincoln a liar. On this basis, the newspaper began a campaign against the instructor. The speaker remonstrated with the editor of the newspaper, who replied, in effect, "I don't care what else you said. You said the Gettysburg Address was propaganda, didn't you?" This appeared to the editor complete proof that Lincoln had been maligned and that the speaker deserved to be discharged from his position at the university. Similar practices may be found in advertisements. A reviewer may be quoted on the jacket of a book as having said, "A brilliant work," while reading of the context may reveal that what he really said was, "It just falls short of being a brilliant work." There are some people who will always be able to find a defense for such a practice in saying, "But he did use the words, 'a brilliant work,' didn't he?"

People in the course of argument very frequently complain about words meaning different things to different people. Instead of complaining, they should accept such differences as a matter of course. It would be startling indeed if the word "justice," for example, were to have the same meaning to each of the nine justices of the United States Supreme Court; we should get nothing but unanimous decisions. It would be even more startling if "justice" meant the same to President Kennedy as to Nikita Khrushchev. If we can get deeply into our consciousness the principle that no word ever has the same meaning twice, we will develop the habit of automatically examining contexts, and this will enable us to understand better what others are saying. As it is, however, we are all too likely, when a word sounds familiar, to assume that we understand it even when we don't. In this way we read into people's remarks meanings that were never intended. Then we waste energy in angrily accusing people of "intellectual dishonesty" or "abuse of words," when their only sin is that they use words in ways unlike our own, as they can hardly help doing, especially if their background has been widely different from ours. There are cases of intellectual dishonesty and the abuse of words, of course, but they do not always occur in the places where people think they do.

In the study of history or of cultures other than our own, contexts take on special importance. To say, "There was no running water or electricity in the house," does not condemn an English house in 1570, but says a great deal against a house in Chicago in 1963. Again, if we wish to understand the Constitution of the United States, it is not enough, as our historians now tell us, merely to look up all the words in the dictionary and to read the interpretations written by Supreme Court justices. We must see the Constitution in its historical context: the conditions of life, the state of the arts and industries and transportation, the current ideas of the time—all of which helped to determine what words went into the Constitution and what those words meant to those who wrote them. After all, the words "United States of America" stood for quite a different-sized nation and a different culture in 1790 from what they stand for today. When it comes to very big subjects, the range of contexts to be examined—verbal, social, and historical—may become very large indeed.

In personal relations, furthermore, those who ignore psychological contexts often make the mistake of interpreting as insults remarks that are only intended in jest.

The Interaction of Words

All this is not to say, however, that the reader might just as well throw away his dictionary, simply because contexts are so important. Any word in a sentence—any sentence in a paragraph, any paragraph in a larger unit—whose meaning is revealed by its context, is itself part of the context of the rest of the text. To look up a word in a dictionary, therefore, frequently explains not only the word itself, but the rest of the sentence, paragraph, conversation, or essay in which it is found. All words within a given context interact upon one another.

Realizing, then, that a dictionary is a historical work, we should understand the dictionary thus: "The word *mother* has most frequently been used in the past among English-speaking people to indicate a female parent." From this we can safely infer, "If that is how it has been used, that is what it *probably* means in the sentence I am trying to understand." This is what we normally do, of course; after we look up a word in the dictionary, we reexamine the context to see if the definition fits. If the context reads, "Mother began to form in the bottle," one may have to look at the dictionary more carefully.

A dictionary definition, therefore, is an invaluable guide to interpretation. Words do not have a single "correct meaning"; they apply to *groups* of similar situations, which might be called *areas of meaning*. It is for defining these areas of meaning that a dictionary is useful. In each use of any word, we examine the particular context and the extensional events denoted (if possible) to discover the *point* intended within the area of meaning.

. . .

Review Questions

1. What is the American attitude toward the dictionary?
2. How do the editors of a dictionary arrive at definitions of words?
3. What is the proper task of the writer of a dictionary?
4. Explain the differences among verbal, social, and physical contexts.
5. Distinguish between extensional and intensional meanings. How are they related to the difference between denotation and connotation?
6. What is a "non-sense argument"?
7. Explain Hayakawa's statement, "No word ever has exactly the same meaning twice."
8. What may be the results of willfully ignoring contexts? In what fields is this practice common?
9. How do dictionary definitions and contexts work together to enable a person to determine the meaning of a word in a passage?

Discussion Questions

1. In the light of Hayakawa's description of how dictionaries are made, what do you think the American attitude toward dictionaries should be?
2. Why is quoting out of context a favorite device of the politician and the adman? Find some examples of out-of-context quotations (perhaps from movie advertisements), consult the context from which they were taken, and determine if the meaning of the complete text has been distorted.
3. Though fallacious, the idea that each word has one definite meaning has many believers. What problems could result from a person believing that such words as "intellectual," "conservative," and "democracy" never vary in meaning?
4. How do children who cannot read dictionaries learn the meaning of unfamiliar words? How much help are parental definitions? If they are attempted, how should they be phrased? How would they differ from dictionary definitions?

CLARENCE L. BARNHART

problems in
editing dictionaries

This paper deals with some of the editorial problems in the
production of commercial English-English dictionaries. Such
dictionaries out of necessity are of a popular nature because they
must depend for their existence upon widespread acceptance
by the general public. The publisher usually determines the audience for which he wishes to make a book. His determination
of the market he would like to reach depends upon the type of
his previous publications. His salesmen are probably trained to
reach only one type of market, and ability to sell in that particular market conditions to a great extent the type of dictionary to
be made. A publisher of schoolbooks will probably start with a
school dictionary; a publisher of trade books with a college dictionary.

It is the function of a popular dictionary to answer the questions that the user of the dictionary asks, and dictionaries on the
commercial market will be successful in proportion to the extent
to which they answer these questions of the buyer. This is the
basis on which the editor must determine the type of information to include. The editor's very first concern, therefore, must
be to determine the probable buyer of a particular book. The
amount of information that the editor can give is limited by the
price that the buyer will pay for a dictionary in a particular
market; his editorial judgment is always limited by the space
available. All of these factors must be considered in order for

Originally entitled, "Problems in Editing Commercial Monolingual Dictionaries," from *Problems in Lexicography* (eds. Fred Householder and
Sol Saporta), Publication Twenty-one of the Indiana University Research Center in Anthropology, Folklore, and Linguistics, pp. 161–181.
Reprinted by permission of the author.

the commercial editor to produce a single dictionary or a series of dictionaries that will enable him to stay in business.

To what extent, then, can the editor answer the questions of any buyer about any word of the English language? This depends to some extent upon the number of words in actual use in the literature (reading matter) of today and in the literature of the past that is widely read and studied today. For the popular dictionary tends to be a dictionary of the standard language and is concerned with slang and various specialized vocabularies only so far as they may appear in current newspapers, magazines, and books.

Some years ago Professor Robert L. Ramsay of the University of Missouri estimated the size of the working vocabulary of the English language—the words which any literate person may encounter and about which he may have questions dealing with spelling, pronunciation, meaning, idiomatic use, synonyms, levels of usage, and origin—to be around 250,000 active words.

The usual desk dictionary of educated people in the United States is a college dictionary containing 120,000 to 150,000 of these words. Unabridged dictionaries may contain as many as 500,000 words and one-volume or two-volume dictionaries may contain 200,000 or 250,000 words but they are priced so high that there is little bookstore market for them. The ordinary college dictionary will contain somewhere between 14,000,0000 and 17,000,000 characters. Since there are five-and-a-half characters to the average word, a college dictionary will contain some three million running words. If the editor attempted to include the complete active vocabulary, he would have to use 500,000 or more words simply to list the entries and the pronunciations. He would have only ten words to define the entry, provide illustrative sentences and phrases, give the etymology, and list synonyms and antonyms. Since there are approximately twice as many meanings as entries put in college dictionaries, this would reduce the amount of space for each definition to about four words a definition and leave only two words for illustrative phrases, etymologies, synonym studies, and so forth. This is obviously an impossible situation. The editors of all college dictionaries are forced, then, to make a selection of the terms which they put in their dictionaries.

Which 125,000–150,000 words should be entered and how should they be treated? This selection of material to be included depends upon the judgment of the editor as to the type of user of his book and the kind and level of information that the user will want. One important market for the college dictionary is the freshman composition market. In 1955 I circulated 108 questionnaires in 99 colleges in 27 states (5 eastern, 8 southern, and 14 western) reporting on the use of the dictionary by some 56,000 students. The teachers were asked to rate six types of information commonly given in college dictionaries according to their importance to the college freshman. Their replies indicate that the college freshman uses his dictionary most frequently for meaning and almost as frequently for spelling. Pronunciation is third with synonym studies and lists, usage notes, and etymologies far behind.

The selection of the 125,000–150,000 terms to be included depends to some extent upon the importance the editor assigns to the six types of information given. An editor of a college dictionary who emphasizes the importance of meaning may consider the omission of all or part of the meanings of such "easy" words as *good* or *bad* or *with*. An editor interested in spelling may give more irregular inflected forms. One interested in usage may omit spellings of irregular inflected forms and undefined run-on entries such as *absolutely* or *badness*. A college dictionary editor interested in pronunciation may give more variant pronunciations than one primarily interested in meaning. The selection of material to be included should depend upon the interests and needs of the buyer and not upon the specialized interest of the editor. For example, it is possibly an editorial mistake to include rare Scottisms as William Allen Neilson did in the last Webster's Unabridged, for they take up at least some of the space of the 70,000 compounds Tom Knott crossed out.

If the interest of the buyer is a primary consideration, certainly spelling would require major consideration, for spelling is one of the principal problems of the users of dictionaries and

one of the principal reasons for buying dictionaries. What are
the spelling difficulties that most people encounter? Where the
difficulty in spelling is in the middle or end of a root word it is
easy to verify the spelling in almost any dictionary. The distinction in spelling between *capital* and *Capitol* or between *principal* and *principle* is easy to find. Treatment of inflected forms
(*antagonize, antagonized, antagonizing; travel, traveled* or *travelled, traveling* or *travelling*) in which the inflected form is not
a simple root + a suffix is handled differently by different dictionaries. If the editor feels that the average buyer of the dictionary knows the rules for dropping *e* or doubling of the consonant
when *-ed* and *-ing* is added he will not list these inflected forms.

One of the principal spelling difficulties with derivative or
run-on entries is the recognition of the root form. Derivative
words in which the root form is clearly recognized (such as *absolutely* or *resolutely*) might well be run-ons unless there is a
meaning or pronunciation problem as there is for *absolutely*. Of
the four major college dictionaries on the market, one omits the
entry entirely, two others enter it as a run-on with pronunciation, and the fourth enters, pronounces, and defines it. *Resolutely* is not entered in one, is spelled out in full as a run-on after
resolute in two, and entered as a *-ly* run-on in the fourth. Those
derivative entries that have some change in the root (e.g., *arbitrarily, atomization, archaistic*) often throwing them out of alphabetical order or making it hard to recognize the root must
either be put in the alphabetical list in the proper place or
run-on. To do this, however, takes a certain amount of space
that cannot be used in defining some rare and difficult word. In
this conflict between the user of the dictionary for spelling and
the one who uses it for the meaning of hard words, the editor
must make a choice unless he has enough space to include both
types of information. His first problem, then, is to choose
whether he will give more importance to information about
spelling or about meaning. Since meaning difficulty outranks
all other uses of the dictionary in importance so far as college
freshmen are concerned, the editor usually compromises and
enters derivatives without meaning difficulty but with simple
spelling or pronunciation difficulty as run-ons instead of as

main entries. *Arbitrarily* is a main entry in one of the four college dictionaries and a run-on in the other three; *atomization* is omitted in two of the college dictionaries and given as a run-on in the other two; *archaistic* is run-on in two of the college dictionaries and defined in the other two. If you are making a dictionary for college freshmen or for secretaries, the dictionary that enters most forms in their proper alphabetical place would be most useful to the buyer.

Having made a fundamental decision whether to define all entries or to have run-ons, the editor is in a position to select the 125,000–150,000 entries to be included in his dictionary. Nearly all college dictionaries agree close to 90 per cent of the time upon the choice of words to be entered and differ largely in the number of abbreviations, geographical names and biographical names to be included. All include all types of entries but differ markedly in the treatment of the basic vocabulary, the inclusion of idioms, the fullness of the definitions of scientific and technical terms, the illustrative sentences, phrases, and quotations used, the type of etymology given, and so forth. In spite of the fact that the real difference of most dictionaries lies in the description of the words entered, there are a few important differences that each editor must face in the selection of entries.

The agreement among the editors of college dictionaries on a basic, common vocabulary of 100,000 terms is due to the fact that we have such a rich storehouse of material from which to choose. The history of English words and meanings is probably fuller than that in any other language. The commercial dictionary editor can turn to the big *Oxford English Dictionary,* to the ten-volume *Century Dictionary,* to the *Dictionary of American English,* and to the *Dictionary of Americanisms* for scholarly information. Quotations for each important sense are abundantly supplied in these dictionaries. When I was corresponding with the compiler of the Hungarian-English dictionary, Professor Ladislás Orszagh, he stated that they had nothing comparable to the OED on which to draw. He had to collect quotations in order to proceed with his book; there was no historical dictionary of the Hungarian language. All dictionary makers owe a great debt to the OED and they owe a similar debt to the big ten-volume

Century prepared by one of the great linguists of the nineteenth century, William Dwight Whitney, who produced a superb descriptive dictionary of the English language and was the first to give adequate treatment to scientific terminology.

Probably no proper survey of the thousands of pages in the OED and the *Century* (there are over 8,000 pages in three columns in this book alone) has ever been made. These mines of information can be read and studied again and again. On my first high-school dictionary a staff of ten editors spent over five years combing the OED. Out of this mass of material we selected the meanings that were to be included in our high-school dictionary. We were aided in this task with a semantic count which Dr. E. L. Thorndike had made of current standard literature that assigned meanings to some 5,000,000 words in running context. In this fashion, we could determine the order in which the meanings of words were used in the current English language in material ranging from children's books to the *Britannica* and through technical literature. This count was of enormous importance in verifying editorial judgment in collecting definitions. . . .

Commercial dictionary editing, however, that depends only upon scholarly dictionaries is out-of-date because the language recorded is out-of-date. The record of English from 1900 to the present should be sampled. In [the table] is a sample of the books in a long-time reading project of standard literature to remedy this lack of a modern record. In order to meet the needs of modern users of the college dictionary it is necessary to sample the reading of the public to which you address your book. If a word or meaning occurs in several different sources over a wide range of magazines and books during a considerable period of time, such a word or meaning may be worth considering for inclusion in a current, college dictionary. Obviously, we must get a wide enough sampling to help the editor decide which words and meanings are important enough to include in a college dictionary. In reading for this purpose, we read for words and meanings normally in an unabridged dictionary but not in current college dictionaries, as well as for new words and meanings making their way into the language. Our selection of new words and meanings depends upon the extent and accuracy of our sampling. Too large a sampling is expensive and serves no purpose if it duplicates information already existing in the OED, the *Old Century*, the *Dictionary of Americanisms*, and the *Dictionary of American English*. Our problem is to add to that material which has been compiled before us. With the commercial resources that we have at hand we need to sample newspapers, popular magazines, literary magazines, and technical magazines, and to keep at this sampling systematically over a period of years. This is expensive. Every quotation that reaches my files costs approximately 30¢. When one considers the vast amount of printed matter probably no sampling would be adequate with fewer than 50,000 quotations a year; 100,000 quotations would be a more adequate sampling. Perhaps reading of such scientific magazines as the *Scientific American, Science News Letter,* the *New Scientist,* and such newspapers as the *Wall Street Journal,* the *Manchester Guardian,* and the *New York Times,* and such general magazines as *Harper's,* the *Atlantic Monthly,* the *Saturday Review,* and the *Listener* will give a fairly good picture of the magazine and newspaper reading of educated people. Reading various annuals and yearbooks as well as a number of important current novels and books will give an adequate basis for the selection of new definitions and entries. In all reading it is important to sample both British and American usage. See [the table] for a partial sample of the standard literature that could be read to bring the record of standard English up-to-date.

Adequate sampling, then, is one of the editor's major considerations, and he can accomplish this with a continuing group of readers who are aware of what is already in the file. A balanced quotation file of perhaps half a million modern quotations that supplements the file of the *Oxford,* the *Century* and the *Dictionary of Americanisms* would be adequate to give authority to the selection of new material. . . .

To select 125,000–150,000 terms to include in a college dictionary means combing the standard scholarly sources such as the *Oxford, Century,* and the two American dictionaries, the using of the counts, and accumulating a modern quotation file which will supplement and amplify the information that has

TABLE

Code: essential *** desirable ** possible *

Author	Title	Date	Type	Nation
Edman, Irwin	Philosopher's Holiday **	1938	Essay	Amer.
Eliot, T. S.	For Lancelot Andrewes ***	1928	Essay	Amer.
	The Sacred Wood ***	1920	Essay	Amer.
Faulkner, Wm.	The Hamlet ***	1940	Novel	Amer.
	Sanctuary **	1931	Novel	Amer.
Fisher, Vardis	No Villain Need Be *	1936	Novel	Amer.
Fitzgerald, F. S.	Tender Is the Night **	1934	Novel	Amer.
	The Crack-up **	1945	Misc.	Amer.
Ford, Ford Madox	No More Parades ***	1925	Novel	Brit.
Forster, E. M.	Howard's End ***	1910	Novel	Brit.
	Abinger Harvest **	1936	Essay	Brit.
Frank, Waldo	City Block *	1922	Novel	Amer.
Galsworthy, J.	The Man of Property *	1906	Novel	Brit.
Garland, Hamlin	A Son of the Middle Border **	1917	Novel	Amer.
Gerould, Katherine F.	Conquistador **	1923	Novel	Amer.
Glasgow, Ellen	They Stooped to Folly	1929	Novel	Amer.
Greene, Graham	The Labyrinthine Ways **	1940	Novel	Brit.
	The Heart of the Matter ***	1948	Novel	Brit.
Hammett, Dashiell	The Maltese Falcon *	1930	Novel	Amer.
Hand, Learned	The Spirit of Liberty **	—	Essay	Amer.
Hemingway, Ernest	Green Hills of Africa **	1935	Essay	Amer.
	Death in the Afternoon **	1932	Essay	Amer.

been collected in the past. This work can only be done by a well-trained staff over a period of years.

However, an editor with this trained staff, a modern quotation file, and the backing of a publisher who seeks a particular market, must make numerous policy decisions involving a great many areas of linguistic knowledge. No single editor can have the necessary knowledge to formulate the policy in matters of pronunciation, etymology, definition, and levels of usage, but one way of acquiring trustworthy advice is to form an editorial advisory committee. The function of a committee is to supplement the experience, training, and information of the editor; it does not do the work of special editors or supervise or direct the work that is done. Such a committee should have members who represent various points of view, and more than one scholar should represent any particular field such as etymology, pronunciation, or usage. Curiously enough, specialists in one particular field often give very useful suggestions in nonrelated fields. A large committee, representing many points of view, is one of the most useful adjuncts to an editor in framing policies. Otherwise policies are very likely to be decided in the seeming commercial interest of the publisher or limited by the narrowness of the editor. Such a committee, however, cannot function by majority vote. To vote democratically about matters of information is not the way to settle an intellectual problem. Some one person, in this case, the editor, must have the power of final decision and this power of final decision should be made on the side of the agreed-upon knowledge of the experts. The function of a general reference book is to make available to the general public in understandable language the knowledge upon which scholars and specialists are agreed. It is the function of the editorial advisory committee to remind the editor of this agreed-upon knowledge. The editor must be able to evaluate his committee and to know when to take the advice of a particular scholar and when not to. The editorial advisory committee makes it possible for the editor to set policies which are in accordance with the advances in knowledge of the day.

What are some of the important policies that an editorial advisory committee, the editor, and his staff must consider? One of the most pressing of these and one that occupies a great deal of time and attention is pronunciation. Opinions on pronunciations are likely to vary violently according to the experience and background of the person who holds them. . . . Which of [the] different kinds of keys are suitable for a college dictionary? This central problem of a key must be faced; and it is more difficult when there is a series of dictionaries involved than when there is only one dictionary.

. . .

Another important problem the editorial committee must consider is the order of definitions. Should the historical order be followed, or should the dictionary be a descriptive dictionary of the current English language and start with the central or core meaning today? If we decide upon the historical method, how are we going to determine the dates of each meaning? Must we rely upon the OED and the *Dictionary of American English* or do we have additional information that we can turn to in our own files to verify dates? What attempt will be made to change the order of the definitions as dates in the OED and the *Dictionary of American English* are corrected by new information? If we have the central or core meaning as the basis of organization, how are we to determine the central or core meaning? Are there any semantic counts that would show what is commonest today? Would the frequency of the modern quotations give some clue?

Are the definitions to be written on the same level or is the editor to make some effort to determine what type of person will look up a particular word or meaning and then frame definitions in language suitable for the person looking them up?

What is to be done with scientific entries, particularly the names of plants and animals? Is the technical name to be given or is it to be excluded as useless and the space devoted to other more important matters? What is to be the differentiation in the treatment of words like *get, with,* and so forth, as over against a word like *aristocracy*? When are illustrative sentences to be used? To what degree are idioms to be covered? . . . Should illustrative sentences be made up, should they be from modern sources, or should they always be quotations of some author? If the latter is given, should chapter and verse be cited in a book for general reference? How much space should be devoted to illustrative sentences? College dictionaries devoted from 54 to 61 per cent of their space to definitions and from .7 to 1.3 per cent to illustrative sentences and phrases. Should more space be devoted to illustrative sentences and less to definitions?

How are various levels of usage to be labeled? Should the

spoken vocabulary be labeled *Colloq.*? Should the formal vocabulary be labeled *Literary*? How can the uniqueness of a spoken word and a formal written word be established? How should we distinguish between informal spoken and informal written? Or should the distinction be between *formal* and *informal*?

Should the current dialects of English be recorded and to what extent? Should we include only those dialectic words that occur in newspapers, magazines, and novels? To what extent should we include South African, Anglo-Indian, and Australian words? What words in different parts of the United States should be included? What about Briticisms? Is Briticism a good restrictive label or should we say "in England"? So also should we use "in India" instead of "Anglo-Indian"?

When is a word or meaning archaic and when is it obsolete? Is a word archaic when it is used only to give an old-fashioned flavor to writing? Can we define *obsolete* as a word that is not used at all? What happens if an obsolete word is revived, say, by Spenser, Scott, or Robert Graves, and becomes current for a while among literary people? Is it then an obsolete word or an archaic word? The same problem, incidentally, arises in dialect words. Of what value is the label *poetic*? Does a poetic language exist?

I have listed some of the policy problems of pronunciation, meaning, and levels of usage so that you may have some idea of the problems that could be submitted to an advisory committee. The process of submitting problems to the committee is illustrated by a questionnaire on derogatory words. Several questions are asked about a list of words which are often used to convey an unfriendly attitude toward or opinion of some person, class, or group of persons. The words included are:

Canuck	guinea
Chinaman	hunky
Chink	Jap
dago	kike
frog	limey
greaser	mammy

mick	spik
nigger	wop
polack	yid
Shylock	

The advisors are first asked to indicate their judgment on the present status of the words under one of three headings: "Always unfriendly, a 'fighting' word"; "Likely to be unfriendly"; or "Relatively Innocuous."

The second question concerns the exclusion of derogatory words ("Always unfriendly") and words which may be derogatory ("Likely to be unfriendly") from school dictionaries at different levels, i.e., whether they should be excluded from all school dictionaries, or whether they should be excluded only from those used up to the sixth grade, in junior high school, or in high school. Those advisors who suggest exclusion of any words at the school level are asked to check the words they would exclude from college-level dictionaries.

For terms which they think should be included, the advisors are asked to suggest a qualifying or restrictive label. A list of typical restrictions used in dictionaries is attached to the questionnaire for help in framing the labels:

A. *Linguistic Labels:*

1. Pop. (= popular usage)
2. Colloq.
3. Slang.
4. Loosely.
5. Local.
6. In the S United States.
7. Americanism, Southern.
8. Esp. in Southern States.

B. *Social Labels:*

1. Unfriendly use.
2. Used in an unfriendly way.
3. In discourteous use.
4. An objectionable usage.
5. Offensive.
6. An offensive usage.
7. Originally a corrupted form of speech; now generally coarse, always offensive.

8. Opprobrious use.
9. A derogatory term.
10. Derogatory.
11. Derogatory use.
12. Usually derogatory.
13. Used chiefly in contempt.
14. Often used familiarly, now chiefly contemptuous.
15. Hostile and contemptuous term.
16. A hostile and contemptuous term.
17. A shortened form often expressing contempt, hostility, etc.

18. A term of contempt or derision.
19. Vulgar term of prejudice and contempt.
20. Now a vulgar usage.
21. A vulgar, offensive term of contempt, as used by Negrophobes.
22. Vulgar term indicating a contemptuous or patronizing attitude.
23. Vulgar, offensive term of hostility and contempt, as used by anti-Semites.

When the questionnaires are returned, the opinions are collected, sifted, analyzed, collated, and often returned to the members of the committee to be reviewed a second time. Finally, a decision is made by the editor.

Once the editor and his committee have settled on the policies for the dictionary, the editor then has the problem of combing the vast amounts of information available to him, selecting it, arranging it, and preparing it for publication. Usually, an office staff prepares the copy for the dictionary in order that everything included may be adjusted to the space that we have and a proper balance between the various types of information presented may be maintained. This involves people who are highly skilled in the art of abstracting, careful and judicious in their judgments, and capable of writing good clear English. Even etymologies and pronunciations are best prepared by a staff.

Assuming that the staff has looked carefully through secondary sources and followed the policies of the editorial advisory committee as set by the editor, there is the problem of checking the accuracy of the facts given in the dictionary. No dictionary should be content to merely abstract secondary sources. There are a great many fields of knowledge. It is very hard to conceive of a dictionary for general use being prepared by a staff inside an office without any special checks of accuracy made by an outside staff. Nowhere is this principle of outside checking more important than in the handling of scientific material. The names of plants and animals, the terms in chemistry, physics, aeronautics, electronics, and so forth should be checked by at least one specialist in each field. Is one specialist enough? Is it better to have both a British and an American critic if we are to have a representative dictionary of the English language?

I have gone into some of the various editorial problems from the standpoint of a statement of policies, the work of the staff, and the work of the special editors. The work of all editors must be coordinated by the general editor and put into a book which the publisher promotes on the general market. The editor has combined the thinking of all of these people and balanced one interest against the other in order to furnish a book which will be acceptable to all the parties concerned, as well as to the general public. He is the interpreter of the linguist to the publisher, the publisher to the linguist, the definer or staff member to the etymologist in the conflicts for space. The editor has given from 54 to 61 per cent of space to definitions, .7 to 1.3 per cent to illustrative phrases, from 5 to 8.5 per cent to etymologies, from 2.1 to 4.4 per cent to synonym studies and lists, and around 28 per cent to entries, pronunciations, parts of speech, inflected forms, usage notes and other material.

I hope from these general observations and from the specific problems that I have listed that you will get at least some idea of the special editorial problems that the editor of a commercial dictionary has. Many of these problems are the same as those of the scholarly dictionary. For any dictionary—commercial or scholarly—is more valuable when it gives the agreed-upon knowledge of the experts, carefully labels opinions as such, and balances the types of information given to meet the needs of its public.

Review Questions

1. What practical matters must the editor of a commercial dictionary consider in order to produce a profitable dictionary or series of dictionaries?
2. Why does a college dictionary only contain about half of the 250,000 active words in the working vocabulary of the English language?
3. How many words are there altogether in the language (at least as reflected in an unabridged dictionary)?
4. How are the interests of the buyer of a college dictionary reflected in the amount of space the editor devotes to spelling, pronunciation, meaning, etymology, usage, and synonym lists?
5. Why are the *Oxford English Dictionary,* the *Century Dictionary,* the *Dictionary of American English,* and the *Dictionary of Americanisms* important to the editor of a college dictionary?
6. What are "semantic counts"?
7. Why do editors sample literature written since 1900? Why do the editors not sample literature written before 1900? What kinds of literature are sampled and why?
8. What is the composition and function of an editorial advisory committee?
9. What kinds of policy problems do the editor, his staff, and the editorial advisory committee face?
10. In the making of a dictionary, what steps occur after the general policies have been determined?

Discussion Questions

1. Barnhart observes that the success of a dictionary is determined by the extent to which it answers the public's questions. He further points out that the interest of the public is a primary consideration and that the book must be acceptable to that public. On the other hand, Barnhart states that the function of a general reference book is to inform the public about agreed-upon knowledge. Recent developments in language study have produced findings that many people do not accept: *Webster's Third,* for example, which stated and then applied many of the new ideas about language, was bitterly criticized by people who believed they represented the "general public." Can a dictionary editor reconcile such differences between the public and the linguists? Should he?

Is it possible to "reform" the thinking of the public about language matters?

2. Barnhart states, "In order to meet the needs of modern users of a college dictionary it is necessary to sample the reading of the public to which you address your book." If we assume that the buyers are college freshmen, what kinds of literature should be sampled? Barnhart offers a list of "standard literature" to be sampled and provides a code to describe their "desirability." Can you discern any pattern as to which sorts of books are essential, desirable, or possible?

3. To discover how college freshmen used their dictionaries, Barnhart polled their teachers. Do you think consulting the students themselves would have produced the same results? What do you and your classmates use your dictionaries for? Do you think student use of the synonym lists, for example, is more prevalent than Barnhart's survey indicates?

4. Does Barnhart's description of the problems of editing dictionaries support or qualify Hayakawa's assertion, "The writer of a dictionary is a historian, not a lawgiver"? Defend your answer.

5. To what extent are there different audiences of dictionary users? Would the needs of a grade-school student be filled by a college dictionary? In what specific ways do you suppose they would and would not? Is there a need for a variety of dictionaries with differing contents and emphases?

MORRIS BISHOP

so to speak

In the beginning was the Word, and the Word was with God, and the Word was God. Now in these latter days the Word is with Man, who doesn't know quite what to do with it.

Words are little creatures, crowding about us, eager for our command. Each word has a physical character, a look, and a personality, an ancestry, an expectation of life and death, a hope of posterity. Some words are beautiful, some ugly, some evil. The word "glory" shines; the common word for excrement smells. There are holy words, like the proper name of God, pronounced only once a year in the innermost chamber of Jerusalem's Temple. (Orthodox Jewish students write "G-d" in their English themes, out of respect or fear.) There are magic words, spells, to open gates and safes, summon spirits, put an end to the world. What are magic spells but magic spellings? Words sing to us, frighten us, impel us to self-immolation and murder. They belong to us; they couple at our order, to make what have well been called the aureate words of poets and the inkhorn words of pedants. We can keep dear words alive, or at our caprice we can kill them—though some escape and prosper in our despite.

Thought makes the word; also the word makes thought. Some psychologists allege that explicit thought does not exist without verbalization. Thought, they say, emerges from our silent secret speech, from the tiny quivers of the speech organs, from the interior monologue we all carry on endlessly. Let us pause a moment and reflect on our thought; we reflect, in words,

Morris Bishop, "So to Speak," *Horizon*, Summer, 1969, and "Good Usage, Bad Usage and Usage," *The American Heritage Dictionary of the English Language*, © copyright 1969, American Heritage Publishing Co., Inc. Reprinted by permission.

on a surge of hurrying words. This hidden turmoil of words is called endophasic speech.

Much of our formless secret thought is, to be sure, idiotic. Before we permit endophasic speech to emerge as spoken words, we must arrange it in patterns of sense and form, accessible to other people. These patterns, this ordered behavior of words, are usage. And usage is the ruler, the governor, the judge of language. Horace said it in his *Ars Poetica: "usus, / Quem penes arbitrium / est, et jus, et norma loquendi."* Or, in the old translation of the passage:

> "Yes, words long faded may again revive;
> And words may fade now blooming and alive,
> If usage wills it so, to whom belongs
> The rule and law, the government of tongues."

Deferring to the rule and law of usage, we may yet order words well or ill, thus creating Good Usage and Bad Usage.

Now the trouble begins. Whose usage is good, whose bad? Is not my usage good for me? Do you have authority over my usage? Does anyone have authority? And if authority exists, is it helpful or hurtful to usage?

We demand freedom for our own usage, authority for others. And we are not above seeking comfort and support from authority. One of our commonest phrases is "look it up in the dictionary." (Not any particular dictionary; just "the dictionary.") Every law court has its big dictionary; the law settles cases, awards millions, rates crimes and misdemeanors, by quoting the definitions of some poor attic lexicographer, "a harmless drudge," as defined by the lexicographer Samuel Johnson. We acclaim freedom, but we love the word "freedom" more than the fact. Most people most of the time would rather be secure than free; they cry for law and order. We know the menaces of freedom. In the matter of usage we know how language may corrupt thought; we know the power of bloody words.

Who, then, shall wield authority? The king, perhaps? The phrase "the king's English" came in, we are told, with Henry VIII, who ruled from 1509 to 1547. He was a poet and a

man of letters when he had the time. The king's English remained standard, even under George I, who could not speak
English. Recent kings and queens of England have not been
noteworthy for an exemplary style. The only royal phrasing that
comes to mind is Edward VIII's "At long last . . . the woman I
love." In America the President's English has never ruled the
citizenry. One notorious presidential venture into lexicography
was Harding's approbation of "normalcy." But he said that he
had looked it up in the dictionary.

The king's English was naturally identified with the spoken
style of gentlemen and ladies of the English court. Similarly in
France the grammarian Vaugelas in 1647 defined good usage as
the speech habits of the sounder members of the court, in conformity with the practice in writing of the sounder contemporary authors. Good usage, then, would represent the practice
of an elite, of breeding, station, and intellect. This contention
has been taken as an axiom until very recent times.

The idea of an elite with authority over language clearly
needed delimitation. In France Cardinal Richelieu, who piqued
himself on his style in verse and prose, authorized in 1635 the
formation of an *Académie française,* composed of writers, book-
ish nobles and magistrates, and amateurs of letters. The *Académie,* the Supreme Court of the French literary world, set itself
the task of preparing a dictionary. It has been working at its
dictionary, off and on, for more than three hundred years.

Lacking an academy, Englishmen appealed to the usage of
good writers to preserve, or fix, general usage. Thence more
trouble. Who are the good writers? Shakespeare, no doubt. But
Shakespeare, with his wild and carefree coinages, his cheery disregard for grammatical agreements, demands our admiration,
not our imitation. The King James Bible? It is inspired, yea
verily, but thou wouldst not follow inspired usage, wouldst
thou? In Latin, a fossilized tongue, the rule is simple: if a locution is in Cicero, it is correct. In English we have no Cicero. The
only writers whom all critics would accept as "best" have been
dead for such a long time that their works are uncertain models
for the living language of our times.

We should, perhaps, make the authority of the best writers

defer to that of professional judges of language, the critics and grammarians. Quintilian, a rhetorician of the first century A.D., appealed to the consensus of the *eruditi*. Ben Jonson said: "Custom is the most certain mistress of language, as the public stamp makes the current money. . . . That I call custom of speech, which is the consent of the learned; as custom of life, which is the consent of the good." In the seventeenth and eighteenth centuries the English grammarians appeared, devoting themselves to "refining, ascertaining, and fixing" the language. They were scholars; aware of linguistic history, they conceived of English usage as a development from primitive barbarism to the harmonious perfection of their own times. They regarded the past as a preparation, the present as a glorious achievement, the future as a threatening decadence. Jonathan Swift was terrified of the coming corruption and invoked governmental authority to fix the language; else, he feared, within two centuries the literary works of his time, including his own, would be unreadable and unread.

The grammarians justified their judgments by appealing not only to history but to reason. They strengthened the concepts Good and Bad to become Right and Wrong. They regarded language as something existing mysteriously apart from man, governed by a universal grammar waiting to be discovered by intrepid scholars. No doubt they were sympathetically fascinated by the story Herodotus tells of the king who isolated two small children with a deaf-and-dumb shepherd to find out what language they would learn to speak (it was Phrygian) thus to identify the original speech of mankind. Rightness was to be achieved by logical analysis of form and meaning, with much use of analogy. Popular usage was scouted, as of its nature corrupt. The grammarians made great play with purity and impurity. Pure English lived in perpetual danger of defloration by the impure. But purity, alas, has now been undone; the very word is uttered with a smile. The Society for Pure English, after a long and brilliant career, has collapsed.

The grammarians did much useful work in rationalizing the language. However, their precepts were often overlogical or based on faulty logic. From them derive many of the distinctions that have ever since tortured scholars young and old. The "shall-will," "should-would" rules are said to be an invention of the seventeenth-century mathematician John Wallis.

Samuel Johnson, whose epoch-making *Dictionary of the English Language* appeared in 1755, shared many of the convictions of the grammarians. He was concerned to fix the language against lowering corruption, for, he said in his preface, "Tongues, like governments, have a natural tendency to degeneration; we have long preserved our constitution, let us make some struggle for our language." He foresaw linguistic calamity. "The tropes of poetry will make hourly encroachments, and the metaphorical will become the current sense: pronunciation will be varied by levity or ignorance, and the pen must at length comply with the tongue; illiterate writers will at one time or other, by publick infatuation, rise into renown, who, not knowing the original import of words, will use them with colloquial licentiousness, confound distinction, and forget propriety." Those who know better must fight on in the hopeless war; "we retard what we cannot repel, we palliate what we cannot cure."

One will have noticed, amid the funeral music of Dr. Johnson's preface, the startling phrase: "the pen must at length comply with the tongue." Though the Doctor deplored the fact, he recognized that speech, not writers, not grammatical logic, must in the end command usage. This idea took shape and found expression in the work of Noah Webster (1758–1843).

Webster was a Connecticut farm boy with a Yale education in a day when colleges did not teach English in course. His series of spelling books and dictionaries actually went far toward fixing the American language. His standard of correctness, however, was the usage of the enlightened members of each community, not that of the "polite part" of city society, which, he believed, consisted largely of coxcombs. "General custom must be the rule of speaking," he said; and "it is always better to be *vulgarly* right than *politely* wrong." He was astonishingly liberal, even radical, in his acceptance of popular usage, giving his approval to "it is me," "who she is married to," and "them horses."

Thus common usage began to assume dominance at the expense of formal grammar. The scholarly Irish archbishop Richard C. Trench in 1857 defined a dictionary as an inventory of the language, a historical monument. "It is no task of the maker of it to select the *good* words of a language. . . . He is an historian of it, not a critic."

This view of language and its use prevailed in the twentieth century. A school of linguistic scientists constituted itself, and in time it found a place on most college faculties, ousting the old-fashioned philologists of the English and foreign language departments. The descriptive, or structural, linguists applied the procedures of science to language, which they would no more criticize than a physicist would criticize an atom or an entomologist a cockroach.

These are the five principles of structural, or descriptive, linguistics: (1) language changes constantly; (2) change is normal; (3) spoken language is *the* language; (4) correctness rests upon usage; (5) all usage is relative.* Speech is no miracle; it is merely a set of noises you make with your face. The written word came late in time and is insignificant in comparison with the spoken language. The written language is just a set of marks you make with your fist. In language there is no such thing as good and bad, better or worse. Anything is "correct" that is acceptable in a given social group. Nothing is "incorrect," for an error becomes correct by the mere fact of its use. Lexicography, then, must be merely descriptive, not prescriptive.

The underlying assumption is that language, by its very nature, is a growing, evolving thing; and that whereas it may be cultivated, one cannot fix it without killing it. Like any other fundamental social activity, it will undergo vicissitudes that to the older generation often seem regrettable. And indeed, some changes in language turn out to be empty fads that are soon forgotten, like some changes in women's fashions. Others are found to be enduringly useful, so that a generation later it becomes hard to imagine how we got along without them.

The lesson that the linguists draw, or that others draw from

* See "Who is Behind the Assault on English," by Lincoln Barnett, July, 1963.

their practice, is that any comprehensible locution is OK, that any spelling in general use is alrite. Only silly purists could object to a nite-club, for a nite-club is more like a nite-club than a night club could be. Anyway, a nite-club does not cater to purists.

A linguists' lexicon refrains, then, from value judgments, from imposed pronunciations and spellings. It classifies usages as standard or substandard, not right or wrong. At most it recommends, it does not command. And the looker-up is likely to turn away uncounseled and uncomforted.

The makers of the AMERICAN HERITAGE *Dictionary,* profiting much by the linguists' researches, have not adopted their doctrines entire. They accept usage as the authority for correctness, but they believe that good usage may be distinguished from bad usage. They maintain that those best fitted to make such distinctions are, as Noah Webster said, the enlightened members of the community, not the scholarly theoreticians, not the instinctive verbalizers of the unlettered mass. The best authorities are those practicing writers who have demonstrated their sensitivity to the language and their power to wield it effectively and beautifully.

The editors therefore constituted a Usage Panel made up of novelists, essayists, poets, journalists, writers on science and sports, public officials, professors. The members of the panel have in common only a recognized ability to write good English. They are not, with one exception, grammarians; they represent roughly Quintilian's consensus of the well-informed, Vaugelas's sounder members of the courtly world, T. R. Lounsbury's "the intellectually good."

The usage panelists accepted their task and turned to it with gusto. They revealed, often with passion, their likes and dislikes, their principles and also their whims and crotchets.

On specific questions put to them they disagreed more than they agreed. In only one case did they register 100 per cent—in disfavor of "simultaneous" as an adverb ("the referendum was conducted simultaneous with the election"). Other scores approached unanimity, as in the following:

Expression	Approved by	Dis- approved by
"ain't I?" in writing		99%
"between you and I" in writing		99%
"dropout" used as a noun	97%	
"thusly"		97%
"debut" as a verb ("the company will debut its new models")		97%
"slow" as an adverb ("drive slow")	96%	
"medias" as a plural (instead of "media")		95%
"their own" referring to the singular ("nobody thinks the criticism applies to their own work")		95%
"but what" ("there is no doubt but what he will try")		95%
"myself" instead of "me" in compound objects, in writing ("he invited Mary and myself to dinner")		95%
"anxious" in the sense of "eager"	94%	
"type" for "type of" ("that type shrub")		94%
"rather unique"; "most unique"		94%

On the whole, the panelists tend toward conservatism, while avoiding overniceness, prissiness. ("Was graduated," says John Bainbridge, is used "by all who write with a quill pen.") Sixty-one per cent of them feel bad about the expression "I feel badly" when they see it in writing; only 45 per cent object when they hear it in speech. Whereas "most unique" was condemned by 94 per cent, "more perfect" was condoned by 65 per cent. More than most people, the panelists know the history of words and have tested the value of idioms. More than most, they have grown tired of overused vogue-words. They dislike "senior citizen" ("I'd as soon use 'underprivileged' for 'poor'—or any other social science Choctaw"—Berton Roueché). "Enthuse" finds little favor; "By God, let's hold the line on this one!" cries Dwight Macdonald. " 'Finalize,' " says Isaac Asimov, "is nothing more than bureaucratic illiteracy." Critics of the critics might rejoin that we have no exact synonyms for "enthuse" and "finalize," that the words are full of life and power.

The panelists are not opposed to all neologisms; they distinguish between the useless, pretentious coinage, such as "commentate," and the creative effort to find a word for an unnamed concept or thing. Lewis Mumford says: "My principle of judgment is to refuse a variant (often vague) when the existing word gives the same meaning . . . I hold that 'meticulous,' by its very sound, indicates an exact, indeed fussy, care that 'careful' does not." And Gilbert Highet: "I have great admiration for the American genius for creating short vivid words (often disyllabic) to express complex ideas: e.g., a collision between a vehicle and another object which is not direct but lateral or oblique, 'sideswipe.' So recently economists talk of the 'takeoff point' in a developing economy."

In general the jurymen are more cordial toward popular, low-level coinages than toward the pomposities of professional jargons. John K. Sherman welcomes "rambunctious" and "rile" as "tangy Americanisms." No one, however, likes business English. The panelists betray a particular spite against advertisese and against Madison Avenue, once a very respectable street, now an avenue of ill fame. Does this spite reveal a professional jealousy? The advertisers are, after all, fecund creators languagewise.

The panelists are more attentive to the practice of their social group than to grammatical logic. They are antipedantic, scornful of the grammarians' effort to ban "it's me." Some (as Theodore C. Sorenson) would throw away the silly rule that the relative "that" must introduce restrictive clauses, "which" nonrestrictive. Dwight Macdonald would drop "whom" altogether, as a needless refinement. John Ciardi, accepting "alternative" as a term applied to more than two choices: "Language abhors a vacuum and English leaves one at this point." Ninety-one per cent of the panelists accept the use of "internecine" to mean "pertaining to civil war or to a struggle within a family, group, organization, nation, or the like." They know, of course, that the Latin *internecinus* just means mutually deadly, but they do not seem to care.

The group is (or are, if you prefer) merciless toward flagrant common errors. Isaac Asimov regards as nauseous those who say "nauseous" when they mean "nauseated." Of "flaunt" for "flout" Walter W. ("Red") Smith writes: "He who flouts grammar flaunts his ignorance. Clout the lout with a knout." Robert Saudek on the use of "bimonthly" in the sense of "semimonthly" says: "No more than I would allow 'double' to mean 'half.'" And summing up, Alistair Cooke well says: "An accumulation of tiny accuracies gives muscle; an accumulation of tiny inaccuracies produces fat."

The panelists have given us the enlightened judgments on usage of a cultivated elite. Their choices represent their own long efforts for precision, reasonableness, and beauty in manipulating English. They are suspicious of innovation. They would presumably reject as barbarisms such useful words as "tenderize," "hospitalize," "roadability." The word "panelist" itself is a new creation that might be called a barbarism. Even the learned scholars are not above making words at need. "Advisee" is standard on our campuses, "tutee" at Harvard.

Our committeemen do not venture beyond their assigned tasks in order to explore the psychology of speech, the mysteries of language. They assume that usage should be clear and cogent, that a brief exact statement is superior to blurry repetitiousness. They are not concerned that most of our speech and much of our writing is time-killing, social noise, "random clucking" that, according to the animal behaviorists, merely reassures the flock of our continuing life and well-being. Even a business letter is likely to be more affective than rational. Should a dun consist merely of the message: "Pay by June 17, or else—"? Indeed no; it should contain a paragraph of apology, a paragraph of summons to pay, and a paragraph of threats ending in expressions of esteem. The recipient expects, and is entitled to, a certain amount of random clucking.

Again, the panelists do not deal with the rhythmical elements of usage. In our casual speech, as in our writing, we make constant choices for euphony, not for significance. In the army we used to feel a subtle dissatisfaction with "Pass the beans" (— ˘ —; a thumping amphimacer). We therefore said commonly: "Pass the goddamn beans" (— ˘ ˘ ˘ —; a paeon primus plus a long). No derogation of the beans was intended; on the contrary, the sentence was merely a polite formula, rhythmically determined.

Nor, finally, do the panelists examine the moral element in usage. Uttering wicked words promotes wickedness; dwelling with pure words makes for purity. Religious ritual uplifts the spirit by the quality of the language; radio commercials degrade. "To use the word gentleman correctly, be one," said Ambrose Bierce. But such themes for reflection lie beyond the scope of the panel's inquiries.

Within their field, the determination of good current usage, the counselors found no absolute standard of rightness. Though naturally believing in their own superiority, they assume no authority. Nor do they accept the authority of others. They bow to no book, least of all to a dictionary. They seem to conclude, without explicit statement, that usage is our own affair. Let that be our conclusion. The duty of determination falls upon us all. By our choices we make usage, good or bad. Let us then try to make good choices, and guard and praise our lovely language and try to be worthy of her.

Review Questions

1. How is usage related to endophasic speech?
2. Who did Vaugelas and Richelieu believe should have authority over language matters?
3. What attitude toward language prevailed in seventeenth- and eighteenth-century England?
4. What is the essential difference between Samuel Johnson's attitude toward language and that of Noah Webster?
5. What are the five principles of structural, or descriptive, linguistics?
6. Why does Bishop believe that a person who consults a linguist's lexicon will turn away "uncounseled and uncomforted"?
7. Whom did the editors of the *American Heritage Dictionary* select to serve on their usage panel? How does the composition of this panel differ from that of the *Académie française*?
8. What is the panel's attitude toward neologisms, business English, and grammatical logic?
9. What linguistic matters were not explored by the usage panel?

Discussion Questions

1. How may language corrupt thought? How may authority create an atmosphere of repression and stifle creativity? How convincing is Bishop's argument for the necessity of authority in language matters?
2. What similarities are there between the usage panel and the *Académie française*? between the attitudes of the editors of the *American Heritage Dictionary* and those of Jonathan Swift and Samuel Johnson? Are the similarities or differences more significant?
3. How fair is Bishop's description of the beliefs of descriptive linguists? How do the short, choppy sentences describing the linguists' beliefs indicate Bishop's attitudes to their approach? Would linguists, who by Bishop's admission consider the appropriateness of usage, agree with his comments about what is "OK" or "alrite"? Would they even endorse his use of these expressions in an essay written for the readers of *Horizon*?
4. Bishop lists examples of the kinds of usage questions the usage panel considered. Look up some of the sample expressions in a recent college dictionary, preferably *Webster's Seventh*, a diction-

ary noted for its linguistic approach. Are the dictionaries in accord about the status of the expressions? How is this matter of consistency relevant to the idea of having a usage panel?

5. Examine carefully the process by which Bishop assumes the existence of what he calls "Bad Usage." How convincing is his demonstration?

WILSON FOLLETT

sabotage in Springfield

Of dictionaries, as of newspapers, it might be said that the
bad ones are too bad to exist, the good ones too good not to be
better. No dictionary of a living language is perfect or ever can
be, if only because the time required for compilation, editing,
and issuance is so great that shadows of obsolescence are falling
on parts of any such work before it ever gets into the hands of a
user. Preparation of *Webster's Third New International Dictionary of the English Language* began intensively in the Springfield
establishment of G. & C. Merriam Company in 1936, but the
century was nine months into its seventh decade before any outsider could have his first look at what had been accomplished.
His first look is, of course, incompetent to acquaint him with
the merits of the new work; these no one can fully discover without months or years of everyday use. On the other hand, it costs
only minutes to find out that what will rank as the great event
of American linguistic history in this decade, and perhaps in
this quarter century, is in many crucial particulars a very great
calamity.

Why should the probable and possible superiorities of the
Third New International be so difficult to assess, the shortcomings so easy? Because the superiorities are special, departmen-
tal, and recondite, the shortcomings general and within the
common grasp. The new dictionary comes to us with a claim of
100,000 new words or new definitions. These run almost over-
whelmingly to scientific and technological terms or meanings
that have come into existence since 1934, and especially to
words classified as ISV (belonging to the international scientific
vocabulary). No one person can possibly use or even compre-
hend all of them; the coverage in this domain, certainly impres-

sive to the nonspecialist, may or may not command the admiration of specialists. It is said that historians of the graphic arts
and of architecture were displeased with the 1934 Webster, both
for its omissions and for some definitions of what it included in
their fields. Its 1961 successor may have disarmed their reserva-
tions; only they can pronounce.

But all of us may without brashness form summary judgments about the treatment of what belongs to all of us—the
standard, staple, traditional language of general reading and
speaking, the ordinary vocabulary and idioms of novelist, essay-
ist, letter writer, reporter, editorial writer, teacher, student, ad-
vertiser; in short, fundamental English. And it is precisely in
this province that Webster III has thrust upon us a dismaying
assortment of the questionable, the perverse, the unworthy, and
the downright outrageous.

Furthermore, what was left out is as legitimate a grievance
to the ordinary reader as anything that has been put in. Think—
if you can—of an unabridged dictionary from which you cannot
learn who Mark Twain was (though **mark twain** is entered as a
leadsman's cry), or what were the names of the apostles, or that
the Virgin was Mary the mother of Jesus of Nazareth, or what
and where the District of Columbia is!

The disappointment and the shock are intensified, of course,
because of the unchallenged position earned by the really unabridged immediate predecessor of this strange work. *Webster's
New International Dictionary*, Second Edition (1934), consum-
mated under the editorship of William Allan Neilson, at once
became the most important reference book in the world to American writers, editors, teachers, students, and general readers—
everyone to whom American English was a matter of serious interest. What better could the next revision do than extend the
Second Edition in the direction of itself, bring it up to date, and
correct its scattering of oversights and errata?

The 1934 dictionary had been, heaven knows, no citadel of
conservatism, no last bastion of puristical bigotry. But it had
made shrewd reports on the status of individual words; it had
taken its clear, beautifully written definitions from fit uses of an
enormous vocabulary by judicious users; it had provided accu-

rate, impartial accounts of the endless guerrilla war between grammarian and antigrammarian and so given every consultant the means to work out his own decisions. Who could wish the forthcoming revision any better fortune than a comparable success in applying the same standards to whatever new matter the new age imposed?

Instead, we have seen a century and a third of illustrious history largely jettisoned; we have seen a novel dictionary formula improvised, in great part out of snap judgments and the sort of theoretical improvement that in practice impairs; and we have seen the gates propped wide open in enthusiastic hospitality to miscellaneous confusions and corruptions. In fine, the anxiously awaited work that was to have crowned cisatlantic linguistic scholarship with a particular glory turns out to be a scandal and a disaster. Worse yet, it plumes itself on its faults and parades assiduously cultivated sins as virtues without precedent.

Examination cannot proceed far without revealing that Webster III, behind its front of passionless objectivity, is in truth a fighting document. And the enemy it is out to destroy is every obstinate vestige of linguistic punctilio, every surviving influence that makes for the upholding of standards, every criterion for distinguishing between better usages and worse. In other words, it has gone over bodily to the school that construes traditions as enslaving, the rudimentary principles of syntax as crippling, and taste as irrelevant. This revolution leaves it in the anomalous position of loudly glorifying its own ancestry— which is indeed glorious—while tacitly sabotaging the principles and ideals that brought the preceding Merriam-Webster to its unchallengeable preeminence. The Third New International is at once a resounding tribute of lip service to the Second and a wholesale repudiation of it—a sweeping act of apology, contrition, and reform.

The right-about-face is, of course, particularly evident in the vocabulary approved. Within a few days of publication the new dictionary was inevitably notorious for its unreserved acceptance as standard of *wise up, get hep* (it uses the second as a definition of the first), *ants in one's pants*, *one for the book, hugeous, nixie, passel, hepped up* (with *hepcat* and *hepster*), *anyplace, someplace,* and so forth. These and a swarm of their kind it admits to full canonical standing by the suppression of such qualifying status labels as *colloquial, slang, cant, facetious,* and *substandard.* The classification *colloquial* it abolishes outright: "it is impossible to know whether a word out of context is colloquial or not." Of *slang* it makes a chary occasional use despite a similar reservation: "No word is invariably slang, and many standard words can be given slang connotations or used so inappropriately as to become slang." *Cornball* is ranked as slang, *corny* is not.

The overall effect signifies a large-scale abrogation of one major responsibility of the lexicographer. He renounces it on the curious ground that helpful discriminations are so far beyond his professional competence that he is obliged to leave them to those who, professing no competence at all, have vainly turned to him for guidance. If some George Ade of the future, aspiring to execute a fable in slang, were to test his attempt by the status labels in Webster III, he would quickly discover with chagrin that he had expressed himself almost without exception in officially applauded English. With but slight exaggeration we can say that if an expression can be shown to have been used in print by some jaded reporter, some candidate for office or his speech writer, some potboiling minor novelist, it is well enough credentialed for the full blessing of the new lexicography.

This extreme tolerance of crude neologisms and of shabby diction generally, however, is but one comparatively trifling aspect of the campaign against punctilio. We begin to sound its deeper implications when we plunge into the definitions and the copious examples that illustrate and support them. Under the distributive pronoun *each* we find, side by side: "(each of them is to pay his own fine) (each of them are to pay their own fine)." Where could anyone look for a neater, more succinct way to outlaw the dusty dogma that a pronoun should agree in number with its antecedent? Here is the same maneuver again under another distributive, *everybody:* "usu. referred to by the third person singular (everybody is bringing his own lunch) but sometimes by a plural personal pronoun (everybody had made up their minds)." Or try *whom* and *whomever:* "(a . . . recruit whom he hoped would prove to be a crack salesman) (people . . . whom you never thought would sympathize) . . . (I go out to talk to whomever it is) . . . (he attacked whomever disagrees with him)." It is, then, all right to put the subject of a finite verb in the accusative case—"esp. after a preposition or a verb of which it might mistakenly be considered the object."

Shall we look into what our dictionary does with a handful of the more common solecisms, such as a publisher might introduce into a cooked-up test for would-be copy editors? Begin with *center around* (or *about*). It seems obvious that expressions derived from Euclidean geometry should make Euclidean sense. A center is a point; it is what things are around, not what is around them; they center *in* or *on* or *at* the point. The Second Edition defined the Great White Way as "That part of Broadway . . . centering about Times Square"—patently an oversight. Is it the same oversight that produces, in the Third: **"heresy . . . 3:** a group or school of thought centering around a particular heresy"? We look up *center* itself, and, lo: "(a story to tell, centered around the political development of a great state) . . . (more scholarship than usual was centered around the main problems)," followed by several equivalent specimens.

Here is *due to.* First we come on irreproachable definitions, irreproachably illustrated, of *due* noun and *due* adjective, and we think we are out of the woods. Alas, they are followed by the manufacture of a composite preposition, *due to,* got up solely to extenuate such abominations as "the event was canceled due to inclement weather." An adjective can modify a verb, then. And here is a glance at that peculiarly incriminating redundancy of the slipshod writer, *equally as:* "equally opposed to Communism as to Fascism." The intolerable *hardly than* or *scarcely than* construction is in full favor: "hardly had the birds dropped than she jumped into the water and retrieved them." The sequence *different than* has the double approbation of editorial use and a citation: conjunctive *unlike* means "in a manner that is different than," and a passage under *different* reads "vastly different in size than it was twenty-five years ago." Adjectival *unlike* and conjunctive *unlike* both get illustrations that implicitly commend the unanchored and grammarless modifier: "so many fine men were outside the charmed circle that, unlike most colleges, there was no disgrace in not being a club man"; "unlike in the gasoline engine, fuel does not enter the cylinder with air on the intake stroke."

This small scattering should not end without some notice of that darling of the advanced libertarians, *like* as a conjunction, first in the meaning of *as,* secondly (and more horribly) in that of *as if.* Now, it is well known to the linguistic historian that *like* was so used for a long time before and after Langland. But it is as well known that the language rather completely sloughed off this usage; that it has long been no more than a regional colloquialism, a rarely seen aberration among competent writers, or an artificially cultivated irritant among defiant ones. The *Saturday Evening Post,* in which *like* for *as* is probably more frequent than in any other painstakingly edited magazine, has seldom if ever printed that construction except in reproducing the speech or tracing the thoughts of characters to whom it might be considered natural. The arguments for *like* have been merely defensive and permissive. Not for centuries has there been any real pressure of authority on a writer to use *like* as a conjunction—until our Third New International Dictionary decided to exert its leverage.

How it is exerted will appear in the following: "(impromptu programs where they ask questions much like I do on the air) . . . (looks like they can raise better tobacco) (looks like he will get the job) (wore his clothes like he was . . . afraid of getting dirt on them) (was like he'd come back from a long trip) (acted like she felt sick) . . . (sounded like the motor had stopped) . . . (the violin now sounds like an old masterpiece should) (did it like he told me to) . . . (wanted a doll like she saw in the store window) . . . (anomalies like just had occurred)."

By the processes represented in the foregoing and countless others for which there is no room here, the latest Webster whittles away at one after another of the traditionary controls until there is little or nothing left of them. The controls, to be sure, have often enough been overvalued and overdone by pedants and purists, by martinets and bigots; but more often, and much more importantly, they have worked as aids toward dignified, workmanlike, and cogent uses of the wonderful language that is our inheritance. To erode and undermine them is to convert the language into a confusion of unchanneled, incalculable williwaws, a capricious wind blowing whithersoever it listeth. And that, if we are to judge by the total effect of the pages under scrutiny—2720 of them and nearly 8000 columns of vocabulary, all compact in Times roman—is exactly what is wanted by the patient and dedicated saboteurs in Springfield. They, if they keep their ears to the ground, will hear many echoes of the despairing cry already wrung from one editorial assistant on a distinguished magazine that still puts its faith in standards: "Why have a Dictionary at all if anything goes?"

The definitions are reinforced, it will have been conveyed, with copious citations from printed sources. These citations occupy a great fraction of the total space. They largely account for the reduction in the number of entries (from 600,000 to 450,000) and for the elimination of the Gazetteer, the Biographical Dictionary, and the condensed key to pronunciation and symbols that ran across the bottoms of facing pages—all very material deprivations. Some 14,000 authors, we are told, are represented in the illustrative quotations—"mostly from the mid-twentieth century."

Can some thousands of authors truly worth space in a dictionary ever be found in any one brief period? Such a concentration can hardly fail to be, for the purposes of a dictionary, egregiously overweighted with the contemporary and the transient. Any very short period, such as a generation, is a period of transition in the history of English, and any great mass of examples drawn primarily from it will be disproportionately focused on transitional and ephemeral elements. To say that recording English *as we find it today* is precisely the purpose of a new dictionary is not much of a retort. For the bulk of the language that we use has come down to us with but minor, glacially slow changes from time out of mind, and a worthy record of it must stand on a much broader base than the fashions of yesterday.

It is, then, a mercy that among the thousands of scraps from recent authors, many of them still producing, we can also find hundreds from Shakespeare, the English Bible, Fielding, Dickens, Hawthorne, Melville, Henry James, Mark Twain, and so on. But the great preponderance of latter-day prose, little of it worth repeating and a good deal of it hardly worth printing in the first place, is likely to curtail by years the useful life of the Third New International.

So much is by the way. When we come to the definitions proper we face something new, startling, and formidable in lexicography. The definitions, all of them conformed to a predetermined rhetorical pattern, may be products of a theory—Gestaltist, perhaps?—of how the receiving mind works. The pattern, in the editor's general preface, is described as follows: "The primary objective of precise, sharp defining has been met through development of a new dictionary style based upon completely analytical one-phrase definitions throughout the book. Since the headword in a definition is intended to be modified only by structural elements restrictive in some degree and essential to each other, the use of commas either to separate or to group has been severely limited, chiefly to elements in apposition or in series. The new defining pattern does not provide for a predication which conveys further expository comment."

This doctrine of the strictly unitary definition is of course formulated and applied in the interest of a logical integrity and a simplification never before consistently attained by lexical definitions. What it produces, when applied with the rigor here insisted on, is in the first place some of the oddest prose ever concocted by pundits. A typical specimen, from the definition of the simplest possible term: **"rabbit punch . . . :** a short chopping blow delivered to the back of the neck or the base of the skull with the edge of the hand opposite the thumb that is illegal in boxing." When the idea, being not quite so simple, requires the one-phrase statement of several components, the definition usually turns out to be a great unmanageable and unpunctuated blob of words strung out beyond the retentive powers of most minds that would need the definition at all. Both theory and result will emerge clearly enough from a pair of specimens, the first dealing with a familiar everyday noun, the second with a mildly technical one:

groan . . . 1: a deep usu. inarticulate and involuntary often strangled sound typically abruptly begun and ended and usu. indicative of pain or grief or tension or desire or sometimes disapproval or annoyance.

kymograph . . . 1: a recording device including an electric motor or clockwork that drives a usu. slowly revolving drum which carries a roll of plain or smoked paper and also having an arrangement for tracing on the paper by means of a stylus a graphic record of motion or pressure (as of the organs of speech, blood pressure, or respiration) often in relation to particular intervals of time.

About these typical definitions as prose, there is much that any good reader might well say. What must be said is that the grim suppression of commas is a mere crotchet. It takes time to read such definitions anyway; commas in the right places would speed rather than slow the reading and would clarify rather than obscure the sense, so that the unitary effect—largely imaginary at best—would be more helped than hurt. In practice, the one-phrase design without further expository predication lacks all the asserted advantages over a competently written definition of the free conventional sort; it is merely more difficult to write, often impossible to write well, and tougher to take in. Compare the corresponding definitions from the Second Edition:

groan . . . A low, moaning sound; usually, a deep, mournful sound uttered in pain or great distress; sometimes, an expression of strong disapprobation; as, the remark was received with *groans*.

kymograph . . . a An automatic apparatus consisting of a motor revolving a drum covered with smoked paper, on which curves of pressure, etc., may be traced.

Everyone professionally concerned with the details of printed English can be grateful to the new Webster for linking

the parts of various expressions that have been either hyphen-
ated compounds or separate words—*highlight, highbrow* and
lowbrow, overall, wisecrack, lowercase and *uppercase,* and so
on. Some of the unions now recognized were long overdue; many
editors have already got them written into codes of house usage.
But outside this small province the new work is a copy editor's
despair, a propounder of endless riddles.

What, for example, are we to make of the common abbreviations *i.e.* and *e.g.?* The first is entered in the vocabulary as **ie**
(no periods, no space), the second as **e g** (space, no periods).
In the preliminary list, "Abbreviations Used in This Dictionary,"
both are given the customary periods. (Oddly, the list translates
its *i.e.* into "that is," but merely expands *e.g.* into "exempli
gratia.") Is one to follow the vocabulary or the list? What point
has the seeming inconsistency?

And what about capitalization? All vocabulary entries are
in lowercase except for such abbreviations as ARW (air raid
warden), MAB (medical advisory board), and PX (post ex-
change). Words possibly inviting capitalization are followed by
such injunctions as *cap, usu cap, sometimes not cap, usu cap
1st A, usu cap A&B.* (One of the small idiosyncrasies is that
"usu.," the most frequent abbreviation, is given a period when
roman, denied it when italic.) From **america,** adjective—all
proper nouns are excluded—to **american yew** there are over 175
consecutive entries that require such injunctions; would it not
have been simpler and more economical to capitalize the entries? A flat *"cap,"* of course, means "always capitalized." But
how often is "usually," and when is "sometimes"? We get dictionaries expressly that they may settle such problems for us.
This dictionary seems to make a virtue of leaving them in flux,
with the explanation that many matters are subjective and that
the individual must decide them for himself—a curious abrogation of authority in a work extrolled as "more useful and authoritative than any previous dictionary."

The rock-bottom practical truth is that the lexicographer
cannot abrogate his authority if he wants to. He may think of
himself as a detached scientist reporting the facts of language,
declining to recommend use of anything or abstention from any-

thing; but the myriad consultants of his work are not going to see him so. He helps create, not a book of fads and fancies and private opinions, but a Dictionary of the English Language. It comes to every reader under auspices that say, not "Take it or leave it," but rather something like this: "Here in 8000 columns is a definitive report of what a synod of the most trustworthy American experts consider the English language to be in the seventh decade of the twentieth century. This is your language; take it and use it. And if you use it in conformity with the principles and practices here exemplified, your use will be the most accurate attainable by any American of this era." The fact that the compilers disclaim authority and piously refrain from judgments is meaningless: the work itself, by virtue of its inclusions and exclusions, its mere existence, is a whole universe of judgments, received by millions as the Word from on high.

And there we have the reason why it is so important for the dictionary maker to keep his discriminations sharp, why it is so damaging if he lets them get out of working order. Suppose he enters a new definition for no better reason than that some careless, lazy, or uninformed scribbler has jumped to an absurd conclusion about what a word means or has been too harassed to run down the word he really wanted. This new definition is going to persuade tens of thousands that, say, *cohort*, a word of multitude, means one associate of crony "(he and three alleged housebreaking cohorts were arraigned on attempted burglary charges)" or that the vogue word *ambivalence*, which denotes simultaneous love and hatred of someone or something, means "continual oscillation between one thing and its opposite (novels . . . vitiated by an ambivalence between satire and sentimentalism)." To what is the definer contributing if not to subversion and decay? To the swallower of the definition it never occurs that he can have drunk corruption from a well that he has every reason to trust as the ultimate in purity. Multiply him by the number of people simultaneously influenced, and the resulting figure by the years through which the influence continues, and a great deal of that product by the influences that will be disseminated through speech and writing and teaching, and you begin to apprehend the scope of the really enormous disaster that can and will be wrought by the lexicographer's abandonment of his responsibility.

Review Questions

1. Why is a perfect dictionary of a living language said to be impossible to produce?
2. What does Follett think the strengths of *Webster's Third* to be? Why are they difficult to assess?
3. According to Follett, what important material is missing from *Webster's Third*?
4. Why does Follett call *Webster's Third* "a fighting document"? How does he think it differs from *Webster's Second*?
5. According to Follett, what major responsibility of the lexicographer have the editors of *Webster's Third* renounced? What evidence is there of abrogation of responsibility?
6. What attitude toward grammar and usage does Follett find expressed in *Webster's Third*? What examples does he give?
7. The definitions in *Webster's Third* are supported by quotations from approximately 14,000 authors. According to Follett, how did the editors of this dictionary err in their selection of authors?
8. Describe the method the editors used in writing definitions. Why does Follett consider it unsatisfactory?
9. What problems relating to abbreviations and capitalization may be found in *Webster's Third*?
10. According to Follett, why cannot the lexicographer abrogate his responsibility even if he wants to?
11. What calamitous results does Follett believe may be caused by the "permissive" attitude of a lexicographer?

Discussion Questions

1. According to Hayakawa, "The writer of a dictionary is a historian, not a lawgiver." Follett would agree that the lexicographer should be a historian, but he would like to have the writer of dictionaries play other roles. Identify the other roles and explain how they are related to some of Follett's criticisms of *Webster's Third*.
2. Compare the attitudes expressed in paragraph 3 with Follett's statements about the sources of the quotations used to buttress the definitions used in *Webster's Third*. Are they contradictory?
3. What period of English language history does Follett want a

dictionary to reflect? Does he seem to feel the need for a new dictionary? What would he consider the function of a new un-abridged dictionary to be?

4. Judging from the attitudes expressed in this essay, do you think that Follett would have been in favor of the usage panel described by Bishop? What would his reaction have been to the inclusion of the many slang terms in the *American Heritage Dictionary*?

5. Would you agree with Follett that the mere presence of a word in the dictionary is an implicit approval of that word as an ac-ceptable part of the English language? Would you agree that most people, as Hayakawa points out, rely on the dictionary as the arbiter of language matters? Do you believe that a dictionary not only records current usage, but determines the direction the language will take?

6. Do you approve of the avoidance of status labels in *Webster's Third*? Is it always, or even often, possible to determine whether a word is slang, colloquial, or standard English? What role does context play in this determination?

7. Is there any contradiction in Follett's apparent willingness to ac-cept usage as the criterion for a word's respectability in Langland's fourteenth-century England, but not in his own twentieth-century America? (Consider his comments on "like" as a conjunction.) If Follett is willing to accept the fact that the language has "sloughed off" a usage, should he also be prepared to accept a usage which the language has *acquired*?

BERGEN EVANS

but what's a
dictionary for?

The storm of abuse in the popular press that greeted the
appearance of *Webster's Third New International Dictionary* is
a curious phenomenon. Never has a scholarly work of this
stature been attacked with such unbridled fury and contempt.
An article in the *Atlantic* viewed it as a "disappointment," a
"shock," a "calamity," "a scandal and a disaster." The New York
Times, in a special editorial, felt that the work would "accelerate
the deterioration" of the language and sternly accused the editors of betraying a public trust. The *Journal* of the American
Bar Association saw the publication as "deplorable," "a flagrant
example of lexicographic irresponsibility," "a serious blow to
the cause of good English." *Life* called it "a non-word deluge,"
"monstrous," "abominable," and "a cause for dismay." They
doubted that "Lincoln could have modelled his Gettysburg
Address" on it—a concept of how things get written that throws
very little light on Lincoln but a great deal on *Life.*

What underlies all this sound and fury? Is the claim of the
G. & C. Merriam Company, probably the world's greatest dictionary maker, that the preparation of the work cost $3.5 mil-
lion, that it required the efforts of three hundred scholars over
a period of twenty-seven years, working on the largest collection
of citations ever assembled in any language—is all this a fraud,
a hoax?

So monstrous a discrepancy in evaluation requires us to
examine basic principles. Just what's a dictionary for? What
does it propose to do? What does the common reader go to a
dictionary to find? What has the purchaser of a dictionary a
right to expect for his money?

Before we look at basic principles, it is necessary to interpose two brief statements. The first of these is that a dictionary is concerned with words. Some dictionaries give various kinds of other useful information. Some have tables of weights and measures on the flyleaves. Some list historical events, and some, home remedies. And there's nothing wrong with their so doing. But the great increase in our vocabulary in the past three decades compels all dictionaries to make more efficient use of their space. And if something must be eliminated, it is sensible to throw out these extraneous things and stick to words.

Yet wild wails arose. The *Saturday Review* lamented that one can no longer find the goddess Astarte under a separate heading —though they point out that a genus of mollusks named after the goddess is included! They seemed to feel that out of sheer perversity the editors of the dictionary stooped to mollusks while ignoring goddesses and that, in some way, this typifies modern lexicography. Mr. Wilson Follett, folletizing (his mental processes demand some special designation) in the *Atlantic,* cried out in horror that one is not even able to learn from the Third International "that the Virgin was Mary the mother of Jesus"!

The second brief statement is that there has been even more progress in the making of dictionaries in the past thirty years than there has been in the making of automobiles. The difference, for example, between the much-touted Second International (1934) and the much-clouted Third International (1961) is not like the difference between yearly models but like the difference between the horse and buggy and the automobile. Between the appearance of these two editions a whole new science related to the making of dictionaries, the science of descriptive linguistics, has come into being.

Modern linguistics gets its charter from Leonard Bloomfield's *Language* (1933). Bloomfield, for thirteen years professor of Germanic philology at the University of Chicago and for nine years professor of linguistics at Yale, was one of those inseminating scholars who can't be relegated to any department and don't dream of accepting established categories and procedures just because they're established. He was as much an anthropologist as a linguist, and his concepts of language were shaped not by Strunk's *Elements of Style* but by his knowledge of Cree Indian dialects.

The broad general findings of the new science are:

1. All languages are systems of human conventions, not systems of natural laws. The first—and essential—step in the study of any language is observing and setting down precisely what happens when native speakers speak it.

2. Each language is unique in its pronunciation, grammar, and vocabulary. It cannot be described in terms of logic or of some theoretical, ideal language. It cannot be described in terms of any other language, or even in terms of its own past.

3. All languages are dynamic rather than static, and hence a "rule" in any language can only be a statement of contemporary practice. Change is constant—and normal.

4. "Correctness" can rest only upon usage, for the simple reason that there is nothing else for it to rest on. And all usage is relative.

From these propositions it follows that a dictionary is good only insofar as it is a comprehensive and accurate description of current usage. And to be comprehensive it must include some indication of social and regional associations.

New dictionaries are needed because English has changed more in the past two generations than at any other time in its history. It has had to adapt to extraordinary cultural and technological changes, two world wars, unparalleled changes in transportation and communication, and unprecedented movements of populations.

More subtly, but pervasively, it has changed under the influence of mass education and the growth of democracy. As written English is used by increasing millions and for more reasons than ever before, the language has become more utilitarian and more informal. Every publication in America today includes pages that would appear, to the purist of forty years ago, unbuttoned gibberish. Not that they are; they simply show that you can't hold the language of one generation up as a model for the next.

It's not that you mustn't. You *can't*. For example, in the issue in which *Life* stated editorially that it would follow the Second

International, there were over forty words, constructions, and meanings which are in the Third International but not in the Second. The issue of the New York *Times* which hailed the Second International as the authority to which it would adhere and the Third International as a scandal and a betrayal which it would reject used one hundred and fifty-three separate words, phrases, and constructions which are listed in the Third International but not in the Second and nineteen others which are condemned in the Second. Many of them are used many times, more than three hundred such uses in all. The Washington *Post,* in an editorial captioned "Keep Your Old Webster's," says, in the first sentence, "don't throw it away," and in the second, "hang on to it." But the old Webster's labels *don't* "colloquial" and doesn't include "hang on to," in this sense, at all.

In short, all of these publications are written in the language that the Third International describes, even the very editorials which scorn it. And this is no coincidence, because the Third International isn't setting up any new standards at all; it is simply describing what *Life,* the Washington *Post,* and the New York *Times* are doing. Much of the dictionary's material comes from these very publications, the *Times,* in particular, furnishing more of its illustrative quotations than any other newspaper.

And the papers have no choice. No journal or periodical could sell a single issue today if it restricted itself to the American language of twenty-eight years ago. It couldn't discuss half the things we are interested in, and its style would seem stiff and cumbrous. If the editorials were serious, the public—and the stockholders—have reason to be grateful that the writers on these publications are more literate than the editors.

And so back to our questions: what's a dictionary for, and how, in 1962, can it best do what it ought to do? The demands are simple. The common reader turns to a dictionary for information about the spelling, pronunciation, meaning, and proper use of words. He wants to know what is current and respectable. But he wants—and has a right to—the truth, the full truth. And the full truth about any language, and especially about American English today, is that there are many areas in which certainty is impossible and simplification is misleading.

Even in so settled a matter as spelling, a dictionary cannot always be absolute. *Theater* is correct, but so is *theatre*. And so are *traveled* and *travelled, plow* and *plough, catalog* and *catalogue,* and scores of other variants. The reader may want a single certainty. He may have taken an unyielding position in an argument, he may have wagered in support of his conviction and may demand that the dictionary "settle" the matter. But neither his vanity nor his purse is any concern of the dictionary's; it must record the facts. And the fact here is that there are many words in our language which may be spelled, with equal correctness, in either of two ways.

So with pronunciation. A citizen listening to his radio might notice that James B. Conant, Bernard Baruch, and Dwight D. Eisenhower pronounce *economics* as ECKuhnomiks, while A. Whitney Griswold, Adlai Stevenson, and Herbert Hoover pronounce it EEKuhnomiks. He turns to the dictionary to see which of the two pronunciations is "right" and finds that they are both acceptable.

Has he been betrayed? Has the dictionary abdicated its responsibility? Should it say that one *must* speak like the president of Harvard or like the president of Yale, like the thirty-first President of the United States or like the thirty-fourth? Surely it's none of its business to make a choice. Not because of the distinction of these particular speakers; lexicography, like God, is no respecter of persons. But because so widespread and conspicuous a use of two pronunciations among people of this elevation shows that there *are* two pronunciations. Their speaking establishes the fact which the dictionary must record.

Among the "enormities" with which *Life* taxes the Third International is its listing of "the common mispronunciation" *heighth*. That it is labeled a "dialectal variant" seems, somehow, to compound the felony. But one hears the word so pronounced, and if one professes to give a full account of American English in the 1960s, one has to take some cognizance of it. All people do not possess *Life's* intuitive perception that the word is so "monstrous" that even to list it as a dialect variation is to merit scorn. Among these, by the way, was John Milton, who, in one of the greatest passages in all literature, besought the Holy Spirit to raise him to the "highth" of his great argument. And even the *Oxford English Dictionary* is so benighted as to list it, in full boldface, right alongside of *Height* as a variant that has been in the language since at least 1290.

Now there are still, apparently, millions of Americans who retain, in this as in much else, some of the speech of Milton. This particular pronunciation seems to be receding, but the *American Dialect Dictionary* still records instances of it from almost every state on the Eastern seaboard and notes that it is heard from older people and "occasionally in educated speech," "common with good speakers," "general," "widespread."

Under these circumstances, what is a dictionary to do? Since millions speak the word this way, the pronunciation can't be ignored. Since it has been in use as long as we have any record of English and since it has been used by the greatest writers, it can't be described as substandard or slang. But it is heard now only in certain localities. That makes it a dialectal pronunciation, and an honest dictionary will list it as such. What else can it do? Should it do?

The average purchaser of a dictionary uses it most often, probably, to find out what a word "means." As a reader, he wants to know what an author intended to convey. As a speaker or writer, he wants to know what a word will convey to his auditors. And this, too, is complex, subtle, and forever changing.

An illustration is furnished by an editorial in the Washington *Post* (January 17, 1962). After a ringing appeal to those who "love truth and accuracy" and the usual bombinations about "abdication of authority" and "barbarism," the editorial charges the Third International with "pretentious and obscure verbosity" and specifically instances its definition of "so simple an object as a door."

The definition reads:

a movable piece of firm material or a structure supported usu. along one side and swinging on pivots or hinges, sliding along a groove, rolling up and down, revolving as one of four leaves, or folding like an accordion by means of which an opening may be closed or kept open for passage into or out of a building, room, or other covered enclosure or a car, airplane, elevator, or other vehicle.

Then follows a series of special meanings, each particularly defined and, where necessary, illustrated by a quotation.

Since, aside from roaring and admonishing the "gentlemen from Springfield" that "accuracy and brevity are virtues," the *Post*'s editorial fails to explain what is wrong with the definition, we can only infer from "so simple" a thing that the writer takes the plain, downright, man-in-the-street attitude that a door is a door and any damn fool knows that.

But if so, he has walked into one of lexicography's biggest booby traps: the belief that the obvious is easy to define. Whereas the opposite is true. Anyone can give a fair description of the strange, the new, or the unique. It's the commonplace, the habitual, that challenges definition, for its very commonness compels us to define it in uncommon terms. Dr. Johnson was ridiculed on just this score when his dictionary appeared in 1755. For two hundred years his definition of a network as "any thing reticulated or decussated, at equal distances, with interstices between the intersections" has been good for a laugh. But in the merriment one thing is always overlooked: no one has yet come up with a better definition! Subsequent dictionaries defined it as a mesh and then defined a mesh as a network. That's simple, all right.

Anyone who attempts sincerely to state what the word *door* means in the United States of America today can't take refuge in a log cabin. There has been an enormous proliferation of closing and demarking devices and structures in the past twenty years, and anyone who tries to thread his way through the many meanings now included under *door* may have to sacrifice brevity to accuracy and even have to employ words that a limited vocabulary may find obscure.

Is the entrance to a tent a door, for instance? And what of the thing that seals the exit of an airplane? Is this a door? Or what of those sheets and jets of air that are now being used, in place of old-fashioned oak and hinges, to screen entrances and exits. Are they doors? And what of those accordion-like things that set off various sections of many modern apartments? The fine print in the lease takes it for granted that they are doors and that spaces demarked by them are rooms—and the rent is computed on the number of rooms.

Was I gypped by the landlord when he called the folding contraption that shuts off my kitchen a door? I go to the Second International, which the editor of the *Post* urges me to use in preference to the Third International. Here I find that a door is

> The movable frame or barrier of boards, or other material, usually turning on hinges or pivots or sliding, by which an entranceway into a house or apartment is closed or opened; also, a similar part of a piece of furniture, as in a cabinet or bookcase.

This is only forty-six words, but though it includes the cellar door, it excludes the barn door and the accordion-like thing.

So I go on to the Third International. I see at once that the new definition is longer. But I'm looking for accuracy, and if I must sacrifice brevity to get it, then I must. And, sure enough, in the definition which raised the *Post*'s blood pressure, I find the words "folding like an accordion." The thing *is* a door, and my landlord is using the word in one of its currently accepted meanings.

We don't turn to a work of reference merely for confirmation. We all have words in our vocabularies which we have misunderstood, and to come on the true meaning of one of these words is quite a shock. All our complacency and self-esteem rise to oppose the discovery. But eventually we must accept the humiliation and laugh it off as best we can.

Some, often those who have set themselves up as authorities, stick to their error and charge the dictionary with being in a conspiracy against them. They are sure that their meaning is the only "right" one. And when the dictionary doesn't bear them out they complain about "permissive" attitudes instead of correcting their mistake.

The New York *Times* and the *Saturday Review* both regarded as contemptibly "permissive" the fact that one meaning of one word was illustrated by a quotation from Polly Adler. But a rudimentary knowledge of the development of any language would have told them that the underworld has been a far more active force in shaping and enriching speech than all the synods that have ever convened. Their attitude is like that of the patriot who canceled his subscription to the *Dictionary of American Biography* when he discovered that the very first volume included Benedict Arnold!

The ultimate of "permissiveness," singled out by almost every critic for special scorn, was the inclusion in the Third International of *finalize*. It was this, more than any other one thing, that was given as the reason for sticking to the good old Second International—that "peerless authority on American English," as the *Times* called it. But if it was such an authority, why didn't they look into it? They would have found *finalize* if they had.

And why shouldn't it be there? It exists. It's been recorded for two generations. Millions employ it every day. Two Presidents of the United States—men of widely differing cultural backgrounds—have used it in formal statements. And so has the Secretary-General of the United Nations, a man of unusual linguistic attainments. It isn't permitting the word but omitting it that would break faith with the reader. Because it is exactly the sort of word we want information about.

To list it as substandard would be to imply that it is used solely by the ignorant and the illiterate. But this would be misrepresentation: President Kennedy and U Thant are highly educated men, and both are articulate and literate. It isn't even a freak form. On the contrary, it is a classic example of a regular process of development in English, a process which has given us such thoroughly accepted words as *generalize, minimize, formalize,* and *verbalize*. Nor can it be dismissed on logical grounds or on the ground that it is a mere duplication of *complete*. It says something that *complete* doesn't say and says it in a way that is significant in the modern bureaucratic world: one usually *completes* something which he has initiated but *finalizes* the work of others.

One is free to dislike the word. I don't like it. But the editor

of a dictionary has to examine the evidence for a word's existence and seek it in context to get, as clearly and closely as he
can, the exact meaning that it conveys to those who use it. And
if it is widely used by well-educated, literate, reputable people,
he must list it as a standard word. He is not compiling a volume
of his own prejudices.

An individual's use of his native tongue is the surest index
to his position within his community. And those who turn to a
dictionary expect from it some statement of the current status of
a word or a grammatical construction. And it is with the failure
to assume this function that modern lexicography has been most
fiercely charged. The charge is based on a naïve assumption that
simple labels can be attached in all instances. But they can't.
Some words are standard in some constructions and not in
others. There may be as many shades of status as of meaning,
and modern lexicography instead of abdicating this function has
fulfilled it to a degree utterly unknown to earlier dictionaries.

Consider the word *fetch*, meaning to "go get and bring to."
Until recently a standard word of full dignity ("Fetch me, I
pray thee, a little water in a vessel"—I Kings 17:10), it has become slightly tainted. Perhaps the command latent in it is
resented as undemocratic. Or maybe its use in training dogs to
retrieve has made some people feel that it is an undignified word
to apply to human beings. But, whatever the reason, there is a
growing uncertainty about its status, and hence it is the sort of
word that conscientious people look up in a dictionary.

Will they find it labeled "good" or "bad"? Neither, of course,
because either applied indiscriminately would be untrue. The
Third International lists nineteen different meanings of the
verb *to fetch*. Of these some are labeled "dialectal," some "chiefly
dialectal," some "obsolete," one "chiefly Scottish," and two "not
in formal use." The primary meaning—"to go after and bring
back"—is not labeled and hence can be accepted as standard,
accepted with the more assurance because the many shades of
labeling show us that the word's status has been carefully considered.

On grammatical questions the Third International tries to be equally exact and thorough. Sometimes a construction is listed without comment, meaning that in the opinion of the editors it is unquestionably respectable. Sometimes a construction carries the comment "used by speakers and writers on all educational levels though disapproved by some grammarians." Or the comment may be "used in substandard speech and formerly also by reputable writers." Or "less often in standard than in substandard speech." Or simply "dial."

And this very accurate reporting is based on evidence which is presented for our examination. One may feel that the evidence is inadequate or that the evaluation of it is erroneous. But surely, in the face of classification so much more elaborate and careful than any known heretofore, one cannot fly into a rage and insist that the dictionary is "out to destroy . . . every vestige of linguistic punctilio . . . every criterion for distinguishing between better usages and worse."

Words, as we have said, are continually shifting their meanings and connotations and hence their status. A word which has dignity, say, in the vocabulary of an older person may go down in other people's estimation. Like *fetch*. The older speaker is not likely to be aware of this and will probably be inclined to ascribe the snickers of the young at his speech to that degeneration of manners which every generation has deplored in its juniors. But a word which is coming up in the scale—like *jazz*, say, or, more recently, *crap*—will strike his ear at once. We are much more aware of offenses given us than of those we give. And if he turns to a dictionary and finds the offending word listed as standard— or even listed, apparently—his response is likely to be an outburst of indignation.

But the dictionary can neither snicker nor fulminate. It records. It will offend many, no doubt, to find the expression *wise up*, meaning to inform or to become informed, listed in the Third International with no restricting label. To my aging ears it still sounds like slang. But the evidence—quotations from the *Kiplinger Washington Letter* and the *Wall Street Journal*—convinces me that it is I who am out of step, lagging behind. If such publications have taken to using *wise up* in serious contexts, with no punctuational indication of irregularity, then it is obviously respectable. And finding it so listed and supported, I can only say that it's nice to be informed and sigh to realize that I am becoming an old fogy. But, of course, I don't have to use it (and I'll be damned if I will! "Let them smile, as I do now, At the old forsaken bough Where I cling").

In part, the trouble is due to the fact that there is no standard for standard. Ideas of what is proper to use in serious, dignified speech and writing are changing—and with breathtaking rapidity. This is one of the major facts of contemporary American English. But it is no more the dictionary's business to oppose this process than to speed it up.

Even in our standard speech some words are more dignified and some more informal than others, and dictionaries have tried to guide us through these uncertainties by marking certain words and constructions as "colloquial," meaning "inappropriate in a formal situation." But this distinction, in the opinion of most scholars, has done more harm than good. It has created the notion that these particular words are inferior, when actually they might be the best possible words in an informal statement. And so—to the rage of many reviewers—the Third International has dropped this label. Not all labels, as angrily charged, but only this one out of a score. And the doing so may have been an error, but it certainly didn't constitute "betrayal" or "abandoning of all distinctions." It was intended to end a certain confusion.

In all the finer shades of meaning, of which the status of a word is only one, the user is on his own, whether he likes it or not. Despite *Life*'s artless assumption about the Gettysburg Address, nothing worth writing is written *from* a dictionary. The dictionary, rather, comes along afterwards and describes what *has been* written.

Words in themselves are not dignified, or silly, or wise, or malicious. But they can be used in dignified, silly, wise, or malicious ways by dignified, silly, wise, or malicious people. *Egghead,* for example, is a perfectly legitimate word, as legitimate as *highbrow* or *long-haired.* But there is something very wrong and very undignified, by civilized standards, in a belligerent dislike for intelligence and education. *Yak* is an amusing word for persistent chatter. Anyone could say, "We were just yakking over a cup of coffee," with no harm to his dignity. But to call a Supreme Court decision *yakking* is to be vulgarly insulting and so, undignified. Again, there's nothing wrong with *confab* when it's appropriate. But when the work of a great research project, employing hundreds of distinguished scholars over several decades and involving the honor of one of the greatest publishing houses in the world, is described as *confabbing* (as the New York *Times* editorially described the preparation of the Third International), the use of this particular word asserts that the lexicographers had merely sat around and talked idly. And the statement becomes undignified—if not, indeed, slanderous.

The lack of dignity in such statements is not in the words, nor in the dictionaries that list them, but in the hostility that deliberately seeks this tone of expression. And in expressing itself the hostility frequently shows that those who are expressing it don't know how to use a dictionary. Most of the reviewers seem unable to read the Third International and unwilling to read the Second.

The *American Bar Association Journal*, for instance, in a typical outburst ("a deplorable abdication of responsibility"), picked out for special scorn the inclusion in the Third International of the word *irregardless*. "As far as the new Webster's is concerned," said the *Journal*, "this meaningless verbal bastard is just as legitimate as any other word in the dictionary." Thirty seconds spent in examining the book they were so roundly condemning would have shown them that in it *irregardless* is labeled "nonstand"—which means "nonstandard," which means "not conforming to the usage generally characteristic of educated native speakers of the language." Is that "just as legitimate as any other word in the dictionary"?

The most disturbing fact of all is that the editors of a dozen of the most influential publications in America today are under the impression that *authoritative* must mean *authoritarian*. Even the "permissive" Third International doesn't recognize this identification—editors' attitudes being not yet, fortunately, those of the American people. But the Fourth International may have to.

The new dictionary may have many faults. Nothing that tries to meet an ever-changing situation over a terrain as vast as contemporary English can hope to be free of them. And much in it is open to honest, and informed, disagreement. There can be linguistic objection to the eradication of proper names. The removal of guides to pronunciation from the foot of every page may not have been worth the valuable space it saved. The new method of defining words of many meanings has disadvantages as well as advantages. And of the half million or more definitions, hundreds, possibly thousands, may seem inadequate or imprecise. To some (of whom I am one) the omission of the label "colloquial" will seem meritorious; to others it will seem a loss.

But one thing is certain: anyone who solemnly announces in the year 1962 that he will be guided in matters of English usage by a dictionary published in 1934 is talking ignorant and pretentious nonsense.

Review Questions

1. How does Evans counter criticism about the lack of proper names in *Webster's Third*?
2. How does Evans explain the difference between *Webster's Second* and *Webster's Third*?
3. What are the four general findings of descriptive linguistics?
4. What major influences have significantly changed English over the past thirty years?
5. Why is it not surprising to find that much of the language in the magazines and newspapers which attacked *Webster's Third* either did not appear in *Webster's Second* or was not "approved" by that dictionary?
6. Why cannot a dictionary be absolute in its treatment of spelling and pronunciation?
7. Why does Evans devote eight paragraphs to the definition of "door"? What point is he making about dictionary definitions?
8. What does Evans see as the relation between current usage and the dictionary? Should a lexicographer judge words on the basis of his own "taste"?
9. How does Evans answer the charge that the editors of *Webster's Third* have abrogated their responsibility of judging the current status of a word or of a grammatical construction?

10. Why did the editors of *Webster's Third* drop the label "colloquial"?
11. Does Evans see any weaknesses in *Webster's Third*?

Discussion Questions

1. Compare the views of Follett and Evans on *Webster's Third*. Their attitudes stem from different notions about the nature of the dictionary and the nature of language. How would you describe their different ideas?
2. Follett sees the dictionary as a dictionary, a grammar book, a biographical dictionary, an atlas, and a book on linguistic etiquette; Evans states that a dictionary need only be concerned with lexicographical matters. What do most people believe the dictionary to be? What do you believe a dictionary should be? Why are people's attitudes toward the dictionary important?
3. How do Evans' ideas about the dictionary and its function compare to Bishop's description of the *American Heritage Dictionary* and the language panel?

ALBERT H. MARCKWARDT

the new Webster dictionary:
a critical appraisal

A complete revision of our largest commercially produced dictionary of the English language has become a regularly recurring event in American life. Upon occasion the time table has varied a bit, but the following listing reveals an astonishing degree of regularity over the past century:

An American Dictionary of the English Language   1864
     (Royal Quarto Edition, Unabridged)
Webster's International Dictionary   1890
Webster's New International Dictionary   1909
Webster's New International Dictionary   1934
     (Second edition)
Webster's Third New International Dictionary   1961

Of the five Webster editions listed above, probably none has called forth such extremes of critical comment as the recent Webster Third. It has been characterized as "a very great calamity." Its general tone has been described as "a dismaying assortment of the questionable, the perverse, the unworthy, the downright outrageous." At the same time, other reviewers speak of the work as "an intellectual achievement of the very highest order," and "a reference work which worthily carries on a tradition of great reference works."

These extremes of praise and blame are reminiscent of the reception of the 1828 edition of *An American Dictionary of the English Language,* compiled by Webster himself and the real parent of the long line of dictionaries which bear his name. At

This paper, which was originally read at a meeting of the Michigan Linguistic Society, is printed by permission of the author.

that time a reviewer in *The Southern Literary Messenger* denounced the treatment of pronunciation as horrible and the orthography as abominable. The English *Quarterly Review* judged it "a decided failure, conducted on perverse and erroneous principles," and, in much the same vein as some of the critics of the Webster Third, complained that "we do not recollect ever to have witnessed in the same compass a greater number of crudities and errors, or more pains taken to so little purpose." But Webster's 1828 work had its admirers as well, particularly among the Germans, who praised the profound learning that it reflected.

The disparate comments on Webster's early work are of interest today only as a historical phenomenon, but those which have been applied to the Webster Third have given rise to considerable confusion. It is scarcely possible for both the critics and the admirers to be right in all that they say, and one may reasonably ask what a more dispassionate evaluation might be.

In approaching such an appraisal, we must understand first of all that the American lexicographer in his concern with current English faces something of a dilemma. He is the inheritor of two traditions clearly in conflict, both of which have their roots in England.

The earlier tradition is that of Samuel Johnson, the compiler of the 1755 *Dictionary of the English Language,* who lent the first touch of sheer genius to English lexicography. In the preface of this great work, he pointed out that "every language has its improprieties and absurdities, which it is the duty of the lexicographer to correct or proscribe." According to him, the function of a dictionary was one, "by which the pronunciation of our language may be fixed and its attainment facilitated; by which its purity may be preserved, its use ascertained, and its duration lengthened." That Johnson was expressing the spirit of his age is shown by comments such as that of Lord Chesterfield, who wrote, "We must have resource to the old Roman expedient in times of confusion and choose a Dictator. Upon this principle I give my vote for Mr. Johnson to fill that great and arduous post."

This concept of the lexicographer as linguistic legislator or arbiter, if not absolute dictator, is still strong in the United States. It is frequently reflected, and indeed encouraged, by the slogans which dictionary publishers—not the editors, let me hasten to say—choose to advertise their wares. The very phrase, "Supreme Authority," which the G. and C. Merriam Company used to employ, supported this view of the dictionary; whether intentionally or not is open to conjecture.

The slightly later and opposed tradition is that of the lexicographer as the objective recorder of the language. For the English-speaking nations this concept was first realized on a substantial scale in what is now known as *The Oxford English Dictionary* but originally entitled *A New English Dictionary on Historical Principles*. Here the purpose is stated as follows:

The aim of this dictionary is to present in alphabetical series the words which have formed the English vocabulary from the time of the earliest records down to the present day, with all the relevant facts concerning their form, sense-history, pronunciation, and etymology. It embraces not only the standard language of literature and conversation, whether current at the moment or obsolete, or archaic, but also the main technical vocabulary, and a large measure of dialetical usage and slang.

Note that this statement contains not one word about fixing the language, about proscription or prescription of any kind. Operating on this basis, the lexicographer contents himself with setting down the record, leaving its interpretation to the reader. Needless to say, the prestige of the *Oxford English Dictionary* is enormous; it is generally conceded to be superior to the corresponding major dictionaries for the other western European languages. The principles on which it is based were formulated as early as 1859.

The conflict of principle which has been pointed out need not necessarily be troublesome. If the language involved is confined as to number of speakers and is the vehicle of a static and stabilized society, there is virtually no problem. But this is not the case with English, which is spoken natively by some two hundred and seventy millions, spread over five continents of the globe. In the United States, at least, the language is that of a highly mobile society, both geographically and up and down the social scale. Under such circumstances, the linguistic reporter and the legislator are more likely to seem to be working at cross purposes.

Nevertheless, it is clearly evident that as the various editions of Webster march down the century, the statements of principle which are to be found in them move steadily away from the Johnsonian or prescriptive concept toward the descriptive position of the Oxford editors. The following excerpt from the front matter of the 1934 edition (p. xxvi) refers specifically to pronunciation, but it is a fair representation of the attitude of its editors toward all language matters:

The function of a pronouncing dictionary is to record as far as possible the pronunciations prevailing in the best present usage, rather than to attempt to dictate what that usage should be. In so far as a dictionary may be known and acknowledged as a faithful recorder and interpreter of such usage, so far and no farther may it be appealed to as an authority.

In the case of diverse usages of extensive prevalence, the dictionary must recognize each of them.

A somewhat broader treatment of the editorial function is to be found in the Introduction (p. xi) to the 1934 Webster:

Both Samuel Johnson and Noah Webster conceived it to be a duty of the dictionary editor to maintain the purity of the standard language. However, with the growth in literacy of the past century, and the increase in fiction and drama, in radio and motion picture, of the use of dialect, slang, and colloquial speech, it has become necessary for a general dictionary to record and interpret the vocabularies of geographical and occupational dialects, and of the livelier levels of the speech of the educated.

It would be difficult to imagine a more cogent or forthright exposition of the descriptive function of the dictionary than these two statements of editorial policy. The first of them apparently satisfied the editors of the Webster Third, for they repeat it in their Introduction (p. 6a) with only one minor expansion: "best present usage" of the earlier edition now reads, "general

cultivated conversational usage, both formal and informal."
This offers additional support for the conclusion that with respect to the conflict between opposing lexicographical concepts,
the descriptive had been accepted, the prescriptive rejected, as
early as 1934. Whatever differences there may be between the
1934 and 1962 editions, they are not matters of policy or principle. They are instead differences in the way in which a principle common to both dictionaries has been realized.

Lexicographical policy is not ordinarily a matter of absorb-
ing interest, but it has been necessary to deal with it at some
length because the Webster Third has been criticized on occasion for repudiating, even sabotaging the principles of the second edition. Such charges serve only to reveal a total lack of
awareness on the part of the critic as to what these principles
were, as well as an inability to distinguish between principle and
practice.

The extremes of public reaction to the new Webster must
therefore be understood in terms of editorial decisions on a
practical rather than a theoretical level. Such an understanding
may best be attained by considering certain of the practical
questions which confronted the editors, what the decisions on
them were, and what the reasons for them may have been.

At the very outset of their preparations, the editors apparently felt an obligation to increase considerably the amount of
evidence upon which the new dictionary was to be based. Dictionary evidence normally exists in the form of citation slips,
the products of an extensive reading program. The citations are
filed under their appropriate headwords, and in the editing process they constitute the raw material for the definitions and in
fact for most of the word treatment.

At the time of the compilation of the second edition, the files
in the Springfield offices held some 1,615,000 citation slips. In
the years intervening between the two editions, as the result of
what must have been a tremendous effort, this figure was nearly
quadrupled. Just under 4,500,000 citations were added, resulting in a total of 6,000,000, a number approximately equalling
the collection for the *Oxford English Dictionary*, but far more
heavily concentrated on the language of the present day. In ad-

dition, the *Dictionary of American English* and the *Dictionary of Americanisms* had both been completed in the years 1944 and 1951 respectively, constituting a further increase in the size of the corpus available to the editors of the Webster Third. As a result, they found themselves with approximately 50,000 new words, that is, words not entered in the Webster Second, and 50,000 new meanings for words already entered.

At this point physical and financial factors enter into consideration. For a number of reasons, undoubtedly based upon a century of business experience, the publishers are firmly committed to a single-volume dictionary. They had made the Webster Second as large, that is to say thick, as any one volume could possibly get and still assure a back that might withstand the rigors of long and constant use, particularly in schools and libraries. Thus it was manifestly impossible to increase the number of pages by the ten or fifteen percent necessary to accommodate the new entries. If these were to be included, something had to come out. The kind of material that was removed forms the basis of some of the criticisms of the present edition.

The first excision consisted of the materials which, in earlier editions, had been placed below the horizontal line running across the page. These included archaisms, dialect forms, variant spellings, and proper names. To quote the editors, "Many obsolete and comparatively useless or obscure words have been omitted. These include, in general, words that had become obsolete before 1755 unless found in well-known major works of a few major writers." Incidentally, the significance of the date 1755 can scarcely escape one's attention. In the first place it was the publication year of Dr. Johnson's dictionary. Moreover, as a deadline for obsolescence, it marks an advance of two centuries and a half over the corresponding date of 1500 for the Webster Second. Thus, in word selection as well as in other matters, the emphasis is clearly placed upon the current state of the language.

Getting rid of the obsolete and the obscure did not in itself solve the space problem. Still other things had to go, and these taken together constitute the parts essential to a peripheral function of the dictionary long cherished by Americans—the encyclopedic function. In the process of elimination, the editors removed among other things:

1. The gazeteer section.
2. The biological section.
3. Titles of written works and works of art.
4. Names of characters in fiction, folklore, and mythology.
5. Names of battles, wars, organizations, cities, and states.
6. Mottoes and other familiar sayings.

There have been further excisions as well. Color plates and illustrations are reduced in a proprotion somewhere between one-fourth and one-third. Even the number of pages has gone down from 3210 to 2720.

This elimination of encyclopedic material has caused anguish. "Think, if you can," complains Wilson Follett, "of an unabridged dictionary from which you cannot learn who Mark Twain was, or what were the names of the apostles, or that the Virgin was Mary, the mother of Jesus of Nazareth, or what and where the District of Columbia is." Actually, this is not at all difficult. The great Oxford comes immediately to mind, as does Henry Cecil Wyld's *Universal Dictionary of the English Language,* or any of the great academy dictionaries of such languages as French or Spanish.

Neverthless, Follett's reaction will be shared by many Americans. In the past, dictionaries published in this country have cheerfully served an encyclopedic as well as a lexicographic function, and ironically enough it was Noah Webster himself who was primarily responsible. His first dictionary, published in 1806, included tables of the moneys of most of the commercial nations in the world, tables of weights and measures, ancient and modern, the divisions of time among the Jews, Greeks, and Romans, and an official list of the post-offices in the United States, to mention only a few of the extra features. Although the editors of the current volume have broken with their progenitor in cutting out these impedimenta, they have not at all departed from the essential principles of lexicography in so doing.

Undoubtedly they felt that the considerable increase in the

number of illustrative citations would readily compensate for the loss of the peripheral material. Such citations do constitute the core of the reportorial dictionary. For instance, there were no citations for the adjective *oratorical* in the second edition; the Third has three. The second edition gave three identified citations for *chase*, verb. In the Third, there are four identified and seven unidentified citations.

According to the Preface of the current edition, "More than 14,000 different authors are quoted for their use of words or for the structural pattern of their words . . ." Many of these are contemporary. The reader is also informed that the verbal illustrations (citations apparently unidentified as to author) are "mostly from the twentieth century."

This innovation has met with something less than universal approval, a reaction not so much attributable to the editorial policy itself as to some of the advertising antics of the business office. The original brochure, announcing this edition as "one of the most remarkable literary achievements of all time," included among the list of authors cited such names as Billy Rose, Fulton Lewis, Jr., Art Linkletter, Dinah Shore, Ted Williams, and Ethel Merman. In addition there were Harry Truman, Dwight D. Eisenhower, John F. Kennedy, and Richard Nixon, whose names were undoubtedly signed to reams of material which they did not compose. To the sympathetic this signalled a conscious attempt to include a wide range of current authors. To the critical it betokened a lack of discrimination and responsibility. Actually, the citations from such sources are few in number and small in proportion.

A point which must be taken into account here is that which was made at the very outset of this essay, namely that the life of a Webster edition is roughly calculated at twenty-five years. Thus, the overriding concern of the dictionary is quite appropriately the language in its current state. It is on these grounds that the editors may logically justify the preponderance of citations from current authors, irrespective of lasting literary merit. It may be assumed that in the 1986 edition many of them will be discarded, to be replaced by others from the 1970's and early 1980's. In this respect the Webster practice will differ sharply from that of the *Oxford English Dictionary*, for which no new edition was contemplated, although certainly only a small proportion of the authors cited in that work are literary giants of lasting reputation.

Another departure in the Webster Third from the practice of earlier editions, which has given rise to considerable criticism, is the treatment of what are called *status labels*. Here again some of the disapproval has its source in misunderstanding. Basically, the editors have developed a terminology which is at once semantically neutral and more precise than that which has been employed in the past. The label *illiterate* has been discontinued. It has become a term of censure rather than a dispassionate indication of the inability to read and write. The current replacements, *substandard* and *nonstandard*, are matter-of-fact rather than pejorative and permit a gradation of acceptability, the latter indicating a wider range of occurrence than the former, although it is applied to a smaller number of words and expressions. American dialect ascriptions represent a great advance in precision over those of the second edition in that they reflect an adaptation of the terminology for the various dialect areas developed by Professor Hans Kurath, editor of the Linguistic Atlas and the most eminent linguistic geographer in the country. It was unfortunate, however, that the editors chose not to indicate those words current in all regions of the United States but not in England or other parts of the English-speaking world.

Another innovation in the Webster Third is the elimination of the label *colloquial*. There are two conceivable reasons for this: In the first place the term is ambivalent, signifying informality on the one hand and the spoken rather than the written medium on the other. It is customary now among students of the language to be somewhat more precise, recognizing not only *colloquial* but *casual* and *intimate* as further gradations of the spoken variety of the language, any of which not only may be but are regularly employed by speakers of unquestioned cultivation.

An even greater objection to the label *colloquial* is the persistence with which an unfavorable connotation has adhered to it. Dictionary users never interpreted the term in the way in which dictionary editors intended. It was not meant as a condemnation either in the Webster Second or in the various abridged dictionaries based upon it. The editors took great pains to say so, both in the prefactory material and in the definition of the word itself, but this went quite unheeded. So for the present edition the staff was faced with the alternative of finding an acceptable substitute less liable to misinterpretation, or of eliminating the label altogether. It chose the latter, partly perhaps because of the unsatisfactory experience of other dictionaries which had experimented with a substitute.

In general the changes in the choice and ascription of labels reflect an endeavor to achieve greater precision and objectivity. The attempt at precision undoubtedly finds some adherents, although there will be disagreements over the application of the labels in specific instances. The attempt at objectivity has, understandably enough, resulted in the disappearance of the censorious tone which, for many, seemed to be part of the proper function of the labels *colloquial* and *illiterate*. To such persons, the lack of censure will be understood as a lowering of standards.

In dealing with pronunciation, the editors of the Webster Third had to contend with two factors which had not faced their predecessors. One was a new electronic development, namely voice amplification. The other was a new concept in the analysis of language, that of the phoneme or meaningful unit of sound.

Voice amplification affected the kind of pronunciation which the dictionary undertook to record. In preloud-speaker days, the second edition of Webster recorded what is called "formal platform speech," the speech of cultivated users of English, speaking formally with a view to being completely understood by their hearers. That there were other types of pronunciation wholly appropriate to less formal situations was readily conceded by the editors, but they evidently felt that their editorial responsibility could be discharged with the greatest amount of effectiveness and least confusion by indicating just the one.

The microphone has changed all this. Certain devices of articulation necessary for clarity when the speaker was forced to depend on lung power to make himself audible to the last row of a large auditorium are no longer necessary. Nor are they often employed today. They have gone, along with the orotund periods of the old-time spellbinder.

This change led the Webster editors into a complete revision of the manner in which evidence on pronunciations was collected. Where Webster Second had attempted a sampling, by means of written questionnaires, of the pronunciation of persons who did a considerable amount of public speaking, the Webster Third staff turned its attention directly to the language itself rather than to opinion about it. They listened to radio, television, and recordings; to speech in all parts of the country and in all types of situations. Again, as with the citations for word occurrences, forms and meanings, the body of evidence was tremendously increased in range and scope, but certainly less skewed toward a single type of pronunciation.

In any English dictionary, and particularly one designed for use in the United States, a decision upon the particular system, or respelling, to indicate pronunciation always poses a problem. For a number of reasons, the American public has been unwilling to accept the International Phonetic Alphabet; nor is this a particularly economical device when a number of variants must be shown. The Webster Second continued with few changes the system of its predecessors, which was cumbersome in that a single sound was indicated by more than one transcription, and confusing in that a single character sometimes covered far more latitude than the user was likely to realize.

The editors of the current edition have attempted to take advantage of a concept basic to present-day linguistic science, that of the phoneme. A cogent discussion of this concept and its impact upon the way in which pronunciations are indicated may be found under the rubric *phonemicity* in the Webster Third *Guide to Pronunciation*. The general result has been the disappearance of a rash of diacritics which made the earlier dictionaries difficult to read and to interpret. Some useful characters have been taken over from the phonetic alphabet, notably the elongated *n* to indicate the usual sound of *ng*, and most important, the inverted *e* or schwa for the neutral vowel used in weakly stressed syllables. The latter, it must be confessed, is an innovation in which Webster followed some of its competitors. At all events, the public will no longer be misled into believing that the final vowel of *caucus* is somehow different from that of *fracas*.

Unfortunately the necessity of economizing on space has led to the excision of the authoritative treatments of the individual sounds of English which lent scholarly distinction to the second edition though perhaps read by only a few. Also, certain innovations of the Webster Third will cause annoyance until the public becomes accustomed to them. One of these may well be the indication of stress by a mark preceding rather than following the syllable. The removal of the pronunciation key from the bottom of the page is another. The use of a modified *d* character to indicate what the editors call, "the usual American pronunciation of *latter*," will seem to the critical like countenancing the slipshod, and it is possible that a *t* with a diacritic might have served quite as well without outraging quite so many sensibilities.

With pronunciation as with countless other features of the dictionary, the editors have attempted to present the facts of the language as they saw them. It is an honest presentation, maintaining the principles and the concept of the dictionary characteristic of previous editions, but carrying them out with greater consistency and basing them upon far more evidence. There have been errors of judgment, more often perhaps with respect to manner of presentation than in the interpretation of the facts which are reported, but this is inevitable in an undertaking of such magnitude.

My comments so far should have suggested, to a degree at least, the reasons for some of the changes which are to be found in the Webster Third. They have not yet given an answer to the question which was initially posed: why the extremes of praise and blame. The encomiums are easy to account for. They represent the approval of those who accept the descriptive principle and find in the current product a generally conscientious and more thorough implementation of it than is otherwise available.

The chorus of protest is somewhat more complex in origin.

It is in part the expression of a desire for linguistic authoritarianism, an attitude which can be explained only in terms of a number of complex and interrelated factors in American cultural history. Added to this is the mistaken notion that the Webster Third represents a change in lexicographical principle, an error which is fostered by the more complete coverage and greater accuracy of the edition. The excision of certain kinds of non-essential material represented a sudden departure from a time-honored practice. Finally, there is, as always, a tendency toward careless reading and inept comparison. Upon occasion a judgment objected to in the third edition was already present in the second, and there is the amusing instance of the critic, writing in a semi-sophisticated weekly, who was outraged by what seemed to him to be undue permissiveness. But some of the matters about which he complained were already present in the 1909 edition.

In the light of all this, one can only say that by a more literal acceptance of its declared function, and by running counter more obviously to what people want or think they want in a dictionary and to what they think they have been getting, the Webster Third represents a calculated risk of $3,500,000. Depending on one's point of view, it is either a courageous or a foolhardy venture into the latter half of the twentieth century. For the staff, who in the face of the public clamor must wonder if it has been at all worthwhile, there is only the dubious comfort in Macaulay's words, "The best lexicographer may well be content if his productions are received by the world in cold esteem."

Review Questions

1. What two conflicting traditions have American lexicographers inherited? What are their sources?
2. What linguistic factors intensify the conflict between the two traditions?
3. What differences are there between *Webster's Second* and *Webster's Third*?
4. Why does *Webster's Third* omit some of the material included in the second edition? What material is deleted in the third edition?

How do the deletions reflect an emphasis on linguistic reporting?

5. Why does *Webster's Third* use more illustrative quotations than did its predecessors? What sorts of authors are cited in *Webster's Third*? Why do the language conservatives object to some of these authors? How may the inclusion of such authors be justified?

6. How are status labels treated in *Webster's Third*? How were they treated in *Webster's Second*? How do the changes from past practice relate to the new linguistic emphasis? Why do the editors depart from the traditional use of status labels?

7. How has the development of voice amplification affected the way lexicographers collect evidence about pronunciation?

8. How have the editors of *Webster's Third* used the phoneme to improve their handling of pronunciation?

9. How does Marckwardt explain the "chorus of protest"?

Discussion Questions

1. Marckwardt calls the encyclopedic material "impediments" and "peripheral material" and certainly feels that its deletion from *Webster's Third* is more than compensated for by the inclusion of additional words and quotations. Why do you suppose Noah Webster included such encyclopedic material in his 1806 dictionary? Do the same reasons still exist? Why do illustrative citations "constitute the core of the reportorial dictionary"?

2. Marckwardt compares the reception accorded *Webster's Third* with that given Noah Webster's *An American Dictionary of the English Language* in 1828 and notes in passing that the Germans admired the profound learning reflected in the earlier work. Why do you think Marckwardt chose to discuss the reception of the 1828 dictionary? How is the quotation from Macaulay related to Marckwardt's thesis?

3. Marckwardt notes that the editors of *Webster's Third* turned their attention to the language itself and to what people actually said, rather than to opinions about language. To Marckwardt, would the usage panel described by Bishop represent a forward or a backward step? Explain fully. Give your own views about the matter, and defend them fully. To which of the two traditions described by Marckwardt does the usage panel of the *American Heritage Dictionary* belong?

4. Review the specific innovations introduced by *Webster's Third*. As a whole, do they reflect a basic change in the lexicographic policy which governed *Webster's Second*, or are they merely

logical and up-to-date extensions of the old policy? That is, are the similarities between the two dictionaries greater than the differences, or not? What *are* the similarities?

5. How may people be educated about the function of a dictionary? What are some of the problems involved?

dialects and usage

Grammar and usage are not always adequately distinguished. Grammar pertains to the internal structure of a language that if violated may result in a lack of communication. If the structure of a language is violated, any native speaker, regardless of the degree of his education, will probably know it, even though he may not be able to define the problem. He will know, to take an extreme case, that the words "Boy two the each with is girls of" do not make sense, but that the combination "Each boy is with two of the girls" does. Not only is word order crucial grammatically in English, but the endings of words and the meaningful use of non-lexical words like "the," "with," and "if" (sometimes called "function words") are also. An individual speaker in a speech community has relatively little choice about his use of these features of the language. Some variation is possible from one dialect to another, but very little is likely among members of the same social and geographical dialect. There is pressure upon the speaker to conform, but it is exerted by the language itself, not by other speakers.

There is also pressure toward conformity in matters of usage, but a greater variety of choice is possible, and the pressure is exerted not from within the language, but from without, and not for linguistic reasons at all, but for social reasons. Matters of usage have to do not so much with grammatical correctness as with social acceptance, not so much with whether something *can* be said as with whether it *ought* to be. The appropriateness of one utterance over another, whether spoken or written, depends upon the social occasion for which it is framed, upon regional practice, and upon the immediate context of the utterance. Usage is closely

associated with rhetoric, that is, with speaking or writing effectively, pleasingly, or convincingly. It is inaccurate to speak of
"correct" or "incorrect" usage, since these terms imply absolutes
which do not exist; instead, we should speak of "varieties of
appropriateness."

A native speaker of a language learns the basic grammar for
himself as a young child listening and responding to other people.
Later, with varying degrees of success, a teacher may try to make
him aware of what he has learned, but this practice is often
about as rewarding as teaching the proverbial centipede the theory
of walking: confusing, uninteresting, and ultimately self-
defeating. The student is not mature enough to be interested in
analyzing language, which he regards pragmatically as a means of
communicating. Too much analysis of the complex system of
language too early may, by calling undue attention to itself,
thwart the young student's natural enthusiasm for using language
in new and interesting ways. In addition, from a purely practical
standpoint, such analysis may not help the student accomplish
what it is so often said to do: improve his speaking or writing
ability. Many college composition instructors, certainly, have found
that a student's ability to analyze a sentence or an essay does not
necessarily help him write much better. One's creative and
one's critical abilities frequently do not correspond very closely,
if at all.

Grammar can have a valid place in the curriculum, however,
when it is taught for its own sake as a manifestation of the intricate
systematizing capacity of the human being, and when the student
is encouraged to personally examine the system of language
inductively and to define for himself some of its principles. The
student should not be forced to follow slavishly a particular self-
contained method (like traditional sentence diagramming), which,
although of some value, tends to cultivate his ability to fit sentences into preconstructed molds. Instead of learning much about
the system of language, the student all too often merely learns
the system of diagramming. It is even possible, in fact, that
grammar per se should only be taught at the advanced college or
university level, perhaps in graduate school, and then only to
language specialists, especially since, of necessity, the grammar

taught in the schools to date has often been so oversimplified and, therefore, so distorted as to be almost entirely inadequate.

Unless the teacher is able to encourage the student to study the system of language itself, it might be more rewarding for them both to concentrate on usage. In fact, this has been the attitude of many teachers for a long while, but their idea of teaching usage is often still to tell the student that such-and-such is better than such-and-such, without adequately, if at all, examining the reason for such an assertion. Actually, the student should be exposed to as many varieties of usage in as large a number of circumstances as possible so that he can see for himself which usage is most appropriate under a given set of circumstances. Thus he should develop a sensitivity to language and its use, and his teacher should show him that what he learns about language should be additive, not corrective. The ghetto speaker, for example, should not be made to feel that the way he speaks at home is bad or inappropriate. At home his speech habits are doubtless entirely appropriate. Any other way of speaking might be completely out of place. What he must be made to realize is that what he learns in school about language, as about anything else, is meant to add to the knowledge he has been acquiring since birth in the necessarily restricted environment of the home. The more he knows about language, the more use he can make of it in a greater variety of social situations.

Altogether too frequently, *ex cathedra* pronouncements from teachers and handbooks tend to be very conservative and, therefore, not realistic or truthful. In fact, if a student is taught always to say and always to expect to hear expressions like "To whom do you wish to speak?" and "It was I who called," the teacher will ensure that he will *not* develop a sensitivity for language. Such decorous expression is sometimes called for, and sometimes not. If the student is unwilling or unable to learn to speak like this consistently and yet feels that he really should, he may learn to feel awkward and uncomfortable about language, and the teacher will be laying the groundwork for some of his contorted writing later in college composition classes. Furthermore, whether knowingly or not, the teacher often insists upon and perpetuates the grossest sort of snob appeal. Instead of explaining about the appropriateness and variety of usage, instead of examining the

advantages—whether social, economic, or whatever—of certain
kinds of responses over others, depending upon the occasion, he is
content to invoke the "authorities" and to encourage all students
to speak and write alike.

Succumbing to what Donald Lloyd calls "our national mania
for correctness," the high-school and college composition teacher
alike, no less than the editor and the dissertation director, often
insist, in fact, that the young writer divest himself not only of
all regionalisms and colorful expression, but of individuality of
whatever sort. When the teacher goes on to ban stale metaphors, triteness, and clichés, the writer is left in a quandary. On the
one hand, he is denied the freshness of natural expression, on the
other, the tried-and-true formulas that he might comfortably fall
back on. At best, then, he learns to write a kind of artificial
literary dialect often called "edited English." One writer's style
becomes no different from another's, and a dull literary blandness
results which is called "good prose." Thus, if the teacher is persistent enough, he gets what he asks for: "correct" but unimaginative essays; and the essays are unimaginative not only in form,
but also in content, since the two matters are so closely related.

Our knowledge about how the English language is actually used
in America is steadily growing. The varieties of usage which
Professors McDavid and Marckwardt discuss have been made
known to us largely through the publication of Hans Kurath's
Linguistic Atlas of New England (1939–1943). The maps of dialect
features were made possible through the efforts of "field workers"
who interviewed individual speakers ("informants") of widely
different ages and educational backgrounds and accurately recorded many features of their speech, including distinctive
pronunciation, the inflection of various parts of speech, and usage.
Similar studies have been made for most areas of the United
States, and we can look forward to their eventual publication and
to still other related books, such as Kurath's *Word Geography*
(already published), mentioned by Marckwardt. In addition, the
systematic survey of American regional English, which Marckwardt
notes the lack of in 1958, is now progressing apace in the form of

a dialect dictionary. The American Dialect Society, in addition to its older journal *Dialect Notes* and its current journal *Publication of the American Dialect Society,* is sponsoring DARE, the *Dictionary of American Regional English,* a project directed by Professor Frederic G. Cassidy of the University of Wisconsin. Not only is regional literature examined for dialect features, but field workers, traveling in "word wagons" (small buses carrying tape recorders and other equipment), collect dialect information directly from the speech of informants. When DARE and the projected *Linguistic Atlas of the United States and Canada* are completed, we will have readily available extensive information on regional dialects for the entire country. Indeed, we already have a great deal of this information, for many important publications have resulted from the unpublished *Linguistic Atlas* materials housed at the University of Michigan. Unfortunately, we know much less about social dialects in the United States, although we can expect much activity in this field soon, largely through the efforts of groups like the National Council of Teachers of English, the American Dialect Society, and the Center for Applied Linguistics.

The variety of usage handbooks available, to be sure, already indicates a great deal about the language habits of many different social groups. To a lesser extent, the handbooks also include regional differences, but problems of usage are more often related to social than to regional dialects. Until recently, however, the handbooks have tended to reflect not the usage of the speakers of the language at all, but the opinions and prejudices of the conservative compilers, who reflect the language practices of a generation or even several generations earlier. Wilson Follett's *Modern American Usage,* published as recently as 1966, is the most conservative and accordingly the least realistic of all. The most distinguished of the traditional handbooks is H. W. Fowler's *A Dictionary of Modern English Usage,* originally published in 1926, and revised in 1965 by Sir Ernest Gowers, but British rather than American in orientation. For American usage, there is Margaret Nicholson's *Dictionary of American-English Usage* (1957), also an updating of Fowler's book. Bergen and Cornelia Evans' *A Dictionary of Contemporary American Usage* (1957) breaks with the conservative tradition and for Americans is clearly the most useful comprehensive handbook yet to appear. The book is securely based on scholarly research, although even these editors seem ultimately guided by their own opinions and preferences. There is no room for subjectivity in Margaret Bryant's *Current American Usage: How Americans Say It and Write It* (1962). This work should be the model for future handbooks. For 240 entries it provides lengthy discussions based entirely on extensive and documented research. The only significant drawbacks are the relatively small number of entries—even so, the book took twelve years to complete—and the heavier reliance on written rather than on spoken usage. For spoken usage, however, future writers of usage handbooks will be able to refer to the *Linguistic Atlas* and the *Dictionary of American Regional English*.

Something of the extent to which our knowledge about dialects and usage has grown in this country is made apparent in the essays that follow. Not only do the essays underscore the bristling activity in language studies during the second and third quarters of this century, but at the same time they inform us about many of the results of this activity and explore some of the fascinating social implications. The first essay, by Professor McDavid, provides a general view of the differences among regional and social dialects, and these differences are discussed at greater length in a later essay by Professor Marckwardt. Both pieces provide valuable examples and detail. McDavid's remarks on "correctness" anticipate Donald Lloyd's spirited attack, immediately afterward, against the widely held American insistence on language con- formity; and his mention of slang as a "functional variety" of English looks forward to Stuart Berg Flexner's essay demonstrating what an important force slang is in the English language and how much there is to be learned about the nature of all language from its study. The concluding essay serves as a coda for the section and for the entire book. Professor Evans' informal remarks gather together the various themes treated in earlier essays and, with much good humor, reflect a healthy and positive view toward language that makes its study rewarding and enjoyable as well.

For Further Reading

Good popular books on words and their use are H. L. Mencken, *The American Language,* 4th ed. (New York: Knopf, 1963), which is especially useful on slang; Thomas Pyles, *Words and Ways of American English* (New York: Random House, 1952), which is noteworthy for its treatment of "Tall Talk, Turgidity, and Taboo" (Chapter 6); Albert H. Marckwardt, *American English* (New York: Oxford University Press, 1958), which contains a fine treatment of what the author calls "The Genteel Tradition and the Glorification of the Commonplace" (Chapter 6); and Geoffrey Wagner, *On the Wisdom of Words* (New York: Van Nostrand-Reinhold, 1968).

A brief survey of American dialects can be found in Albert C. Baugh, *A History of the English Language,* 2nd ed. (New York: Appleton-Century-Crofts, 1957), pp. 436–446. Other introductory treatments are Carroll E. Reed, *Dialects of American English* (Cleveland: World Publishing, 1967), and Roger W. Shuy, *Discovering American Dialects* (Champaign, Ill.: National Council of Teachers of English, 1967). Also see, "Lexicography and Dialect Geography," in Neil Postman and Charles Weingartner, *Linguistics: A Revolution in Teaching* (New York: Dell, 1966), pp. 154–175. Two readily available phonograph records are John Muri and Raven I. McDavid, Jr., *Americans Speaking: A Dialect Recording Prepared for the National Council of Teachers of English* (Champaign, Ill.: National Council of Teachers of English, 1967), and Evelyn Gott and Raven I. McDavid, Jr., *Our Changing Language* (St. Louis: Webster Division, McGraw-Hill, 1965).

For additional treatments of usage, see "Recent British and American English," in Thomas Pyles, *The Origins and Development of the English Language* (New York: Harcourt, Brace & World, 1964), pp. 217–261; "Usage: Varieties, Levels, and Styles" and "Usage: Finding and Interpreting the Facts," in Albert H. Marckwardt, *Linguistics and the Teaching of English* (Bloomington, Ind.: Indiana University Press), pp. 27–47 and pp. 48–65, respectively; and "Usage," in Neil Postman and Charles Weingartner, *Linguistics: A Revolution in Teaching, op. cit.,* pp. 87–121.

Finally, the little periodical publication called *Word Watching* (Springfield, Mass.: G. & C. Merriam Co.)—known until recently as *Word Study*—regularly contains discussions both about individual words and expressions and about usage and lexicographical matters in general. The following essays are especially recommended:

Philip B. Gove, "Telling the Truth about Words" (April, 1968).
John S. Kenyon, "Ignorance Builds a Language" (April, 1964).

Patrick E. Kilburn, "Labeling the Language" (October, 1968).

James B. McMillan, "Dictionaries and Usage" (February, 1964).

Allen Walker Read, "Is American English Deteriorating?" (October, 1965).

Paul Stoaks, "The Vexed Problem of English Usage" (March, 1967).

RAVEN I. MCDAVID, JR.

usage, dialects, and functional varieties

Since language is the most habitual form of human behavior, the details of usage often become class markers. Social anthropologists have noted that the more ostensibly "open" a society happens to be, the more tolerant it is of the rise of its members to higher class status and the more subtle are the values used for setting one group above another. In the United States, where it is accepted that the grandsons of immigrants and laborers may fill the highest offices in the land, concern with acquiring certain forms of usage as indications of social status is likely to replace the slow acculturation to upper-class mores that has characterized older and more traditionally oriented societies.

Although actually there are subtle distinctions in usage which will determine the appropriateness of a given form on a particular occasion, and which can be appreciated only by long observation and intuitive experience, the prevailing public attitude is that certain forms of usage are "correct" and others are "incorrect." Teachers, especially of English, are supposed to know the difference between "right" and "wrong" in language. And entrepreneurs who make fortunes out of public anxieties stand ready to provide what the schools haven't given, by warning against "common mistakes" in the language of even the best educated. Furthermore, "right" usage is supposed to be stable, as opposed to "wrong" usage which is changing, while in fact some widely spread forms, favored by authoritarians, are clearly innovations and are still regarded by many cultivated speakers as pretentious affectations of the half-educated.

The cold fact about usage in natural languages is that it is diverse and is subject to change. Essentially, in the usage of native speakers, whatever is, is right; but some usages may be more appropriate than others, at least socially. It is not merely the number of speakers and writers that determines the appropriateness, but their age, education, sophistication, and social position. Within any living language there will be varieties of usage associated with geographical origin (*regional dialects* or simply *dialects*), social status (*social dialects* or *social levels*), and relationships (*styles* or *functional varieties*), as well as such special varieties as *slang, argot,* and *technical language.* All of these arise out of the normal interactions of human beings in a complex society.

Regional dialects originate in a variety of ways. Most commonly they come about from settlement, whether old, as of the Germanic tribes between the Rhine and the Elbe, or recent, as of Southern Englishmen in eastern Virginia and Ulster Scots (more commonly called Scotch-Irish) west of the Blue Ridge. Dialects spread along routes of migration and communication. For example, words and pronunciations characteristic of western New England mark the progress of Yankees across New York State and the Great Lakes Basin. In this Northern dialect area we find such grammatical forms as *dove* for the past tense of *dive,* "sick *to* the stomach" for "nauseated," and *darning needle* as the popular name of the dragonfly. Settlements by speakers of other languages may leave their mark. In the Hudson Valley, which was settled by the Dutch, *stoop,* derived from *stoep,* is commonly used for "porch." In Pennsylvania and settlements elsewhere by Pennsylvania Germans, *smearcase,* modified from *Schmierkäse,* denotes "cottage cheese" or any soft cheese suitable for spreading. The Scandinavian loan translation, to *cook coffee,* is used in place of to *make, brew,* or *fix* it in the Upper Midwest. The Spanish *frijoles,* plural of *frijol,* is used to denote the kidney beans widely used in Texas and other parts of the Southwest.

A dialect area with an important cultural center, whose characteristic speech forms tend to spread, is a *focal area.* Older focal areas in the United States are southeastern New England

(Boston), the Delaware Valley (Philadelphia), the Upper Ohio Valley (Pittsburgh), the Virginia Piedmont (Richmond and its neighboring cities), and the South Carolina Low Country (Charleston). Among newer focal areas that have been identified are the Carolina-Georgia Piedmont (Atlanta-Charlotte), Metropolitan Chicago, New Orleans, Salt Lake City, and the San Francisco Bay area. Others are in process of developing, even as older areas like Richmond and Charleston have lost their preeminence.

An area lacking an important center, whose characteristic speech forms are preserved mainly by the older and less educated, is a *relic area*. Among the more noticeable relic areas are northeastern New England (Maine and New Hampshire), Delmarva (the eastern shore of Chesapeake Bay), the North Carolina Coast, and the Southern Appalachians. Similar regional dialects are found in other parts of the English-speaking world. They are much more sharply defined in the British Isles, much less sharply in Australia. In Canada, as in the United States, regional and local differences are sharpest in the older coastal settlements (New Brunswick, Nova Scotia, Prince Edward Island, and especially in Newfoundland), least sharp in the prairie and Rocky Mountain areas where there was almost no permanent settlement before the building of the transcontinental railroads. But no geographic region is without its local subtypes, and in the United States there is nothing that qualifies as a mythically uniform General American Speech.

Cutting across regional distinctions are social ones. In every linguistic community there are certain people whose speech and writing is admired as a model of *cultivated usage,* because of their wealth, education, family connections, or social position. In sharp contrast is the usage of those with little formal education, experience acquired from travel, or other marks of sophistication, and this we would call *folk usage.* In between is *common usage.* How distant from each other the three types are depends, essentially, on the social structure of a particular community.

What is standard usage may sometimes be determined by an official body charged with setting the standard. In England in the 17th and 18th centuries there was a movement toward

setting up an academy for the English language, a manifestation of the appeal of the idea of linguistic legislation to the neo-
classical era. The movement drew its strength in part from the
classical model of Plato's Academy, but more from the example
of the extant academies on the Continent, the Italian Academia
della Crusca (1592) and especially the Académie Française
(1635), founded by Richelieu. Other academies developed in
Europe, notably in Spain and Russia, but no English academy
ever arose. Although Dryden, Defoe, Pope, Swift, and Addison
and Steele, among others, viewed with alarm the "decay" of the
English language and agreed that only an academy could set
things right, they could not agree on who was to head it, and
the Royal Society, the one learned body that might have assumed the role, confined its interest to the physical sciences.
Samuel Johnson originally proposed to set himself up as the arbiter of the English language through his dictionary, but the
result of his labors was to convince him that such a role was
impracticable.

Nevertheless, the learned of Johnson's day vested in his dictionary the authority of the academy that Johnson had es-
chewed, and established the Anglo-American tradition of dictionary worship, which assumes that a dictionary must and does
include within its covers more accurate information on any
word than any layman could possibly have. The yearning for an
academy is not a thing of the past; laymen are far less likely to
criticize a dictionary or a grammar for unwarranted assumptions of authority than for abdicating its responsibility to make
decisions the public are bound to obey.

Academies usually select one local variety of educated
speech to impose as an official standard: Roman-Florentine in
Italy, Parisian in France, Castilian in Spain, and Moscovian in
Russia. Their legislative power induces a conservatism that prevents their decisions from accurately representing cultivated
usage. If the Académie Française overlooks or rejects a word or
meaning at its weekly meeting, no reconsideration is possible
for several decades, until the rest of the dictionary has been revised and the same part of the alphabet comes up again. As a
result, there is a growing split between academic usage, sub-

servient to the Academy, and popular educated usage, defiant of it.

Inasmuch as the academy-sponsored prestige dialects of Italy, France, Spain, and Russia had achieved their positions before the academies were set up, essentially the academies merely recognized accomplished facts. In Great Britain the grammar and pronunciation used by educated men from the south of England, called Received Standard, have informally achieved highest status without an academy. Fostered by the "public schools," Winchester, Eton, and the like, and by the two great universities, Oxford and Cambridge, Received Standard has long been a badge of office for those who handle the affairs of church and state. Used normally by upper-class families, Received Standard as taught in the public schools to children of the newly rich has been one of the ways for the established order to accommodate the new wealth. A merchant or manufacturer who has risen in society cannot acquire the accent or forms of usage of his new class, but his children can—and the status that goes with it. Yet even in its heyday Received Standard was never uniform or unchanging. Observers have commented on many changes over the past two generations. Today, with the expansion of education under the welfare state, it is no longer possible to bestow Received Standard on every recruit to the intellectual elite, and it has consequently lost much of its glamour.

Until the 1920's, Received Standard was the usual model for teaching English to native speakers of other languages. It is the basis for the local varieties of English that have arisen in the new nations developing out of the Commonwealth in Asia and Africa. The educational systems of these countries have been modeled on British practice, and some of their institutions of higher education are still affiliated with British universities. In Europe there is still a notion in some quarters that Received Standard is "better" or "more elegant" than any variety of American English. However, as overseas students come to the United States in increasing numbers, and as American commercial and educational operations develop overseas, the prestige of Received Standard is no longer unquestioned.

The American criteria for separating standard from nonstandard usage are of yet another sort. On the one hand, a predominantly middle-class society, believing in the importance of formal education, is likely to accept authoritarian judgments; on the other, Americans have inherited traditions of democratic individualism, and are likely to resent the proscription of habitual pronunciations, words, and even grammatical forms. But contributing most to the American multivalued standard is the history of strong local cultural traditions. Before the American Revolution and for some time thereafter, communication between the colonies, or the new states, was difficult. In Boston, New York, Philadelphia, Richmond, and Charleston, indigenous cultivated English developed in different ways. In the new cities to the west similar developments took place. In some rural areas and in a few cities, notably New York, the rapid assimilation of large numbers of immigrants with languages other than English has almost swamped traditional local educated usage and pronunciation.

Throughout the English-speaking world and particularly in America, the grammar of the educated is much more uniform than their pronunciation. In fact, grammar is the surest linguistic index of a speaker's education and general culture. There are almost no structural differences from region to region. The familiar use of such verb phrases as *might could* and *used to could* by educated Southerners stands almost alone. Even in matters of incidence there are few regional differences in the grammar of educated people. One of these is the Northern use of *dove* (dov) for the past tense of *dived*.

As we might expect, grammatical variations are greater in folk and common usage than among the cultivated. Alongside the standard past tense *saw* we find *see, seed*, and *seen*. The last is common everywhere but in New England, the two others are restricted regionally. Beside the standard *climbed*, we have *clam, clim, clom, clome, cloom*, and *clum*, with fairly clear regional patterns, though the last is the most common.

In vocabulary, the sharpest regional distinctions concern matters of humble and rustic life before the mechanization of agriculture. Many such words are only faintly remembered as supermarkets and mass advertising substitute national terms for local ones. But at the same time, new local and regional terms are developing. A dry-cleaning establishment is a *cleanser* in Boston; a rubber band is a *rubber binder* in Minnesota. The grass strip between sidewalk and street is a *boulevard* in Minneapolis, a *devil strip* in Akron, a *tree lawn* in Cleveland, and a *tree belt* in Springfield, Massachusetts; a sandwich of many ingredients, in a small loaf of bread, is a *poor boy* in New Orleans, a *submarine* in Boston, a *hoagy* in Philadelphia, a *hero* in New York City, and a *grinder* in upstate New York.

Regional and social differences are not to be confused with style. Both educated and uneducated usage, wherever encountered, have formal and informal modes though the educated speaker has more gradations at his command. Informal usage is neither better nor worse than the formal usage of the same speaker. What really matters is that each usage should be appropriate for the situation. An educated speaker will transfer from informal *haven't* to formal *have not*. The uneducated speaker who informally uses *I seen* or *I done gone* may adjust to the formal mode with *I have saw* and *I have went*.

Slang is usually but not inevitably associated with the informal style. Characterized by novelty and impermanence, it is used to indicate that one is up to date, but it often merely indicates that one is dated. Within a few years *hot* as a general adjective of approbation gave way to *cool*, and *cool* in turn to *boss*. Recently, however, old slang terms have been temporarily revivified by the rerunning of old movies on television.

Slang was once a synonym for argot, the ingroup language used by those who participate in a particular activity, especially a criminal one. In fact, much slang still derives from small, specialized groups, some of it nursed along tenderly by press agents. Popular musicians have originated many slang expressions now in general use. The word *jazz* itself is a good example: a Southern term meaning to copulate, it was used by the musicians who entertained in New Orleans brothels to describe their kinds of musical improvisations and soon came into general use despite the horror of Southerners who had previously known the word as a taboo verb. Today much slang originates with narcotic addicts, spreads to popular musicians, and then gains vogue among the young, while falling into disuse among its inventors. Other argot, however, is restricted to the practitioners of a particular field: *boff*, meaning variously "a humorous line," "a belly laugh," or "a box-office hit," seems restricted in its use to theatrical circles; *snow*, as it means "cocaine or heroin," is a common term only among drug addicts.

The fate of slang and argot terms is unpredictable. Most of them disappear rapidly, some win their way into standard use, and still others remain what they were to begin with. *Mob*, deplored by Swift and other purists of 1700, would never be questioned today, but *moll*, meaning "a prostitute" or "the mistress of a gangster," has been in use since the early 1600's, and is still slang.

Technical terms arise because it is necessary for those who share a scientific or technical interest to have a basis for discussion. The difference between scientific and popular usage may be seen most strikingly in the biological sciences. A Latin term like *Panthera leo* (lion) has a specific reference, while *cougar* may refer to any large wild American feline predator, or *partridge* may designate the bobwhite quail, a kind of grouse, or some other game bird, according to local usage. Common words may be used with specific reference in a given field: *fusion* denotes one thing in politics, another in nuclear physics. As a field of inquiry becomes a matter of general interest, its technical terms will be picked up and used with less precision. Because of popular interest in Freudian psychology, such terms as *complex, fixation,* and *transference* are bandied about in senses Freud would never have sanctioned.

Despite some yearnings for authorities who would prescribe how people should use their language, the tendency in the English-speaking world is toward teaching based on objective description of the language. This does not mean an abandonment of standards. Indeed, in some situations this approach may call for rigorous drill so as to make habitual the features which everywhere set off standard usage from other varieties. It may also lead to systematic and rigorous drill to impart a fuller command of the rhetorical possibilities of standard English. At the same time, it should provide a more flexible attitude, an acceptance of varieties of cultivated speech other than one's own, and an understanding of the ways in which varieties of a language arose.

Review Questions

1. Describe and comment on the prevailing public attitude toward usage. What are the "cold facts" about usage?
2. How does McDavid qualify his comment, "In the usage of native speakers, whatever is, is right"?
3. How do regional dialects originate?
4. Define "focal area" and "relic area" and give examples.
5. Name and describe the three varieties of social usage.
6. Why do Englishmen and Americans worship the dictionary?
7. What are some of the problems caused by national academies which set the standard of usage?
8. Describe Received Standard and comment on its history.
9. What factors have contributed to the American multivalued standard in usage matters?
10. What is the relation between variations in grammar and the three varieties of social usage?
11. What are the two characteristics of slang? What groups are the principle sources of our slang? What determines the fate of slang and argot words?
12. Why are technical terms created? Why do they sometimes pass into common usage?
13. McDavid writes, "The tendency in the English-speaking world is toward teaching based on objective description of the language." What does McDavid believe the results of this tendency will be?

Discussion Questions

1. How would you account for the existence of relic areas? What do the ones that McDavid lists have in common? How do they appear to differ from focal areas?
2. How does McDavid's explanation of American dictionary worship compare to Marckwardt's? How does his attitude toward language "academies" compare to Bishop's?
3. Has there ever been an American counterpart to the British Received Standard? What social and cultural factors affect the creation of an "accepted" mode of speech?
4. McDavid insists that usage be appropriate to the situation. Give

some examples of situations in which cultivated usage would be inappropriate. There are also situations in which members of a socially elite class deliberately affect the usages of less prestigious social classes. Why do politicians sometimes behave in this way? Does the "mucker pose," as this strategy is called, reflect a democratic or a condescending attitude toward an audience?

5. Although McDavid states that the trend in English is toward the objective description of the language, he also implies that English teachers are conservative and resist giving up notions about "right" and "wrong" in matters of usage. What were the views of your high-school English teachers toward language? Do you see any reason for some English teachers' obsession with "correctness" in usage matters?

6. Being as precise as you can, discuss the kinds of differences in speech that one will and will not encounter when exposed to different regional dialects. Compare these kinds of differences with those among speakers of different social status in the same region or city. Which, if either, seems more significant: the differences in geography or in social status?

7. Give examples of your everyday speech habits as they are influenced by functional varieties of usage. In the written expression of language, would you include the same sort of usages in a letter to your favorite elderly aunt that you would in a note to a roommate? What relationship do you perceive between usage and "tone" in a piece of writing?

8. Under what circumstances would it be advantageous for a person to be able to speak with facility the dialect of more than one geographical area and of more than one social group? Would you say that a person with this sort of versatility in language—and who can vary his speech with appropriate varieties of usage— knows more about language than a punctilious teacher or an unsophisticated student who always speaks in the same manner?

DONALD J. LLOYD

our national mania
for correctness

Every now and then the editors of the university presses let out a disgruntled bleat about the miserable writing done by scholars, even those who are expert in literary fields; and from time to time there are letters and editorials in our national reviews bewailing some current academic malpractice with the English language. At present, even *PMLA* (the Publications of the Modern Language Association), traditionally the repository of some of the worst writing done by researchers, is trying to herd its authors toward more lucid exposition. And at two recent meetings of the august Mediaeval Academy, one at Boston and one at Dumbarton Oaks, bitter remarks were passed about the failure of specialists in the Middle Ages to present their findings in some form palatable to the general reader, so that he can at least understand what they are writing about.

Even admitting that a really compelling style is the result of years of cultivation, much scholarly writing is certainly worse than it needs to be. But it is not alone in this. Generally speaking, the writing of literate Americans whose primary business is not writing but something else is pretty bad. It is muddy, backward, convoluted and self-strangled; it is only too obviously the product of a task approached unwillingly and accomplished without satisfaction or zeal. Except for the professionals among us, we Americans are hell on the English language. I am not in touch with the general run of British writing by non-professionals, but I suspect that it is nothing to make those islanders smug, either.

From *American Scholar*, XXI (Summer, 1952), 283–289. Reprinted by permission of the author.

Furthermore, almost any college professor, turning the spotlight with some relief from himself and his colleagues to his students, will agree that their writing stinks to high heaven, too. It is a rare student who can write what he has to write with simplicity, lucidity and euphony, those qualities singled out by Somerset Maugham; far more graduating seniors are candidates for a remedial clinic than can pass a writing test with honors. And freshman writing is forever the nightmare of the teachers of composition, as it would be of their colleagues if the latter could not escape to the simple inanities of their objective tests.

Yet it was not always so. I have on my desk a little manuscript from the fourteenth century written by an unknown author, which I am in the process of editing. When I read it to one of my classes, as I occasionally do, with no more modernization than my own Great Lakes pronunciation and the substitution of a word for one which has become obsolete, it is a simple, clear and engaging document. "Where is any man nowadays that asketh how I shall love God and my fellow-Christians?" it begins. "How I shall flee sin and serve God truly as a true Christian man should? What man is there that will learn the true law of God, which he biddeth every Christian man to keep upon pain of damnation in hell without end? . . . Unnethe [scarcely] is there any lewd man or lewd woman that can rightly well say his Pater Noster, his Ave Maria, and his Creed, and sound the words out readily as they should. But when they play Christmas games about the fire, therein will they not fail. Those must be said out without stumbling for dread of smiting. But if a lewd man should be smited now for each failing that he maketh in saying of his Pater Noster, his Ave Maria, and his Creed, I trowe he should be smited at the full." And so on, to the beautiful poetic line, "Then think it not heavy to dwell with thy mother in her wide house, thou that laist in the strait chamber of her womb." The spelling in the original is hectic, and the capitalization and punctuation sporadic, to say the least.

Yet there was a man who knew what he had to say and set out about saying it, with no nonsense and no fumbling. He aimed for his audience and, judging by the dog-ears and sweat-marks on the book, which is about the size of one of our pocket books, he hit it. Why cannot we do as well in our time? Indeed, the eighteenth century was about the last age in which almost any man, if he was literate at all, could set down his thoughts— such as they were—so that they did not have to be excavated by the reader. We have an abundance of letters, diaries, pamphlets, and other papers from that period, and they are well written. It was the age, we may recall, not only of Boswell and Johnson, but of Pepys and Franklin as well, and of a host of other men whose main legacy to us was a simple, direct, workmanlike style, sufficient to the man and to the occasion, which said what it had to say and said it well. With the end of that century we go into the foggy, foggy darkness, and God knows whether we shall ever find our way out of it—as a people, that is, as a nation of thinking men and women with something to say.

Nevertheless, there is no question what makes our writing bad, or what we shall have to do to better it. We shall simply have to isolate and root out a monomania which now possesses us, which impedes all language study and inhibits all mastery of our native tongue—all mastery, that is, on paper; for as speakers of English, we Americans are loving and effective cultivators of our expression. I recall the gas station attendant who was filling my car. The gasoline foamed to the top of the tank, and he shut off the pump. "Whew!" I said, "that nearly went over." "When you see whitecaps," he replied, "you better stop." "You better had," I said, lost in admiration. But if you had given him a pencil, he would have chewed the end off before he got one word on paper.

The demon which possesses us is our mania for correctness. It dominates our minds from the first grade to the graduate school; it is the first and often the only thing we think of when we think of our language. Our spelling must be "correct"—even if the words are ill-chosen; our "usage" must be "correct"—even though any possible substitute expression, however crude, would be perfectly clear; our punctuation must be "correct"—even though practices surge and change with the passing of years, and differ from book to book, periodical to periodical. Correct!

That's what we've got to be, and the idea that we've got to be correct rests like a soggy blanket on our brains and our hands whenever we try to write.

This mania for correctness is another legacy from the eighteenth century, but it did not get a real grip on us until well into the nineteenth. Its power over us today is appalling. Among my other tasks, I teach advanced courses in the English language to students preparing to teach. Most of these are seniors and graduate students, and in the summer especially, there is a sprinkling of older men and women, experienced teachers, who are sweating out a master's degree. They have had courses in "English" throughout their schooling. But of the nature and structure of the English language, the nature of language habits, the relation of speech to writing, and the differences in usage which arise from dialect and from differing occupational and educational demands—of all these, they know nothing at all. Nor do they come to me expecting to learn about these. They want to know two things: what correct usage is and how you beat it into the kids' heads. That there are other considerations important to an English teacher is news to many of them. What they get from me is a good long look at their language.

To trace this monolithic concentration on usage is to pursue a vicious circle, with the linguists on the outside. The literate public seems to get it from the English teachers, and the teachers get it from the public. The attitudes and pronouncements on language of a Jacques Barzun, a Wilson Follett, a Bernard De Voto, or a Norman Lewis ("How Correct Must Correct English Be?") mean more to English teachers than anything said by the most distinguished professional students of language—such as Leonard Bloomfield, Robert Hall or Charles Carpenter Fries. Correct usage is pursued and discussed, furthermore, without much reference to the actual writing of literary men. Now and again I amuse myself by blue-penciling a current magazine such as the *Saturday Review* or *Collier's* against the rules. I have to report that error is rampant, if variation is to be considered error. The boys just don't seem to pay attention to the rules. Moreover, having seen some of their first drafts, I am pretty sure that what conformity they do display is the work of their wives, secretaries, editors, proofreaders and typesetters, rather than their own. It takes a determined effort to beat the old Adam out of a readable manuscript.

Thus it is only the determined, consciously creative professional who can build his work on the actual language of men. In a recent issue of the *Saturday Review,* I stumbled on a quotation from Wolfgang Langewiesche. "Well, it isn't crowned by no castle, that's for sure," he wrote, "and by no cathedral either." My eyes popped, and I read it again. I liked it. It looked right; it sounded right; it had a fine Chaucerian swing to it. But I bet it cost him some blood and a fifth of Scotch to get it into print. In my own limited publication, I find "a historical" changed to "an historical," all my "further's" changed to "farther" and all my "farther's" to "further," "than us" watered down to "than we," and many, many more. How E. M. Forster got by with "the author he thinks," and got it reprinted in a freshman handbook a few pages along from the prohibition of such locutions baffles me. A phony standardization of usage appears in print, the work of editors unconscious of the ultimate meaning of what they do.

The result of all this is that a wet hand of fear rests on the heart of every nonprofessional writer who merely has a lot of important knowledge to communicate. He writes every sentence with a self-conscious horror of doing something wrong. It is always a comfort to him if he can fit himself into some system, such as that of a business or governmental office which provides him with a model. It is thus that gobbledegook comes into being. I once braced a distinguished sociologist, a student of occupational myths and attitudes, about the convoluted, mainly nominal turgidity of his writing. He apparently admitted verbs into his sentences the way we admit DP's into the United States, reluctantly and with pain. In speech he was racy, confident and compelling, a brilliant lecturer. "It's the only way I can get my work into the periodicals," he told me blandly. "If it's clear and simple, they don't think it's scholarly." With what relief the pedagogues subside into pedagese!

If we really want to get good writing from people who know things, so that we can come to learn what they know as easily as we learn from their talk, we can do it in a generation or so.

In school and out, in print and out, we can leave usage to its natural nurse, the unforced imitation of the practices which are actually current among educated people. We can use our English courses in school and college, not to give drill on questionable choices among common alternatives, demanding that one be taken as right and the others as wrong, but to give practice in reading and writing. We can learn to read and write for the idea, and go for the idea without regard for anything else. Then our young people will come to maturity confidently using their pencils to find out what they think and get it down on paper; then our scholars will come to write simply, clearly and brilliantly what they brilliantly know.

In our speech we have arrived, I think, at a decency of discourse which is conducive to effective expression. We listen, with a grave courteous attention, to massive patterns of speaking different from our own because they come from differences in dialect and social status; we listen without carping and without a mean contempt. Furthermore, we participate; we go with a speaker through halts and starts, over abysses of construction, filling in the lacunae without hesitation; we discount inadvertencies and disregard wrong words, and we arrive in genial good will with the speaker at his meaning. In this atmosphere, our speech has thrived, and the ordinary American is in conversation a confident, competent expressive being. In writing he is something else again.

No one flourishes in an atmosphere of repression. It is possible, of course, for a person with special aptitudes and a special drive to bull his way past the prohibitions and achieve an individual style. But with the negative attitude that attends all our writing, those whose main interest lies elsewhere are inhibited by fear of "error" and the nagging it stirs up from setting pen to paper, until the sight of a blank white page gives them the shakes. It is no wonder that their expression is halting and ineffective. They cannot fulfill the demands of a prissy propriety and trace the form of an idea at the same time. They thus arrive at adulthood victims of the steely eye of Mr. Sherwin Cody, whose bearded face stares at them from the countless ads for his correspondence school, demanding, "Do YOU make these mistakes in English?" The locutions he lists are not mistakes, and Mr. Cody knows they are not; but his readers do not know it, and they do not know that they don't matter anyway.

For usage doesn't matter. What matters is that we get done what we have to do, and get said what we have to say. Sufficient conformity is imposed upon us by the patterns of our language and by the general practices of its users so that we do not have to run the idea of conformity into the ground by carping about trivial erratics in expression. Why in this matter of language alone complete conformity should be considered a virtue—except to typists, printers and typesetters—it is difficult to see (unless, perhaps, we are using it as a covert and pusillanimous means of establishing our own superiority). In our other concerns in life, we prize individuality; why in this one matter we should depart from a principle that otherwise serves us well is a puzzle for fools and wise men to ponder, especially since there is no general agreement on what to conform to, and one man's correctness is another's error. Not until we come to our senses—teachers, editors, writers and readers together—and stop riding each other's backs, will the casual, brisk, colorful, amused, ironic and entertaining talk of Americans find its way into print. We should all be happy to see it there.

Review Questions

1. Why does Lloyd discuss the fourteenth-century manuscript? What points does he make about "style"?
2. What was the last century in which men could express themselves simply and directly? Which writers in this age excelled at writing?
3. Does our "mania for correctness" apply to our writing or to our speaking, or does it apply to both?
4. The "English" courses that teachers traditionally take fail to cover what aspects of language? What are teachers often interested in learning about "English"?
5. What does Lloyd mean when he states, "To trace this monolithic concentration on usage is to pursue a vicious circle, with the linguists on the outside"?
6. Does Lloyd believe that there is any relation between correctness

and the writing of "literary men"? What evidence does he offer to support his argument?

7. What is the attitude of editors toward usage?
8. Why does the nonprofessional writer lapse into gobbledegook?
9. What does Lloyd believe should be taught in high-school and college English courses?
10. Are Americans more capable in speech or in writing? Why?
11. What does Mr. Sherwin Cody represent? Why is he mentioned?
12. What, according to Lloyd, should be the relation between speaking and writing?

Discussion Questions

1. Lloyd mentions Maugham's requirements for good writing: simplicity, lucidity, and euphony. Elsewhere in the essay, Lloyd praises the fourteenth-century manuscript as a "simple, clear and engaging document," refers to the "simple, direct, workmanlike style" of eighteenth-century writers, and hopes that our scholars will write "simply, clearly and brilliantly." These comments imply the presence of an audience. Explain what Maugham's requirements mean and how they relate to the writer and his audience. What, then, does Lloyd believe the purpose of writing to be?
2. Lloyd states, "No one flourishes in an atmosphere of repression." What forces and influences in our society have produced this "atmosphere"?
3. Lloyd implies that we should write more or less as we speak. At least we should not consciously try to divest our writing of all traces of individuality and strive to write in a special and contrived "literary" manner. Do you think that the student might thus be able to pay more attention to the content of his compositions? Do you think this would help alleviate the frequently heard complaint of the student that the instructor grades an essay too much on form and not enough on content? Discuss the matter with your instructor.
4. If the student makes little or no distinction between his speaking and writing styles, can you think of problems which might result? How is this matter related to tone? to audience? to the first, second, or third drafts of out-of-class themes?
5. Is it true, as Lloyd states in the last paragraph, that "usage doesn't matter"? Does usage matter in speech? What does Lloyd mean when he denies the importance of usage? What is the relation between his assertion and the style of the essay as a whole?

regional and social variations

The English language is spoken natively in America by no less than 145 million persons over an area of some three million square miles. Various parts of the United States differ considerably from each other with respect to climate, topography, plant and animal life, economic conditions, and social structure. Sociologists and historians recognize at least six regional cultures within the continental borders of the country. The same a priori grounds that led us to assume the existence of a series of differences between British and American English at the outset of this work will justify the inference that the language is likely not to be uniform throughout the country. The American novelist John Steinbeck in his *Grapes of Wrath* offers convincing evidence of the plausibility of this assumption:

'I knowed you wasn't Oklahomy folks. You talk queer kinda— That ain't no blame, you understan'.'

'Ever'body says words different,' said Ivy. 'Arkansas folks says 'em different, and Oklahomy folks says 'em different. And we seen a lady from Massachusetts, an' she said 'em differentest of all. Couldn' hardly make out what she was sayin'.'

Early travelers to America and native commentators on the language agree on the existence of regional differences at an early period in our national history. Mrs. Anne Royal called attention to various Southernisms in the works which she wrote during the second quarter of the nineteenth century, and as early as 1829, Dr. Robley Dunglison had identified many of the Americanisms, in the glossary he compiled, with particular portions of the country. Charles Dickens recognized regional differences in the English he encountered in his first tour of the United States, and William Howard Russell, reporting on Abraham Lincoln's first state banquet, at which he was a guest, mentions his astonishment at finding 'a diversity of accent almost as great as if a number of foreigners had been speaking English.'

A number of other observers, however, were sufficiently impressed by the uniformity of the language throughout the country to make this a matter of comment. De Tocqueville, in a rather extended treatment of the language of the young republic, flatly declared, 'There is no patois in the New World,' and John Pickering, along with Noah Webster, easily the most distinguished of our early philologists, also remarked on the great uniformity of dialect through the United States, 'in consequence,' as he said, 'of the frequent removals of people from one part of our country to another.'

There is truth in both types of comment. People in various parts of the United States do not all speak alike, but there is greater uniformity here than in England or in the countries of Western Europe, and this makes the collection of a trustworthy body of information upon the regional variations in American English a somewhat difficult and delicate matter.

The gathering of authentic data on the dialects of many of the countries of Western Europe began in the latter decades of the nineteenth century. The *Atlas linguistique de la France* followed closely upon the heels of the *Sprachatlas des deutschen Reichs,* and the activities of the English Dialect Society were initiated about the same time. In 1889 a group of American scholars organized the American Dialect Society, hoping that the activities of this organization might result in a body of material from which either a dialect dictionary or a series of linguistic maps, or both, might be compiled. The society remained relatively small, however, and although some valuable information appeared in its journal *Dialect Notes*, a systematic survey of the regional varieties of American English has not yet resulted from its activities.

The past quarter of a century, however, has seen the development of such a survey. Beginning in 1928, a group of re-

searchers under the direction of Professor Hans Kurath, now of
the University of Michigan, undertook the compilation of a *Linguistic Atlas of New England* as the first unit of a projected
Linguistic Atlas of the United States and Canada. The New England atlas, comprising a collection of some 600 maps, each
showing the distribution of a single language feature throughout the area, was published over the period from 1939 to 1943.
Since that time, field work for comparable atlases of the Middle
Atlantic and of the South Atlantic states has been completed,
and the materials are awaiting editing and publication. Field
records for atlases of the North Central states and the Upper
Middle West are virtually complete, and significant beginnings
have been made in the Rocky Mountain and the Pacific Coast
areas. Surveys in Louisiana, in Texas, and in Ontario are also
under way. It is perhaps not too optimistic to predict that within
the next twenty-five years all of the United States and Canada as
well will have been covered in at least an initial survey.

For a number of reasons it is not easy to collect a body of
valid and reliable information on American dialects. The wide
spread of education, the virtual extinction of illiteracy, the extreme mobility of the population—both geographically and from
one social class to another—and the tremendous development of
a number of media of mass communication have all contributed
to the recession of local speech forms. Moreover, the cultural in-
security of a large portion of the American people has caused
them to feel apologetic about their language. Consequently, they
seldom display the same degree of pride or affection that many
an English or a European speaker has for his particular patois.
Since all dialect research is essentially a sampling process, this
means that the investigator must take particular pains to
secure representative and comparable samples from the areas
which are studied. Happily, the very care which this demands
has had the result of developing the methodology of linguistic
geography in this country to a very high level.

In general, the material for a linguistic atlas is based upon
the natural responses of a number of carefully selected individuals representing certain carefully chosen communities, which
in themselves reflect the principal strains of settlement and fac-

ets of cultural development in the area as a whole. Since the spread of education generally results in the disappearance of local or regional speech forms, and since the extension of schooling to virtually all of the population has been an achievement of the past seventy-five years, it became necessary for the American investigator to differentiate between the oldest generation, for whom schooling beyond the elementary level is not usual, and a middle-aged group who is likely to have had some experience with secondary schools. In addition, it is highly desirable to include some representatives of the standard or cultivated speech in each region, that their language may serve as a basis of comparison with the folk speech. Accordingly, in the American atlases, from each community represented, the field worker will choose at least two, and sometimes three representatives, in contrast to the usual practice of European researchers, who may safely content themselves with one. Moreover, it is equally necessary to make certain that the persons chosen in any community have not been subject to alien linguistic influences; consequently, only those who have lived there all of their lives, and preferably those who represent families who have long been identified with the area in question, are interviewed, although as one moves westward into the more recently settled areas this is not always possible.

Since complete materials are available only for the eastern seaboard and for the area north of the Ohio River as far west as the Mississippi, tentative conclusions relative to the regional variations in American English can be presented only for the eastern half of the country. The principal dialect areas presented in Kurath's *Word Geography of the Eastern United States*, are indicated on the accompanying map.

The three major dialect boundaries, it will be noted, cut the country into lateral strips and are labeled by Professor Kurath *Northern*, *Midland*, and *Southern* respectively. The line which separates the Northern and Midland areas begins in New Jersey a little below Sandy Hook, proceeds northwest to the east branch of the Susquehanna near Scranton, Pennsylvania, then goes westward through Pennsylvania just below the northern tier of counties. In Ohio the boundary dips below the Western Reserve,

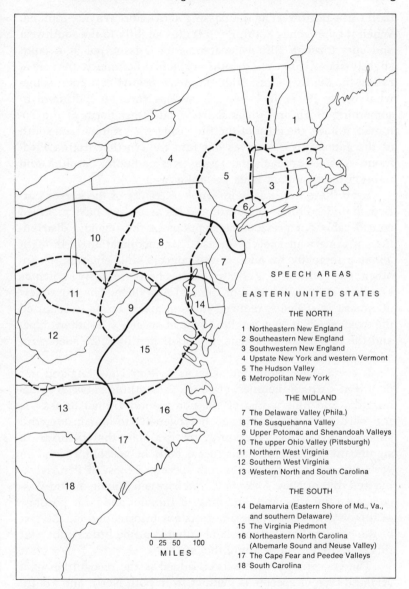

SPEECH AREAS

EASTERN UNITED STATES

THE NORTH

1 Northeastern New England
2 Southeastern New England
3 Southwestern New England
4 Upstate New York and western Vermont
5 The Hudson Valley
6 Metropolitan New York

THE MIDLAND

7 The Delaware Valley (Phila.)
8 The Susquehanna Valley
9 Upper Potomac and Shenandoah Valleys
10 The upper Ohio Valley (Pittsburgh)
11 Northern West Virginia
12 Southern West Virginia
13 Western North and South Carolina

THE SOUTH

14 Delamarvia (Eastern Shore of Md., Va.,
   and southern Delaware)
15 The Virginia Piedmont
16 Northeastern North Carolina
   (Albemarle Sound and Neuse Valley)
17 The Cape Fear and Peedee Valleys
18 South Carolina

0 25 50   100
MILES

Figure 3 from Hans Kurath, *A Word Geography of the Eastern United States* (1949). Reprinted by permission of the University of Michigan Press.

then turns northwest again, passing above Fort Wayne, Indiana. When it approaches South Bend it dips slightly to the southwest and cuts through Illinois, reaching the Mississippi at a point slightly above Quincy. The other principal boundary, that separating the Southern and Midland areas, begins at a point somewhat below Dover in Delaware, sweeps through Baltimore in something of an arc, turns sharply southwest north of the Potomac, follows the crest of the Blue Ridge in Virginia, and south of the James River swerves out into the North Carolina Piedmont. As we approach the lower part of South Carolina and Georgia the boundary is as yet unknown.

Even these necessarily incomplete results of the survey carried on under Professor Kurath and his associates have modified considerably our previous conceptions of the regional distribution of American speech forms. This modification is brought about principally by adding one concept and eliminating another. The concept thus eliminated has been variously known as Middle Western, Western, or General American. The older view of American dialects, reduced to its simplest terms, recognized the existence of a New England type of speech, a Southern type, and the remainder was generally blanketed by some such term as General American.

It seems clear now that what is neither New England nor Southern—which includes, of course, something between three-quarters and nine-tenths of the continental United States—is far too diverse and lacking in homogeneity to be considered a single major dialect. We know, for example, that there are a significant number of differences, both in vocabulary and in verb inflections, between the folk speech of most of Pennsylvania and that of New York state, and between Michigan and Wisconsin on the one hand, and most of Indiana and large portions of Illinois and Ohio on the other. As our information for the rest of the country becomes available, there can be little doubt that this conclusion will be strengthened.

The concept which has been added is the recognition of a Midland type of speech as distinct from both North and South. An examination of the evidence which Professor Kurath presents in his *Word Geography* leaves no doubt that the speech of this area, though it is by no means uniform, is sufficiently differentiated from both North and South to justify its classification as a major dialect area. This conclusion is supported not only by Atwood's study of the verb forms in the eastern portion of the country but by the available materials from the North Central States.

The map shown on page 183 includes also a few, but not all, of the sub-dialect areas which merit recognition. In the North the principal area is that which separates coastal New England from western New England, New York state, and the territory to the west. In general, this boundary follows the line of the Green Mountains, the Berkshire Hills, and the Connecticut River. The Metropolitan New York area consists of a broad circle with the city itself at the center; the Hudson Valley area encompasses the original Dutch settlements in New York and northern New Jersey, spreading into northeastern Pennsylvania. The Midland area is divided into northern and southern sub-areas, the line of demarcation being just a little south of the Old National Road in Ohio, Indiana, and Illinois. Within the Southern dialect region, the Virginia Piedmont and the Delmarva peninsula constitute distinct sub-areas.

Thus far it is the lexical materials gathered in connection with the various atlas projects which have been analyzed most extensively, and as the title of Professor Kurath's work indicates, his plotting of the major dialect areas is based upon vocabulary evidence. For example, characteristic Northern expressions that are current throughout the area include *pail, swill, whiffletree* or *whippletree, comforter* or *comfortable* for a thick quilt, *brook, co-boss* or *come-boss* as a cow call, *johnnycake, salt pork,* and *darning needle* for a dragonfly. In the Midland area we find *blinds* for roller shades, *skillet, spouting* or *spouts* for eaves, a *piece* for food taken between meals, *snake feeder* for a dragonfly, *sook* as the call to calves, *armload* for an armful of wood; and one *hulls* beans when he takes off the shells. A quarter *till* the hour is a typical Midland expression, as is the elliptical *to want off,* or *out,* or *in.* The South has *lightwood* as the term for kindling, a *turn* of wood for an armful; stringbeans are generally *snap beans; hasslet* is the term for the edible inner organs of a pig, *chittlins* for the small intestine; and in this area cows are said to *low* at feeding time.

The sub-dialect areas also have their characteristic forms. In coastal New England, for instance, *pigsty* is the normal term for pig-pen, *bonny clapper* for curdled sour milk, *buttonwood* for a sycamore, and *pandowdy* for a cobbler type of dessert. Eastern Virginia has *cuppin* for a cowpen, *corn house* for a crib. *Lumber room* survives as the term for a storeroom. A grasshopper is known as a *hopper grass,* and *batter bread* is used for a soft cornbread containing egg.

As far as the sectors of the American lexicon which reflect regional differences are concerned, the matter is trenchantly summarized in Kurath's *Word Geography,* where the author points out first of all that the vocabularies of the arts and sciences, of industries, commercial enterprises, social and political institutions, and even many of the crafts, are national in scope because the activities they reflect are organized on a national basis. He then goes on to say:

Enterprises and activities that are regionally restricted have, on the other hand, a considerable body of regional vocabulary which, to be sure, may be known in other parts of the country, even if it is not in active use. The cotton planter of the South, the tobacco grower, the dairy farmer, the wheat grower, the miner, the lumberman, and the rancher of the West have many words and expressions that are strictly regional and sometimes local in their currency.

Regional and local expressions are most common in the vocabulary of the intimate everyday life of the home and the farm—not only among the simple folk and the middle class but also among the cultured . . . Food, clothing, shelter, health, the day's work, play, mating, social gatherings, the land, the farm buildings, implements, the farm stocks and crops, the weather, the fauna and flora—these are the intimate concern of the common folk in the countryside, and for these things expressions are handed down in the family and the neighborhood that schooling and reading and a familiarity with regional or national usage do not blot out.

It is not only in the vocabulary that one finds regional differences in American speech. There are pronunciation features as well. Throughout the Northern area, for example, the distinction between [o] and [ɔ] in such word pairs as *hoarse* and *horse,* *mourning* and *morning* is generally maintained; [s] regularly occurs in *grease* (verb) and *greasy,* and *root* is pronounced by many with the vowel of *wood.* Within the Northern area such sub-dialects as coastal New England and Metropolitan New York also show many characteristic forms; the treatment of the vowel of *bird* is only one of these, and words of the *calf, pass, path, dance* group constitute another. In the Midland area speakers fail to distinguish between *hoarse* and *horse.* Rounding is characteristic of the vowels of *hog, frog, log, wasp* and *wash,* and in the last of these words an *r* often intrudes in the speech of the not too highly educated. The vowels of *due* and *new* will resemble that of *food* rather than *feud.* In the South, *r* is 'lost' except before vowels, as it is in eastern New England and New York City but not in the Northern area generally. Words like *Tuesday, due,* and *new* have a y-like glide preceding the vowel, and final [z] in *Mrs.* is the normal form.

Among the older, relatively uneducated group and even to some extent among the middle-aged informants who have had some secondary schooling there are also regional differences in inflectional forms and syntax. For example, *hadn't ought* for 'oughtn't,' *see* as a past tense form, *clim* for 'climbed' among the oldest sector of the population, *wan't* for 'wasn't,' *be* in such expressions as *How be you?,* and the choice of the preposition *to* in *sick to his stomach* are all characteristic of the Northern area. *Clum* for 'climbed,' *seen* for 'saw,' *all the further* and *I'll wait on you* are to be found in the Midlands, whereas *belongs to be,* *heern* for 'heard,' *seed* as the past tense of 'to see,' *holp* for 'helped,' *might could* and *mought have* are characteristic of the South.

All of this raises the question as to how the regional forms of American English developed in our three and one-half centuries of linguistic history. The first factor which must be taken into account is settlement history. Where did our earliest settlers come from, and what dialects did they speak? At the time of the earliest settlements, English local and regional dialects were in a stronger position than they are today in that they constituted the natural speech of a greater portion of the English-speaking population and were in customary use farther up the social scale.

Moreover, it is quite unlikely that any single local settlement, even at the outset, ever consisted entirely of speakers of the same dialect. Of ten families of settlers gathered in any one place, two might well have spoken London English, three or four others one of the southern or southeastern county dialects. There would be in addition a couple of families speaking northern English and another two or three employing a western dialect. In the course of their being in constant contact with each other, compromises for the everyday terms in which their dialects differed would normally have developed, and one could reasonably expect to find a southern English term for a water receptacle, a northern word for earthworm, and a western designation for sour milk. Matters of pronunciation would eventually, perhaps after a slightly longer time, be compromised in much the same manner. Moreover, the resultant compromises for various localities would be different. In the first place, no two localities would have had exactly the same proportions of speakers of the various English dialects, and even if they had, the two localities would not have arrived at precisely the same set of compromises. Thus, early in our history we developed, at various points on the Atlantic seaboard, a number of local cultures, each with distinctive social characteristics of its own— including a dialect which was basically a unique blend of British types of speech, supplemented in its vocabulary by borrowings from the Indians and from Dutch and German neighbors.

With the beginning of the nineteenth century, three changes occurred which were to have a profound effect upon the language situation in America. First, the industrial revolution resulted in the growth of a number of industrial centers, uprooting a considerable proportion of the farm population and concentrating it in the cities. The development of the railroad and other mechanical means of travel increased greatly the mobility of the average person. The large-scale migrations westward also resulted in some resettlement and shifting, even among those who did not set out on the long trek. All of this resulted in a general abandonment of narrowly local speech forms in favor of fewer, more or less general, regional types. Some local speech forms have remained even to the present day. These are usually known as relics, particularly when they are distributed in isolated spots over an area rather than in concentration. *Open stone peach,* for example, is a relic for freestone peach, occurring in Maryland. *Smurring up,* 'getting foggy,' survives as a relic in eastern Maine and more rarely on Cape Cod and Martha's Vineyard.

Even prior to the shifts in population and changes in the culture pattern, certain colonial cities such as Boston, Philadelphia, and Charleston had acquired prestige by developing as centers of trade and foci of immigration. They became socially and culturally outstanding, as well as economically powerful, thus dominating the areas surrounding them. As a consequence, local expressions and pronunciations peculiar to the countryside came to be replaced by new forms of speech emanating from these centers. A fairly recent instance of this is to be found in the New England term *tonic* for soda water, practically co-extensive with the area served by Boston wholesalers. Professor Kurath considers the influence of these centers as second only to the influence of the original settlement in shaping the regional types of speech on the Atlantic seaboard and in determining their geographic boundaries.

Nor was the general process of dialect formation by any means completed with the settlement of the Atlantic seaboard. As the land to the west came to be taken up in successive stages (for example, western New York, Michigan, Wisconsin in the North; southern Ohio, Indiana, and southern Illinois in the Midland area) the same mixtures of speech forms among the settlers were present at first, and the same linguistic compromises had to be worked out. The same processes occurred in the interior South, in Texas, and later on in the Far West. Consequently, the complete linguistic history, particularly with respect to regional forms, of the United States will not be known until all of the facts concerning the present regional distribution of speech forms have been collected, and until these facts have been collated with the settlement history of the various areas and the speech types employed by the settlers at the time they moved in. In its entirety this would necessitate a greater knowledge of the local dialects of seventeenth-century England than we have at present.

Moreover, such environmental factors as topography, climate, and plant and animal life also play their parts in influencing the dialect of an area, just as they did in the general transplanting of the English language to America. The complexity and size of the network of fresh-water streams will affect the distribution and meaning of such terms as *brook, creek, branch,* and *river.* In parts of Ohio and Pennsylvania, for example, the term *creek* is applied to a much larger body of water than in Michigan. It is even more obvious that in those parts of the country where snow is a rarity or does not fall at all, there will be no necessity for a battery of terms to indicate coasting face down on a sled. It is not surprising that those areas of the country where cows can be milked outside, for at least part of the year, will develop a specific term for the place where this is done: witness *milk gap* or *milking gap* current in the Appalachians south of the James River. The wealth of terms for various types of fences throughout the country is again dependent, in part at least, on the material which is available for building them, be it stones, stumps, or wooden rails.

Different types of institutions and practices which developed in various parts of the country also had their effect upon regional vocabulary. Those settlements which did not follow the practice of setting aside a parcel of land for common grazing purposes had little use for such terms as *green* or *common.* The meaning of *town* will vary according to the place and importance of township and county respectively in the organization of local government. The same principle applies equally well to foods of various kinds, which reflect not only materials which are readily available but folk practices as well. The German custom of preparing raised doughnuts as Lenten fare survives in the Pennsylvania term *fossnocks,* shortened from *Fastnachtskuchen.*

Finally, a new invention or development introduced into several parts of the country at the same time will acquire different names in various places. The baby carriage, for example, seems

to have been a development of the 1830's and '40's, and this is
the term which developed in New England. Within the Philadelphia trade area, however, the article became known as a *baby
coach,* whereas *baby buggy* was adopted west of the Alleghenies
and *baby cab* in other regions throughout the country. Nor have
we necessarily seen an end to this process. Within the last two
decades the building of large, double-lane, limited-access automobile highways has been undertaken in various parts of the
country, yet the terminology for them differs considerably. In
eastern New York, Connecticut, and Rhode Island these are
parkways, but *turnpikes* in Pennsylvania, New Jersey, New
Hampshire, Maine, Massachusetts, Ohio, and Indiana. In New
York *thruway* is used, and they are *expressways* in Michigan
and *freeways* in California. These would seem to be regionalisms in the making.

It is of interest also to look at the dialect situation from the
point of view of various words which are employed in various
parts of the country for the same concept. One of the most interesting and instructive distributions is to be found in connection with the terms used for *earthworm.* This word is used by
cultivated speakers in the metropolitan centers. *Angleworm* is
the regional term in the North, *fishworm* in the Midland area,
and *fishing worm* in the coastal South. *Fish bait* and *bait worm*
occupy smaller areas within the extensive *fishworm* region, but
are also distributed over a wide territory.

In addition, there is a large number of local terms, many of
which are used principally by the older and less-educated in-
habitants. The Merrimack Valley, in New Hampshire, and Essex
County, Massachusetts, have *mud worm. Eace worm* is used in
Rhode Island. *Angle dog* appears in upper Connecticut, and
ground worm on the Eastern Shore of Virginia. *Red worm* is
used in the mountains of North Carolina, and an area around
Toledo, Ohio, uses *dew worm.* Scattered instances of *rainworm*
appear on Buzzards Bay in Massachusetts, throughout the Pennsylvania German area, and in German settlements in North Carolina, Maine, and Wisconsin. We have, thus, a wealth of older
local terms, three distinct regional words, and the cultivated
earthworm appearing in addition as a folk word in South Caro-

lina and along the North Carolina and Virginia coast. Where and how did the various terms originate, and what can be determined about their subsequent history?

Earthworm itself is not an old word; it appears to have been compounded only shortly before the earliest English migrations to America. The earliest *Oxford English Dictionary* citation of the word in its present form is 1591; it appears also as *yearth worm* some thirty years earlier. The various regional terms all seem to have been coined in America; the dictionaries either record no British citations or fail to include the words at all.

The local terms have a varied and interesting history. *Mud worm* seems to occur in standard British English from the beginning of the nineteenth century on. *Eace worm*, as a combined form, goes back at least to Middle English; the first element was a term for 'bait' as early as Aelfric; it is used today in a number of southern counties in England from Kent to Gloucester. *Angle dog* is used currently in Devonshire. *Ground worm*, though coined in England, was transferred to North Carolina and Maryland in the eighteenth century. *Red worm* appears first in England in 1450 and continues through to the mid-nineteenth century, though chiefly in books on fishing, as does *dew worm*, which goes back even farther, to the late Old English period. *Rainworm*, though it appears in Aelfric as *renwyrm*, may be a reformation, even in British English, on the pattern of *Regenwurm* in German, for there is a gap of seven centuries in the citations in the *Oxford English Dictionary* and there is reason to believe that its revival in 1731 was influenced by the German form. Moreover, with but one exception, it has been cited for the United States only in areas settled by Germans.

Thus we have in the standard cultivated term one of relatively recent British formation. Apparently the regional terms were compounded in America, whereas the local terms represent survivals either of dialect usage or anglers' jargon and one loan translation. It is worth noting that the common Old English term, *angle twicce*, surviving as *angle twitch* in Cornwall and Devon, seems not to have found its way to America, and there are, furthermore, such other English formations as *tag worm*, *marsh worm,* and *garden worm* which have not been recorded in America.

At times, too, changes in meaning seem to have entered into the dialect situation, as is illustrated by the development of the regional terms *skillet* and *spider,* the former current in the Midland and the Virginia Piedmont, the latter in the North and in the Southern tidewater area. *Frying pan* is the urban term and is slowly supplanting the others. *Spider* was originally applied to the cast-iron pan with short legs, from which the name was presumably derived, but it was ultimately transferred to the flat-bottomed pan as well. This would seem also to explain the local term *creeper,* used in Marblehead, Massachusetts. *Skillet,* a term of doubtful etymology, first appears in English in 1403, when it was applied to a long-handled brass or copper vessel used for boiling liquids or stewing meat. It is still so used in dialects throughout England. The shift in meaning to a frying pan took place only in America, but an advertisement of 1790, offering for sale 'bakepans, spiders, skillets,' would suggest that even as late as this a distinction between the two was recognized. The examples above have been offered only as a suggestion of the various language processes which have played a part in the distribution and meaning of some of our dialect terms. It is quite obvious that no definitive conclusions about these matters can be reached until the actual facts of dialect distribution are better known than they are at present.

Thus far our concern has been only with regional dialects or speech differences, although we have recognized these as occurring particularly on certain social levels. This raises the question of the extent to which social dialects occur in American English. Is there a so-called vulgate which has reasonably uniform characteristics throughout the country, and if so, what is it?

For the most part, the language of the uncultivated will be recognized in terms of its inflectional characteristics, or at any rate it is this aspect of the language for which the most authentic information is available. Before these matters are taken up in detail, therefore, one or two points about the operation of inflections should be clearly understood.

First, we must recognize that our inflectional endings are in reality a series of patterns which are applied quite automatically whenever a situation demanding their use occurs. Even in highly inflected languages, such as Modern Finnish or Ciceronian Latin, the speaker does or did not find it necessary to recite a paradigm to determine the proper case ending. Second, throughout the history of the language, there are two forces constantly at work upon the inflectional system: sound change, which often introduces irregularities or disturbances in the system, and analogy, which tends to simplify or to straighten these out by extending the scope of the already existing pattern. As we look at some of the features of present-day substandard English, we shall see how these forces operate.

Possibly the one inflectional form most characteristic of the nouns in substandard American English is the unchanged plural after numbers: *six mile down the road, five foot tall,* and similarly applied to *month, year,* and *gallon.* Actually this is the preservation of an old partitive genitive plural after numbers, which resisted the analogical extension of the *-s* inflection to cases other than the nominative and accusative. The lesson to be learned from this is that the substandard language frequently preserves linguistically older forms than Standard English, a fact not too surprising when it is recalled that substandard English depends entirely on oral transmission from one generation to another.

Certain of the pronoun inflections, however, demonstrate precisely the contrary tendency: the development of innovations or new forms and patterns in substandard English. This is true, for example, of the possessive pronoun in its so-called absolute form, which in the standard language represents a strange and inconsistent mixture of patterns indeed. *Mine* and the archaic *thine* are formed from the adjectival form by adding *-n. Hers, ours, yours,* and *theirs,* on the other hand, add *-s* to the adjectival form, probably on the pattern of the noun genitive. *His* and *its* are indistinguishable so far as their secondary and absolute forms are concerned. In contrast, the substandard *mine, yourn, hisn, hern, ourn, theirn* present a perfectly regular pattern formed by an analogical extension of *mine* and *thine* to the third person singular and to the plural forms. At one time or another, several of these forms appeared in Standard English, but they seem never to have caught on and were, as we have seen, replaced in part by the -s forms. But the substandard language carried out the innovation completely and consistently except for *its*, which is virtually never used in the absolute form anyway.

A further point worth mentioning is that although speakers of the substandard language are rarely trained in school grammar, their language observes its own laws—not those of Standard English—in a thoroughly rigorous manner. *Hisn*, for example, is the absolute, not the secondary or adjectival form, and the two are never confused. Most speakers of the substandard language might be expected to say *the book is hisn;* no speaker of substandard English would ever say *hisn book*.

The reflexive pronouns give us another instance of a more regular operation of analogy on the substandard level than on the standard. In Standard English, *myself, yourself, ourselves,* and *yourselves* are combinations of the genitive pronoun plus the singular or plural of the -*self* form; *himself* and *themselves* employ the object form of the pronoun, whereas *herself* and *itself* could be either. Substandard English, in substituting *hisself* and *theirself* in the third person and adhering to the singular of *self* in *ourself* and *yourself* (plural), is not only more consistent but more economical in that the latter combinations signal the plural only once and avoid the tautology of the plural -*selves*. The only ambiguity is in the second person, but the second personal pronoun has lost its distinctions between singular and plural anyway, except for the Southern form *you all*.

One curious feature of the substandard pronoun is the substitution of the object for the subjective form in such sentences as *Us girls went home, John and her was married, Me and him was late.* This seems to occur principally when the subject is compound or when one or more words intervene between the pronominal subject and verb, as in *us girls*. Postverbally the reverse type of substitution (subject for object form) is often found, as in *She gave it to mother and I, She took all of we children.* Since these locutions are found considerably higher up the social and educational scale than those previously mentioned, it is possible, at least, that they are the result of overcorrection.

Space does not permit an exhaustive treatment of all the inflectional forms of substandard English, but a few that are typical deserve brief mention. *Them* as a demonstrative adjective (*them books*) probably harks back to the days when the English article and the demonstrative *that* (dative ðǣm) were one and the same form. The multiple negative was also a regular and accepted feature of older English, as was the so-called flat adverb, without the *-ly* derivative suffix. However, since the standard and substandard languages are undoubtedly farthest apart with respect to verb forms, some features of the verbs of the vulgate, as they were once called by the late Robert Menner, should be described.

First of all, with respect to the present tense, there is some tendency to dispose of the distinctive inflection for the third person singular, either by eliminating it in such forms as *he want, she write*, etc., or by extending the peculiar form of the third person to the first and second—*I has some good friends, You is in lots of trouble*.

It is in the preterit and past participle forms, chiefly of those verbs which are somewhat irregular in Standard English, that the widest deviations occur. Again one may recognize here the two opposing tendencies: the retention of older forms and the simplification of irregularities through analogical processes.

The older forms retained in the substandard language owe their origin chiefly to the fact that the so-called strong verb in earlier stages of the language had four principal parts, a past tense singular as well as a past tense plural, in addition to the infinitive and present participle. Thus *writ* as a past tense of *write* represents an older preterit plural form, as do *begun* and *swum*.

On the other hand, the overwhelming tendency in English verb development throughout the last seven or eight centuries has been toward an aggrandizement of the regular or weak inflection at the expense of the older minor conjugations. This is in effect a tendency toward a two-part verb, the infinitive or present stem opposed to an identical past tense and past participle. In general, this has been brought about through analogical processes. Deviant substandard forms are usually the result of analogies which have not operated in Standard English and which take one of two directions: either the extension of the weak past inflections to such irregular verbs as *know* and *see* (*knowed, seed*) or the amalgamation of the strong preterit or past participle with the complementary form (*I taken, he done* as preterits; *have gave, have wrote, has went* as past participial forms).

In one sense, therefore, the differences between the grammatical systems of standard and substandard English represent a difference in the direction and rapidity of inflectional changes. Unquestionably the easy transition from one social class to another in the United States has resulted in a very hazy line of demarcation between what is acceptable and what is considered illiterate. According to the most rigorous schoolbook standard, some of the language employed in American legislative councils and in business life would not pass muster. The awareness of this, combined with an unrealistic treatment of language in our schools, has resulted at times in a defiance of these questionable standards. More often it has given people a guilt complex about the language they use. James West, in his community study entitled *Plainville, U.S.A.* makes a pertinent comment upon this very point:

'Inferior' English has been selected as a primary and almost universal trait for apology because the school teacher, the press, and the radio have all cooperated to arouse self-consciousness concerning dialect forms, phrases, and phonetics. All but the 'most backwoodsy' speakers frequently ridicule and parody the stratum or strata of speech beneath or older than their own, and at the same time feel uncertain about their own usages.

Consequently, few Americans, even among the well-educated, are confident and assured of the essential aptness and correctness of their speech. It will take at least a half-century of a more enlightened attitude toward language in the public schools to bring about any perceptible change in this state of affairs. In the meantime, what is sadly needed is an entertaining, yet scientific, treatment of vulgate speech to demonstrate how interesting a phenomenon it really is.

Review Questions

1. Why is it difficult to collect valid and reliable information about American dialects?
2. What are some of the problems involved in securing representative and comparable samples from the areas which are studied?
3. Kurath's research established three major dialect areas and also disproved the existence of another dialect. Identify the dialects concerned.
4. Kurath's plotting of the major dialect areas is based on vocabulary evidence. In what areas of human experience are regional variations most likely to be found? Why?
5. One finds regional differences not only in vocabulary, but in what two other areas of language study?
6. Many of our earliest settlers were Englishmen who spoke a variety of dialects. What effect did this have on the development of regional dialects?
7. Which three nineteenth-century changes profoundly affected the American language?
8. How did cities such as Boston, Philadelphia, and Charleston come to exert great influence on the speech of their areas? Did the prestige result from nonlinguistic considerations?
9. How do environmental factors like topography, climate, and plant and animal life influence the vocabulary of an area?
10. Why does Marckwardt discuss regional variations for "earthworm" and "skillet"?
11. The "language of the uncultivated" is most apparent in its inflectional characteristics, but before Marckwardt discusses inflections, he makes two points about how they operate. What are they?
12. Many of the grammatical "mistakes" made by speakers of the "vulgate" are the result of what two opposing tendencies in language?
13. What forces have produced a national "guilt complex" about language, and how may it be "cured"?

Discussion Questions

1. Do your vocabulary and pronunciation clearly place you in one of the three dialect areas described by Marckwardt? What differences do you find between your vocabulary and pronunciation and those of your dialect area? What might explain the differences?

2. Despite the advantages of college educations, extensive traveling, and mass communications, some people, such as comedians and politicians, consciously cling to their native dialects. Why? Can you think of related examples?

3. Is there a single standard dialect in the United States? Why? What does the term "standard" in this sense mean? What are the connotations of the term? Do speakers in Charleston try to speak the way Philadelphians do? Should they? In the term "standard dialect," what does "dialect" refer to: pronunciation? grammatical features? vocabulary? Unless a person leaves his native dialect area, what chance does he have of changing his dialect features?

4. Is an English teacher in the schools more likely to be concerned in the classroom with conformity in regional dialect matters or in social dialect matters? Why is the teacher more concerned with one than with the other? Is an English teacher in New York City likely to speak with the "accent" of an English teacher in Cleveland? Explain. What would happen if the two teachers exchanged classrooms? Would the benefits outweigh the problems?

5. Do you think it would be easier for you to change your social or your regional dialect? Why?

STUART BERG FLEXNER

slang

American slang, as used in the title of this dictionary [*Dictionary of American Slang*], is the body of words and expressions frequently used by or intelligible to a rather large portion of the general American public, but not accepted as good, formal usage by the majority. No word can be called slang simply because of its etymological history; its source, its spelling, and its meaning in a larger sense do *not* make it slang. Slang is best defined by a dictionary that points out who uses slang and what "flavor" it conveys.

I have called all slang used in the United States "American," regardless of its country of origin or use in other countries.

In this preface I shall discuss the human element in the formation of slang (what American slang is, and how and why slang is created and used).

The English language has several levels of vocabulary:

Standard usage comprises those words and expressions used, understood, and accepted by a majority of our citizens under any circumstances or degree of formality. Such words are well defined and their most accepted spellings and pronunciations are given in our standard dictionaries. In standard speech one might say: *Sir, you speak English well.*

Colloquialisms are familiar words and idioms used in informal speech and writing, but not considered explicit or formal enough for polite conversation or business correspondence. Un-

Retitled, originally appeared as Preface to *Dictionary of American Slang*, compiled and edited by Harold Wentworth and Stuart Berg Flexner. Copyright © 1967, 1960 by Thomas Y. Crowell Company, New York, publishers, and reprinted with their permission.

like slang, however, colloquialisms are used and understood by nearly everyone in the United States. The use of slang conveys the suggestion that the speaker and the listener enjoy a special "fraternity," but the use of colloquialisms emphasizes only the informality and familiarity of a general social situation. Almost all idiomatic expressions, for example, could be labeled collo-quial. Colloquially, one might say: *Friend, you talk plain and hit the nail right on the head.*

Dialects are the words, idioms, pronunciations, and speech habits peculiar to specific geographical locations. A dialecticism is a regionalism or localism. In popular use "dialect" has come to mean the words, foreign accents, or speech patterns associ-ated with any ethnic group. In Southern dialect one might say: *Cousin, y'all talk mighty fine.* In ethnic-immigrant "dialects" one might say: *Paisano, you speak good the English,* or *Landsman, your English is plenty all right already.*

Cant, jargon, and *argot* are the words and expressions pecul-iar to special segments of the population. *Cant* is the conversa-tional, familiar idiom used and generally understood only by members of a specific occupation, trade, profession, sect, class, age group, interest group, or other sub-group of our culture. *Jar-gon* is the technical or even secret vocabulary of such a sub-group; jargon is "shop talk." *Argot* is both the cant and the jar-gon of any professional criminal group. In such usages one might say, respectively: *CQ-CQ-CQ . . . the tone of your trans-mission is good; You are free of anxieties related to interper-sonal communication;* or *Duchess, let's have a bowl of chalk.*

Slang is generally defined above. In slang one might say: *Buster, your line is the cat's pajamas,* or *Doll, you come on with the straight jazz, real cool like.*

Each of these levels of language, save standard usage, is more common in speech than in writing, and slang as a whole is no exception. Thus, very few slang words and expressions (hence very few of the entries in this dictionary) appear in standard dictionaries.

American slang tries for a quick, easy, personal mode of speech. It comes mostly from cant, jargon, and argot words and expressions whose popularity has increased until a large number of the general public uses or understands them. Much of this slang retains a basic characteristic of its origin: it is *fully* intelligible only to initiates.

Slang may be represented pictorially as the more popular portion of the cant, jargon, and argot from many sub-groups (only a few of the sub-groups are shown below). The shaded areas represent only general overlapping between groups:

Eventually, some slang passes into standard speech; other slang flourishes for a time with varying popularity and then is forgotten; finally, some slang is never fully accepted nor com-

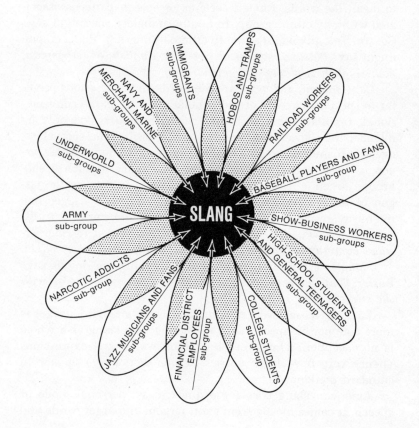

pletely forgotten. *O.K.*, *jazz* (music), and *A-bomb* were recently considered slang, but they are now standard usages. *Bluebelly*, *Lucifer*, and *the bee's knees* have faded from popular use. *Bones* (dice) and *beat it* seem destined to remain slang forever: Chaucer used the first and Shakespeare used the second.

It is impossible for any living vocabulary to be static. Most new slang words and usages evolve quite naturally: they result from specific situations. New objects, ideas, or happenings, for example, require new words to describe them. Each generation also seems to need some new words to describe the same old things.

Railroaders (who were probably the first American subgroup to have a nationwide cant and jargon) thought *jerk water town* was ideally descriptive of a community that others called a *one-horse town*. The changes from *one-horse town* and *don't spare the horses* to a *wide place in the road* and *step on it* were natural and necessary when the automobile replaced the horse. The automobile also produced such new words and new meanings (some of them highly specialized) as *gas buggy*, *jalopy*, *bent eight*, *Chevvie*, *convertible*, and *lube*. Like most major innovations, the automobile affected our social history and introduced or encouraged *dusters*, *hitch hikers*, *road hogs*, *joint hopping*, *necking*, *chicken* (the game), *car coats*, and *suburbia*.

The automobile is only one obvious example. Language always responds to new concepts and developments with new words.

Consider the following:

wars: *redcoats, minutemen, bluebelly, over there, doughboy, gold brick, jeep.*

mass immigrations: *Bohunk, greenhorn, shillalagh, voodoo, pizzeria.*

science and technology: *'gin, side-wheeler, wash-and-wear, fringe area, fallout.*

turbulent eras: *Redskin, maverick, speak, Chicago pineapple, free love, fink, breadline.*

evolution in the styles of eating: *applesauce, clambake, luncheonette, hot dog, coffee and.*

dress: *Mother Hubbard, bustle, shimmy, sailor, Long Johns, zoot suit, Ivy League.*

housing: *lean-to, bundling board, chuckhouse, W.C., railroad flat, split-level, sectional.*

music: *cakewalk, bandwagon, fish music, long hair, rock.*

personality: *Yankee, alligator, flapper, sheik, hepcat, B.M.O.C., beetle, beat.*

new modes of transportation: *stage, pinto, jitney, kayducer, hot shot, jet jockey.*

new modes of entertainment: *barnstormer, two-a-day, clown alley, talkies, d.j., Spectacular.*

changing attitudes toward sex: *painted woman, fast, broad, wolf, jailbait, sixty-nine.*

human motivations: *boy crazy, gold-digger, money-mad, Momism, Oedipus complex, do-gooder, sick.*

personal relationships: *bunky, kids, old lady, steady, ex, gruesome twosome, John.*

work and workers: *clod buster, scab, pencil pusher, white collar, graveyard shift, company man.*

politics: *Tory, do-nothing, mug-wump, third party, brain trust, fellow traveler, Veep.*

and even hair styles: *bun, rat, peroxide blonde, Italian cut, pony tail, D.A.*

Those social groups that first confront a new object, cope with a new situation, or work with a new concept devise and use new words long before the population at large does. The larger, more imaginative, and useful a group's vocabulary, the more likely it is to contribute slang. To generate slang, a group must either be very large and in constant contact with the dominant culture or be small, closely knit, and removed enough from the dominant culture to evolve an extensive, highly personal, and vivid vocabulary. Teen-agers are an example of a large subgroup contributing many words. Criminals, carnival workers, and hoboes are examples of the smaller groups. The smaller groups, because their vocabulary is personal and vivid, contribute to our general slang out of proportion to their size.

Whether the United States has more slang words than any

other country (in proportion to number of people, area, or the number of words in the standard vocabulary) I do not know.[1] Certainly the French and the Spanish enjoy extremely large slang vocabularies. Americans, however, do use their general slang more than any other people.

---

[1] The vocabulary of the average American, most of which he knows but never uses, is usually estimated at 10,000–20,000 words. Of this quantity I estimate conservatively that 2,000 words are slang. Slang, which thus forms about 10 per cent of the words known by the average American, belongs to the part of his vocabulary most frequently *used*.

The English language is now estimated to have at least 600,000 words; this is over four times the 140,000 recorded words of the Elizabethan period. Thus over 450,000 *new words or meanings* have been added since Shakespeare's day, without counting the replacement words or those that have been forgotten between then and now. There are now approximately 10,000 slang words in American English, and about 35,000 cant, jargon, and argot words.

Despite this quantity, 25 per cent of all communication is composed of just nine words. According to McKnight's study, another 25 per cent of all speech is composed of an additional 34 words (or: 43 words comprise 50 per cent of all speech). Scholars do differ, however, on just which nine words are the most popular. Three major studies are: G. H. McKnight, *English Words and Their Background*, Appleton-Century-Crofts, Inc., 1923 (for spoken words only); Godfrey Dewey, "Relative Frequency of English Speech Sounds," *Harvard Studies in Education*, vol. IV, 1923 (for written words only); and Norman R. French, Charles W. Carter, and Walter Koenig, Jr., "Words and Sounds of Telephone Conversations," *Bell System Technical Journal*, April, 1930 (telephone speech only). Their lists of the most common nine words are:

McKnight's speech	Dewey's written	Bell Telephone conversations
	a	a
and	and	
be		
have		
	in	
		I
	is	is
it	it	it
		on
of	of	
	that	that
the	the	the
to	to	to
will		
you		you

American slang reflects the kind of people who create and use it. Its diversity and popularity are in part due to the imagination, self-confidence, and optimism of our people. Its vitality is in further part due to our guarantee of free speech and to our lack of a national academy of language or of any "official" attempt to purify our speech. Americans are restless and frequently move from region to region and from job to job. This hopeful wanderlust, from the time of the pioneers through our westward expansion to modern mobility, has helped spread regional and group terms until they have become general slang. Such restlessness has created constantly new situations which provoke new words. Except for a few Eastern industrial areas and some rural regions in the South and West, America just doesn't look or sound "lived in." We often act and speak as if we were simply visiting and observing. What should be an ordinary experience seems new, unique, or colorful to us, worthy of words and forceful speech. People do not "settle down" in their jobs, towns, or vocabularies.

Nor do we "settle down" intellectually, spiritually, or emotionally. We have few religious, regional, family, class, psychological, or philosophical roots. We don't believe in roots, we believe in teamwork. Our strong loyalties, then, are directed to those social groups—or sub-groups as they are often called—with which we are momentarily identified. This ever-changing "membership" helps to promote and spread slang.

But even within each sub-group only a few new words are generally accepted. Most cant and jargon are local and temporary. What persists are the exceptionally apt and useful cant and jargon terms. These become part of the permanent, personal vocabulary of the group members, giving prestige to the users by proving their acceptance and status in the group. Group members then spread some of this more honored cant and jargon in the dominant culture. If the word is also useful to non-group members, it is on its way to becoming slang. Once new words are introduced into the dominant culture, via television, radio, movies, or newspapers, the rapid movement of individuals and rapid communication between individuals and groups spread the new word very quickly.

For example, consider the son of an Italian immigrant living in New York City. He speaks Italian at home. Among neighborhood youths of similar background he uses many Italian expressions because he finds them always on the tip of his tongue and because they give him a sense of solidarity with his group. He may join a street gang, and after school and during vacations work in a factory. After leaving high school, he joins the navy; then he works for a year seeing the country as a carnival worker. He returns to New York, becomes a longshoreman, marries a girl with a German background, and becomes a boxing fan. He uses Italian and German borrowings, some teen-age street-gang terms, a few factory terms, slang with a navy origin, and carnival, dockworkers, and boxing words. He spreads words from each group to all other groups he belongs to. His Italian parents will learn and use a few street-gang, factory, navy, carnival, dockworker's, and boxing terms; his German in-laws will learn some Italian words from his parents; his navy friends will begin to use some of his Italian expressions; his carnival friends a few navy words; his co-workers on the docks some carnival terms, in addition to all the rest; and his social friends, with whom he may usually talk boxing and dock work, will be interested in and learn some of his Italian and carnival terms. His speech may be considered very "slangy" and picturesque because he has belonged to unusual, colorful sub-groups.

On the other hand, a man born into a Midwestern, middle-class, Protestant family whose ancestors came to the United States in the eighteenth century might carry with him popular high-school terms. At high school he had an interest in hot rods and rock-and-roll. He may have served two years in the army, then gone to an Ivy League college where he became an adept bridge player and an enthusiast of cool music. He may then have become a sales executive and developed a liking for golf. This second man, no more usual or unusual than the first, will know cant and jargon terms of teen-age high-school use, hot-rods, rock-and-roll, Ivy League schools, cool jazz, army life, and some golf player's and bridge player's terms. He knows further a few slang expressions from his parents (members of the Jazz Age of the 1920s), from listening to television programs, seeing both

American and British movies, reading popular literature, and from frequent meetings with people having completely different backgrounds. When he uses cool terms on the golf course, college expressions at home, business words at the bridge table, when he refers to whiskey or drunkenness by a few words he learned from his parents, curses his next-door neighbor in a few choice army terms—then he too is popularizing slang.

It is, then, clear that three cultural conditions especially contribute to the creation of a large slang vocabulary: (1) hospitality to or acceptance of new objects, situations, and concepts; (2) existence of a large number of diversified sub-groups; (3) democratic mingling between these sub-groups and the dominant culture. Primitive peoples have little if any slang because their life is restricted by ritual; they develop few new concepts; and there are no sub-groups that mingle with the dominant culture. (Primitive sub-groups, such as medicine men or magic men, have their own vocabularies; but such groups do not mix with the dominant culture and their jargon can never become slang because it is secret or sacred.)

But what, after all, are the advantages that slang possesses which make it useful? Though our choice of any specific word may usually be made from habit, we sometimes consciously select a slang word because we believe that it communicates more quickly and easily, and more personally, than does a standard word. Sometimes we resort to slang because there is no one standard word to use. In the 1940's, *WAC, cold war,* and *cool* (music) could not be expressed quickly by any standard synonyms. Such words often become standard quickly, as have the first two. We also use slang because it often is more forceful, vivid, and expressive than are standard usages. Slang usually avoids the sentimentality and formality that older words often assume. Taking a girl to a *dance* may seem sentimental, may convey a degree of formal, emotional interest in the girl, and has overtones of fancy balls, fox trots, best suits, and corsages. At times it is more fun to go to a *hop.* To be *busted* or without a *hog* in one's *jeans* is not only more vivid and forceful than being penniless or without funds, it is also a more optimistic state. A *mouthpiece* (or *legal beagle*), *pencil pusher, sawbones, bone-yard, bottle washer* or a course in *biochem* is more vivid and forceful than a lawyer, clerk, doctor, cemetery, laboratory assistant, or a course in biochemistry—and is much more real and less formidable than a legal counsel, junior executive, surgeon, necropolis (or memorial park), laboratory technician, or a course in biological chemistry.

Although standard English is exceedingly hospitable to polysyllabicity and even sesquipedalianism, slang is not. Slang is sometimes used not only because it is concise but just because its brevity makes it forceful. As this dictionary demonstrates, slang seems to prefer short words, especially monosyllables, and, best of all, words beginning with an explosive or an aspirate.[2]

We often use slang *fad* words as a bad habit because they are close to the tip of our tongue. Most of us apply several favorite but vague words to any of several somewhat similar situations; this saves us the time and effort of thinking and speaking precisely. At other times we purposely choose a word because it is vague, because it does not commit us too strongly to what we are saying. For example, if a friend has been praising a woman, we can reply "she's *the bee's knees*" or "she's a real *chick*," which can mean that we consider her very modern, intelligent, pert, and understanding—or can mean that we think she is one of many nondescript, somewhat confused, followers of popular fads. We can also tell our friend that a book we both have recently read is *the cat's pajamas* or *the greatest*. These expres-

---

[2] Many such formations are among our most frequently used slang words. As listed in this dictionary, *bug* has 30 noun meanings, *shot* 14 noun and 4 adjective meanings, *can* 11 noun and 6 verb, *bust* 9 verb and 6 noun, *hook* 8 noun and 5 verb, *fish* 14 noun, and *sack* 8 noun, 1 adjective, and 1 verb meaning. Monosyllabic words also had by far the most citations found in our source reading of popular literature. Of the 40 words for which we found the most quotations, 29 were monosyllabic. Before condensing, *fink* had citations from 70 different sources, *hot* 67, *bug* 62, *blow* and *dog* 60 each, *joint* 59, *stiff* 56, *punk* 53, *bum* and *egg* 50 each, *guy* 43, *make* 41, *bull* and *mug* 37 each, *bird* 34, *fish* and *hit* 30 each, *ham* 25, *yak* 23, *sharp* 14, and *cinch* 10. (Many of these words, of course, have several slang meanings; many of the words also appeared scores of times in the same book or article.)

sions imply that we liked the book for exactly the same reasons that our friend did, without having to state what these reasons were and thus taking the chance of ruining our rapport.

In our language we are constantly recreating our image in our own minds and in the minds of others. Part of this image, as mentioned above, is created by using sub-group cant and jargon in the dominant society; part of it is created by our choice of both standard and slang words. A sub-group vocabulary shows that we have a group to which we "belong" and in which we are "somebody"—outsiders had better respect us. Slang is used to show others (and to remind ourselves of) our biographical, mental, and psychological background; to show our social, economic, geographical, national, racial, religious, educational, occupational, and group interests, memberships, and patriotisms. One of the easiest and quickest ways to do this is by using counter-words. These are automatic, often one-word responses of like or dislike, of acceptance or rejection. They are used to counter the remarks, or even the presence, of others. Many of our fad words and many student and quasi-intellectual slang words are counter-words. For liking: *beat, the cat's pajamas, drooly, gas, George, the greatest, keen, nice, reet, smooth, super, way out,* etc. For rejection of an outsider (implying incompetence to belong to our group): *boob, creep, dope, drip, droop, goof, jerk, kookie, sap, simp, square, weird,* etc. Such automatic counters are overused, almost meaningless, and are a substitute for thought. But they achieve one of the main purposes of speech: quickly and automatically they express our own sub-group and personal criteria. Counter-words are often fad words creating a common bond of self-defense. All the rejecting counters listed above could refer to a moron, an extreme introvert, a birdwatcher, or a genius. The counters merely say that the person is rejected—he does not belong to the group. In uttering the counter we don't care what the person is; we are pledging our own group loyalty, affirming our identity, and expressing our satisfaction at being accepted.

In like manner, at various periods in history, our slang has abounded in words reflecting the fear, distrust, and dislike of people unlike ourselves. This intolerance is shown by the many derogatory slang words for different immigrant, religious, and racial groups: *Chink, greaser, Heinie, hunkie, mick, mockie, nigger, spik.* Many counters and derogatory words try to identify our own group status, to dare others to question our group's, and therefore our own, superiority.

Sometimes slang is used to escape the dull familiarity of standard words, to suggest an escape from the established routine of everyday life. When slang is used, our life seems a little fresher and a little more personal. Also, as at all levels of speech, slang is sometimes used for the pure joy of making sounds, or even for a need to attract attention by making noise. The sheer newness and informality of certain slang words produces a pleasure.

But more important than this expression of a more or less hidden esthetic motive on the part of the speaker is slang's reflection of the personality, the outward, clearly visible characteristics of the speaker. By and large, the man who uses slang is a forceful, pleasing, acceptable personality. Morality and intellect (too frequently not considered virtues in the modern American man) are overlooked in slang, and this has led to a type of reverse morality: many words, once standing for morally good things, are now critical. No one, for example, though these words were once considered complimentary, wants to be called a *prude* or *Puritan*. Even in standard usage they are mildly derisive.

Moreover, a few of the many slang synonyms for drunk are derogatory or critical. To call a person a standard drunk may imply a superior but unsophisticated attitude toward drinking. Thus we use slang and say someone is *boozed up, gassed, high, potted, stinking, has a glow on,* etc., in verbal attempt to convey our understanding and awareness. These slang words show that we too are human and know the effects of excessive drinking.

In the same spirit we refer to people sexually as *big ass man, fast, John, sex pot, shack job, wolf,* etc., all of which accept unsanctioned sexual intercourse as a matter of fact. These words are often used in a complimentary way and in admiration or envy. They always show acceptance of the person as a "regular guy." They are never used to express a moral judgment. Slang has few complimentary or even purely descriptive words for "virgin," "good girl," or "gentleman." Slang has *bag, bat, ex, gold digger, jerk, money mad, n.g., old lady, square,* etc.; but how many words are there for a good wife and mother, an attractive and chaste woman, an honest, hard-working man who is kind to his family, or even a respected elderly person? Slang—and it is frequently true for all language levels—always tends toward degradation rather than elevation. As slang shows, we would rather share or accept vices than be excluded from a social group. For this reason, for self-defense, and to create an aura (but not the fact) of modernity and individuality, much of our slang purposely expresses amorality, cynicism, and "toughness."

Reverse morality also affects slang in other ways. Many use slang just because it is not standard or polite. Many use slang to show their rebellion against *boobs, fuddy-duddies, marks,* and *squares.* Intellectuals and politicians often use slang to create the "common touch" and others use slang to express either their anti-intellectualism or avant-garde leanings. Thus, for teenagers, entertainers, college students, beatniks, jazz fans, intellectuals, and other large groups, slang is often used in preference to standard words and expressions. Slang is the "official" modern language of certain vociferous groups in our population.

In my work on this dictionary, I was constantly aware that most American slang is created and used by males. Many types of slang words—including the taboo and strongly derogatory ones, those referring to sex, women, work, money, whiskey,[3] politics, transportation, sports, and the like—refer primarily to male endeavor and interest. The majority of entries in this dictionary could be labeled "primarily masculine use." Men belong to more sub-groups than do women; men create and use occupational cant and jargon; in business, men have acquaintances who belong to many different sub-groups. Women, on the other hand, still tend to be restricted to family and neighborhood

[3] It would appear that the word having the most slang synonyms is *drunk.*

friends. Women have very little of their own slang.[4] The new
words applied to women's clothing, hair styles, homes, kitchen
utensils and gadgets are usually created by men. Except when
she accompanies her boy friend or husband to *his* recreation
(baseball, hunting, etc.) a woman seldom mingles with other
groups. When women do mingle outside of their own neighborhood and family circles, they do not often talk of the outside
world of business, politics, or other fields of general interest
where new feminine names for objects, concepts, and view-
points could evolve.

Men also tend to avoid words that sound feminine or weak.
Thus there are sexual differences in even the standard vocabularies of men and women. A woman may ask her husband to set
the table for dinner, asking him to put out the *silver, crystal,*
and *china*—while the man will set the table with *knives, forks,
spoons, glasses,* and *dishes.* His wife might think the *table linen*
attractive, the husband might think the *tablecloth* and *napkins*
pretty. A man will buy a *pocketbook* as a gift for his wife, who
will receive a *bag.* The couple will live under the same roof, the
wife in her *home,* the man in his *house.* Once outside of their
domesticity the man will begin to use slang quicker than the
woman. She'll get into the *car* while he'll get into the *jalopy* or
Chevvie. And so they go: she will learn much of her general
slang from him; for any word she associates with the home, her
personal belongings, or any female concept, he will continue to
use a less descriptive, less personal one.

Males also use slang to shock. The rapid tempo of life, combined with the sometimes low boiling point of males, can evoke
emotions—admiration, joy, contempt, anger—stronger than our
old standard vocabulary can convey. In the stress of the moment
a man is not just in a standard "untenable position," he is *up
the creek.* Under strong anger a man does not feel that another
is a mere "incompetent"—he is a *jerk* or a *fuck-off.*

---

[4] Women who do work usually replace men at men's jobs, are less involved in business life than men, and have a shorter business career
(often but an interim between school and marriage). The major female
sub-groups contributing to American slang are: airline stewardesses,
beauty-parlor operators, chorus girls, nurses, prostitutes, and waitresses.

Men also seem to relish hyperbole in slang. Under many situations, men do not see or care to express fine shades of meaning: a girl is either a *knockout* or a *dog*, liquor either *good stuff* or *panther piss*, a person either has *guts* or is *chicken*, a book is either *great* or nothing but *crap*. Men also like slang and colloquial wording because they express action or even violence: we *draw pay, pull a boner, make a score, grab some sleep, feed our face, kill time*—in every instance we tend to use the transitive verb, making ourselves the active doer.

The relation between a sub-group's psychology and its cant and jargon is interesting, and the relation between an individual's vocabulary and psychological personality is even more so. Slang can be one of the most revealing things about a person, because our own personal slang vocabulary contains many words used by choice, words which we use to create our own image, words which we find personally appealing and evocative—as opposed to our frequent use of standard words merely from early teaching and habit. Whether a man calls his wife *baby, doll, honey, the little woman, the Mrs.*, or *my old lady* certainly reveals much about him. What words one uses to refer to a mother (*Mom, old lady*), friend (*buddy, bunkie, old man*), the bathroom (*can, John, little boy's room*), parts of the body and sex acts (*boobies, gigi, hard, laid, score*), being tired (*all in, beat*), being drunk (*clobbered, high, lit up like a Christmas tree, paralyzed*), and the like, reveal much about a person and his motivations.[5]

The basic metaphors, at any rate, for all levels of language depend on the five senses. Thus *rough, smooth, touch; prune, sour puss, sweet; fishy, p.u., rotten egg; blow, loud; blue, red, square*. In slang, many metaphors refer to touch (including the sense of heat and cold) and to taste.

Food is probably our most popular slang image. Food from the farm, kitchen, or table, and its shape, color, and taste suggest many slang metaphors. This is because food can appeal to

[5] For just the last example, *clobbered* may indicate that a drinker is punishing himself, *high* that he is escaping, *lit up like a Christmas tree* that he is seeking attention and a more dominant personality, and *paralyzed* that he seeks punishment, escape or death.

taste, smell, sight, and touch, four of our five senses; because
food is a major, universal image to all people, all sub-groups; because men work to provide it and women devote much time to
buying and preparing it; because food is before our eyes three
times every day.

Many standard food words mean money in nonstandard use:
cabbage, kale, lettuce. Many apply to parts of the body: *cabbage
head, cauliflower ear, meat hooks, nuts, plates of meat.* Many
food words refer to people: *apple, cold fish, Frog, fruitcake,
honey, sweetie pie.* Others refer to general situations and attitudes: to *brew* a plot, to receive a *chewing out*, to find oneself
in a pickle or something *not kosher*, to be unable to *swallow*
another's story, to ask *what's cooking?* Many drunk words also
have food images: *boiled, fried, pickled;* and so do many words
for nonsense: *applesauce, banana oil, spinach.* Many standard
food words also have sexual meanings in slang. The many food
words for money, parts of the body, people, and sex reveal that
food means much more to us than mere nourishment. When a
good egg brings home the bacon to his *honey*, or when a *string
bean* of a *sugar daddy* takes his *piece* of *barbecue* out to get
fried with his hard-earned *kale*, food images have gone a long
way from the farm, kitchen, and table.

Sex has contributed comparatively few words to modern
slang,[6] but these are among our most frequently used. The use
of sex words to refer to sex in polite society and as metaphors in
other fields is increasing. Sex metaphors are common for the
same conscious reasons that food metaphors are. Sex appeals to,
and can be used to apply to, most of the five senses. It is common
to all persons in all sub-groups, and so we are aware of it continually.

Slang words for sexual attraction and for a variety of sexual
acts, positions, and relationships are more common than standard words. Standard non-taboo words referring to sex are so
scarce or remote and scientific that slang is often used in re-

---

[6] Many so-called bedroom words are not technically slang at all, but
are sometimes associated with slang only because standard speech has rejected them as taboo. However, many of these taboo words do have further
metaphorical meanings in slang: *fucked, jerk, screw you,* etc.

ferring to the most romantic, the most obscene, and the most humorous sexual situations. Slang is so universally used in sexual communication that when "a man meets a maid" it is best for all concerned that they know slang.[7] Slang words for sex carry little emotional connotation; they express naked desire or mechanical acts, devises, and positions. They are often blunt, cynical and "tough."

The subconscious relating of sex and food is also apparent from reading this dictionary. Many words with primary, standard meanings of food have sexual slang meanings. The body, parts of the body, and descriptions of each, often call food terms into use: *banana, bread, cheese cake, cherry, jelly roll, meat,* etc. Beloved, or simply sexually attractive, people are also often called by food names: *cookie, cup of tea, honey, peach, quail, tomato,* etc. This primary relation between sex and food depends on the fact that they are man's two major sensuous experiences. They are shared by all personalities and all sub-groups and they appeal to the same senses—thus there is bound to be some overlapping in words and imagery. However, there are too many standard food words having sexual meanings in slang for these conscious reasons to suffice. Sex and food seem to be related in our subconscious.

Also of special interest is the number of slang expressions relating sex and cheating. Used metaphorically, many sex words have secondary meanings of being cheated, deceived, swindled, or taken advantage of, and several words whose primary meaning is cheating or deceiving have further specific sexual meanings: *cheating, fucked, make, royal screwing, score, turn a trick,* etc. As expressed in slang, sex is a trick somehow, a deception, a way to cheat and deceive us. To curse someone we can say *fuck you* or *screw you,* which expresses a wish to deprive him of his good luck, his success, perhaps even his potency as a man.[8]

---

[7] On the other hand, Madame de Staël is reported to have complimented one of her favorite lovers with "speech is not his language."

[8] See F. P. Wood, "The Vocabulary of Failure," *Better English,* Nov., 1938, p. 34. The vocabulary of failure is itself very revealing. Failure in one's personality, school, job, business, or an attempted love affair are all expressed by the same vocabulary. One gets the *brush off,* the *gate,* a

Sex is also associated with confusion, exhausting tasks, and disaster: *ball buster, screwed up, snafu,* etc. It seems clear, therefore, that, in slang, success and sexual energy are related or, to put it more accurately, that thwarted sexual energy will somehow result in personal disaster.

Language is a social symbol. The rise of the middle class coincided with the period of great dictionary makers, theoretical grammarians, and the "correct usage" dogma. The new middle class gave authority to the dictionaries and grammarians in return for "correct usage" rules that helped solidify their social position. Today, newspaper ads still implore us to take mail-order courses in order to "learn to speak like a college graduate," and some misguided English instructors still give a good speaking ability as the primary reason for higher education.

The gap between "correct usage" and modern practice widens each day. Are there valid theoretical rules for speaking good English, or should "observed usage" be the main consideration? Standard words do not necessarily make for precise, forceful, or useful speech. On the other hand, "observed usage" can never promise logic and clarity. Today, we have come to depend on "observed usage," just as eighteenth- and nineteenth-century social climbers depended on "correct usage," for social acceptance.

Because it is not standard, formal, or acceptable under all conditions, slang is usually considered vulgar, impolite, or boorish. As this dictionary shows, however, the vast majority of slang words and expressions are neither taboo, vulgar, derogatory, nor offensive in meaning, sound, or image. There is no reason to avoid any useful, explicit word merely because it is

kiss off, or *walking papers* in both business and personal relationships. As the previous discussion of counter-words demonstrates, slang allows no distinction or degree among individual failures. Incompetence does not apply to just one job or facet of life—either one belongs or is considered unworthy. This unworthiness applies to the entire personality, there are no alternate avenues for success or happiness. One is not merely of limited intelligence, not merely an introvert, not merely ugly, unknowing, or lacking in aggression—but one is a failure in all these things, a complete *drip, jerk,* or *square.* The basic failure is that of personality, the person is not a mere failure—he is an outcast, an untouchable; he is taboo.

labeled "slang." Our present language has not decayed from some past and perfect "King's English," Latin, Greek, or pre-Tower of Babel tongue. All languages and all words have been, are, and can only be but conventions mutually agreed upon for the sake of communicating. Slang came to America on the Mayflower. In general, it is not vulgar, new, or even peculiarly American: an obvious illustration of this is the polite, old French word *tête,* which was originally slang from a Latin word *testa*—cooking pot.

Cant and jargon in no way refer only to the peculiar words of undesirable or underworld groups. Slang does not necessarily come from the underworld, dope addicts, degenerates, hoboes, and the like. Any cultural sub-group develops its own personal cant and jargon which can later become general slang. All of us belong to several of these specific sub-groups using our own cant and jargon. Teen-agers, steel workers, soldiers, Southerners, narcotic addicts, churchgoers, truck drivers, advertising men, jazz musicians, pickpockets, retail salesmen in every field, golf players, immigrants from every country, college professors, baseball fans—all belong to typical sub-groups from which slang originates. Some of these sub-groups are colorful; most are composed of prosaic, average people.

Many people erroneously believe that a fundamental of slang is that it is intentionally picturesque, strained in metaphor, or jocular. Picturesque metaphor (and metonymy, hyperbole, and irony) does or should occur frequently in all levels of speech. Picturesque metaphor is a frequent characteristic of slang, but it does not define slang or exist as an inherent part of it. The picturesque or metaphorical aspect of slang is often due to its direct honesty or to its newness. Many standard usages are just as picturesque, but we have forgotten their original metaphor through habitual use. Thus slang's *jerk* and *windbag* are no more picturesque than the standard *incompetent* and *fool. Incompetent* is from the Latin *competens* plus the negating prefix *in-* and = "unable or unwilling to compete"; *fool* is Old French, from the Latin *follis* which actually = "bellows or wind bag"; slang's *windbag* and the standard *fool* actually have the same metaphor.

As for picturesque sounds, I find very few in slang. Onomato-poeia, reduplications, harsh sounds and pleasing sounds, even rhyming terms, exist on all levels of speech. Readers of this dictionary will find no more picturesque or unusual sounds here than in a similar length dictionary of standard words. Many slang words are homonyms for standard words.

As has been frequently pointed out, many slang words have the same meaning. There seems to be an unnecessary abundance of counter-words, synonyms for "drunk," hundreds of fad words with almost the same meaning, etc. This is because slang introduces word after word year after year from many, many sub-groups. But slang is a scatter-gun process; many new words come at the general public; most are ignored; a few stick in the popular mind.

Remember that "slang" actually does not exist as an entity except in the minds of those of us who study the language. People express themselves and are seldom aware that they are using the artificial divisions of "slang" or "standard." First and forever, language is language, an attempt at communication and self-expression. The fact that some words or expressions are labeled "slang" while others are labeled "jargon" or said to be "from the Anglo-Saxon" is of little value except to scholars. Thus this dictionary is a legitimate addition to standard dictionaries, defining many words just as meaningful as and often more succinct, useful, and popular than many words in standard dictionaries.

. . .

* Several new or changing aspects of American life and the American language are evident from the new slang encountered since 1960. Our society is becoming fragmented into more and more cultural sub-groups. There are more individually self-aware occupational, recreational, intellectual, social, and personality groups than in 1960, and each adds to the general

* The last five paragraphs are reprinted from Flexner's 1967 Preface to the Supplement to the *Dictionary of American Slang*, p. 670.

slang vocabulary. Each new spacecraft launching seems to launch several words into the language from the vocabulary of aerospace technicians. The war in Vietnam is again putting Armed Forces slang into our daily newspapers and vocabulary. Continuing affluence in our society has caused a growth in the comparatively new groups of skiers, skin divers, surfers, sports car enthusiasts, hot rodders, etc., and an increase in the general popularity of their terms (*baggies, ho-dad, baldy,* etc.).

The slang of homosexual sub-groups has also become increasingly familiar to the general population. In the past six years Yiddish borrowings (*chuzpa, klutz, megillah, shtick,* etc.) have entered the language in growing numbers. The slang vocabulary of the big city Negro ghettos (not the older slang of jazz musicians, hepcats, and other Negro stereotypes) has now become widespread among Negroes from coast to coast and has been popularized into the general white culture.

Not unexpectedly, a great number of new terms in the Supplement [to the *Dictionary* of *American* Slang] are coinages of the 17–24 age group, which popularizes more slang than any other. This is our largest cultural sub-group, and it is the most eagerly receptive to new ideas, attitudes, and styles. Slang from this group gains wide currency rapidly because older Americans seek to be, act, and think young.

The most obvious trend found while compiling this Supplement is an increasing awareness of and experimentation with marijuana (*grass, Mexican red,* etc.) and hallucinogenic drugs (*acid, cube, DMT,* etc.), esp. by teen-agers and college students. Much of this vocabulary passes from the addict and habitual user through teen-agers and college students into the middle-class home as general slang.

The emergence of new sub-groups and interests is reflected in the Supplement by the use of new group labels, such as *Aerospace use* (*A-OK*), *glitch, go,* etc.; *Vietnam Armed Forces use* (*ARVN, birdfarm, friendly, hard hat,* etc.); *Homosexual use* (*camp it up, evil, marge, rough trade,* etc.); *Negro use* (*blood brother, nitty-gritty, soul, Whitey,* etc.); and *Addict and Student use* or *Student and habitual users' use* (*bag, straight, trip, turn* [*someone*] *on,* etc.).

Review Questions

1. Define each of the following terms: "slang," "standard usage," "colloquialism," "dialecticism," "cant," "jargon," and "argot."
2. Why do slang words evolve, and what may be their fate?
3. What accounts for the vitality, diversity, and popularity of American slang?
4. How do cant and jargon terms acquire slang status?
5. What three cultural conditions help to produce a large slang vocabulary?
6. Why do people use slang? What are its advantages?
7. Why should people avoid using "fad words"?
8. What are "counter-words"?
9. How may a person's choice of slang words reflect his personality?
10. Why does slang always tend toward degradation rather than elevation?
11. Why is most American slang created and used by men? What characterizes male slang expressions?
12. Why is food our most popular slang image? What subjects frequently are expressed in slang words concerning food?
13. What attitudes toward sex are revealed through slang expressions?
14. "There is no reason to avoid any useful, explicit word merely because it is labeled 'slang.' " Explain.
15. What social phenomena of the 1960s does slang reflect?
16. What age group especially uses slang terms? Why?
17. What new subgroups and interests does recent slang reveal?

Discussion Questions

1. List your own campus slang words that are related to academic life. Can you make any generalizations about their origin? Are they abbreviations, variations of standard words, metaphors, rhyming expressions? What do they reveal about student attitudes toward academic life?
2. Why is the slang vocabulary of the average college student unusually large? What subgroups may the student belong to during the course of an academic year? Why is the slang of one college campus sometimes quite different from that of another?
3. Has the middle-class concern with social status affected our attitudes toward the use of slang? If so, how? Do you see any

similarities between American attitudes toward slang and those toward the function of the dictionary?

4. Flexner contends that his dictionary is a "legitimate addition to standard dictionaries." What worthwhile functions do you think his dictionary may perform; that is, what kinds of things can we learn from slang about our language and how it changes?

5. To what extent has Flexner been influenced by the findings of the linguists? (See Marckwardt's essay on *Webster's Third.*)

6. Make a short list of the most outstanding characteristics of slang, and see if you can account for each of them. Discuss especially the extent to which images and metaphors are important and the reasons for their importance.

BERGEN EVANS

editor's choice—
you couldn't do woise

I am greatly honored at being asked to address so august and influential a body as the Managing Editors of The Associated Press and I would be embarrassed at the flippant aggressiveness of the title of my talk were it not that first, it was selected from among more dignified titles by one of your own officers, and second, the press itself exploits sensationalism and stirs up aggressiveness so consistently and recklessly that it can't complain if a little of it bounces back, but most of all because the absurdity of the title makes it plain, I hope, that I do not regard myself as a Delphic oracle or intend to do any thundering out of Zion.

I want to lay down a few postulates or axioms just to save time. First, speech is the most important thing life has produced. The brilliance of speech, the amazingness of it is something that those of us who use it don't bother to stop to think about. There are no organs of speech. Man invented speech. It is purely parasitic upon organs that have other physiologic functions. Second, speech is spoken. This is so basic, so fundamental to any discussion of speech that, although it seems almost idiotic to state it, it has to be stated over and over again. The ordinary person will talk more in one good, gabby, excited day when he has some real dirt to dish out and meets enough people to listen, or he is angry about something, than he will write in his entire lifetime. Now this doesn't apply to people who, like ourselves, make a living of writing, but we'll do pretty well.

Originally given at the 1963 annual convention of the Associated Press Managing Editors, the speech was printed in the *APME Redbook* and then in a pamphlet published by the G. & C. Merriam Company. The speech is reprinted here by permission of the author.

Man's speech is a living thing; hence, it is constantly changing. Speech is organic and hence, in relation to speech, the word *correct,* which one so often hears, and so often asks about, is utterly meaningless. If you found a mouse, and took it to a mousologist of some kind, and you said to him, "Is this a correct mouse?" he would think you were balmy or something. He would say, "It is a mouse of this species, it seems to be a mouse of this age, it's a mouse of this sex, it's a mouse of this weight, it seems to have had a hard winter." He could go on talking about it all day, but he can't tell you that it's a correct mouse or an incorrect mouse.

The third postulate is that grammar is simply a description of any language. This is not obvious immediately in your own language where status is so much involved and one's ego is at stake, but all you have to do is to translate it to another language to see this at once. Suppose you and I decide for some reason that we want to write an Eskimo grammar. All we can do is go where Eskimos are and write down what they say. If somebody is with us who takes correctness very seriously and he says to you, "Yeh, yeh, yeh, but is this correct Eskimo?" the answer is "I don't know." He says, "Well, look, this is the way they talk here in Baffin Bay but over in Greenland I heard different sounds." All you can say is, "This is Baffin Bay Eskimo—that's Greenland Eskimo," and in your grammar, if somebody is willing to finance a hundred-volume grammar on Eskimo, then you will make these distinctions.

The fourth postulate is that use and custom alone—and here I know many people disagree—determine what each generation and each locality finds acceptable. If in the South they say *clean* and in the North they say *clear*—you went *clean through town* and so on—you cannot say one is wrong and one is right. Forty million people have a right to speak their own language, whether it be southern French, Romanian, or anything else. And incidentally, everybody used to say *clean.* Many of the things that people find wrong are old forms. They never recognize the really new as wrong at all. They are so much a part of it that they don't really realize the language has been actually changed.

The last postulate I want to state is that there are many

forms of English. And no one of them can be unconditionally claimed to be good English to the total exclusion of the others. What passes for rules of grammar—this phrase we often hear—is usually simply half a dozen shibboleths that assert status. That is, they simply are part of the great game of oneupmanship. Somebody learns half a dozen forms—when he hears any deviation from them, he likes to pull rank and usually it terrifies people.

Now there is no way you can scare a man quicker than by using such horrendous words as *pluperfect, future indicative, clausitory subjunctive, nonrestrictive clause, mood, passibles,* and the like. The minute you hit a man with something like this, he crumbles. He heard stuff like this in high school and he wasn't listening, and in the innocence of his heart, he assumes that other people were listening. And it doesn't enter his mind that for the most part they were meaningless and the teacher herself hadn't the faintest idea what they meant, and that not listening to them was a highly salutary exercise.

The ordinary man is annoyed and he says, "Come on, you guys, cut it out." He has employed two colloqualisms, a verb in the imperative, the third person singular pronoun and he's made an idiomatic application of an adverb. Well, he'd be startled to be told all this, because all of these horrendous words merely describe what this man is doing.

Speech is incredibly subtle. You just don't know how clever you are to be able to speak. Speech is infinitely more subtle than writing. Writing is a poor, numb, stumbling, inadequate, approximate thing compared to speech, and always must be. The only one way you could hope to equate speech and writing would be if you could orchestrate it. So much of our meaning in speech is conveyed by emphasis, pause, rising or falling voice, and so on and so on. "He gave her *dog* biscuits." "He gave her dog *biscuits.*" I've exaggerated a bit there. In ordinary speech you wouldn't even make that sharp an emphasis to make two wholly different meanings. "The car stopped with a jerk at the wheel." The very slightest emphasis conveys totally different meaning.

This year I teach a course at Northwestern in Literature and in the course we read from the Bible and I had been lecturing about the Beatitudes. In reading an examination paper of an otherwise intelligent boy, I found a reference to the "B attitudes." Now this boy must have thought, "What are the A attitudes?" That is, he must have gone on, you know, on a totally different thing. The slighest shift of emphasis could reduce meaning to nonsense.

Now people get very excited about problems of grammar. They're not really problems of grammar at all; they are actually very excited about the challenging of their own status somewhere or they're determined to pull rank, and I just want to go into one or two of these statements with you.

Here is a nervous explosion from the *Christian Science Monitor* quite recently entitled "Cheap and Childish." It's objecting to the use of what they call incorrect English and attacking some wicked place called Madison Avenue. The *Monitor* is blowing up because the language is being corrupted. Says the *Monitor:* "To read or to listen, in advertisements in particular, one would get the impression that the American people is a race of semi-illiterates that neither speaks correct English nor is interested. . . . The ineffable monstrosity of Madison Avenue is the substitution of *like* for *as;* we are now told that a certain type of bread is baked just like Mother baked it." Then the editorial concludes by saying: "It is a fact, long noted by Europeans and a fact which has done nothing to increase their opinion of American cultural standards, that the United States is one of the few countries in the world in which public indignation is not stirred by offenses to the language. In most European countries quick and strong resentment is shown whenever the priceless heritage of the national speech is abused." You couldn't get more balderdash in fewer words.

Let me for a moment go into this business of *like* as a conjunction, since not only the *Monitor*, but many other papers, including the *New York Times*, made an issue of this. Most half-educated people, or three-quarters-educated, well, I'll be generous, $9/10$-educated people, will tell you with very great assurance, that *like* cannot be used as a conjunction when introducing a clause and they look you right in the eye when they say this. And most people, not being quite sure what a conjunction is, usually wilt at this point.

But let me show you how complex the problem really is by giving you four examples of the use of *like* as a conjunction in sentences each one of which has a status different from the other. "He takes to it like a duck to water." Here the clause verb *does* has been suppressed. Now sentences of this kind are not only acceptable but preferable. If anyone said, "He takes to it as a duck to water," you'd move your seat over a few inches away from him. This is a little lofty for my taste at least.

Now take what we are told is the most monstrous debauch of the English language ever known. "Winstons taste good like a cigarette should." Madison Avenue, that wicked place, couldn't believe its luck when they got so much mileage out of that. Here where the clause verb is actually expressed, *like* and *as* have long been competing forms.

When this advertisement was stirring up all this furor that it caused, my sister and I were completing our book on the American language and we amused ourselves by questioning and cross-questioning people who got excited about things like this. I met one of my colleagues one day who said, "By God, I'll never smoke another Winston." "Why?" "They're corrupting the language." Then I said to him, "What's wrong with it, what's wrong with 'Winstons taste good like a cigarette should'?" And the answer almost invariably was the same "What's wrong with it? My God, what's wrong with it?" "Yep, what's wrong with it?" "What do you mean, what's wrong with it?" "What's wrong with it?" Then they start to splutter. Finally they may be trapped into saying *like* should not be used as a conjunction. We found many people, when you press them, thought in some way something was wrong with *good*.

Now, what are the facts? *Like* is found in sentences of this kind as far back as 1579. For 300 years some people have used *like* and some have used *as* and steadily and consistently, and within this century in a very rapidly ascending curve, *like* has dominated. About the middle of the 19th century, not until then, somebody decided that the use of *as* in these constructions marked you as a very superior person. This person and his or her followers, whom I call the *ases,* have been very militant on this point, and they have done you in any time they could.

However, for the moment, *like* is certainly in the ascendency. The use of *as* in constructions like "He takes to it as a duck to water" puts you in the minority. You may say you are the correct minority, but if you are enough of a minority, you cannot go on even claiming to be correct. I would say at the moment that the *ases* have lost the battle and that the *likeables* have won.

Now take another use of *like* as a conjunction. "Life is hard for a girl like I." This is from Anita Loos' *Gentlemen Prefer Blondes.* The use of the nominative *I,* implying the suppressed *am* makes this *like* a conjunction. Had it been *me,* it would have been a preposition. Now this sentence differs from "He takes to it like a duck to water" only in the fact that *like* is here followed by a pronoun instead of a noun. Yet nonetheless this construction is substandard. That is, the use of this construction would mark you as an uneducated person. You could not hold a job requiring a normal education if you used this construction. Why? Because usage says accept one, not the other.

Then take a fourth. "You act like you are a combination of Socrates and Napoleon." Is this right or wrong? You try it on people and they are puzzled. They don't know—they are uneasy. What it is, actually, is a regional matter. You will hear this in the South. This is acceptable in the South—it is not acceptable in the North and East.

All I meant with these *likes* is to demonstrate that the use of *like* as a conjunction is a very involved matter. If you just arbitrarily say you can't use it as a conjunction, you're not representing the English language as it is spoken and has been spoken for centuries. You cannot say, "Well, everybody was wrong for 400 years and I'm right." Well, you can say it, but you don't earn vast respect by saying that.

When I did, with Mr. John Mason Brown, a TV show called *The Last Word,* which ran on the Columbia network for three years, by giving away a Britannica among other bait, we got an enormous amount of mail—we got 2,000 letters a day. We got over a million and a half letters, and I read well over 50,000 to 60,000 letters myself.

One of the things that emerged was how passionately the North disapproves of the South's speech, and how supremely indifferent to the North the South is. I don't believe we got a single letter from the South saying "Why do these ignorant damnyankees talk this way?" I think the feeling is they are scum anyway and what does it matter—why do you expect people like that to talk English? But the North is very much on the defensive. We got more angry letters because people said "It's real hot today" instead of saying *very*. *Real* simply means "very." *Very* simply means "real." "Thou art the very God," the Bible says. Yet nonetheless, people assumed in the North the one thing was absolutely criminal and you better call out the militia again.

Now people who talk about rules of grammar, unless they are grammarians, are talking for the most part pretentious nonsense. You cannot understand the rules of English. English is so enormous a language. So amazingly complex. You can't understand it by rules. Fortunately, you have to understand it before you can even go to the kindergarten. You couldn't be admitted to kindergarten if you were not already fairly conversant with the English language; and the great place for learning English in the school system is the schoolyard. This teaches you a great deal more than you get in school. One sneer in the schoolyard will do more to correct the deviation from the norm of that group than any amount of parental thundering.

My children both said *tooken,* and I never correct anybody's speech unless he pays me, and they didn't pay, and we let them go, and they don't say *tooken* now. They are grown up; they are both in college. Somewhere along the line somebody snickered, or some one of their contemporaries in the schoolyard said "yea, yea, yea, tooken, tooken, tooken." That'll do it—that'll do it far better than talking about regular past forms, the present, or gerundive, believe me.

When we were on the air in *The Last Word,* a schoolteacher wrote from Atlanta. She was obviously on the verge of a complete nervous breakdown and needed a sedative very badly. She wrote: "Can you give me some simple rules for teaching my students to use the word *the* properly?" Well, obviously, she had reached the point that all teachers and parents reach, the feeling of getting nowhere. You pick out some trifle like, "You will pick up your clothes tonight," or "You will close the garage door." Concentrate on this one or you are always licked—you never get anywhere. She decided apparently she couldn't teach them anything, but she could pick one simple word and some way they would learn to use that.

Well, I wrote her a letter—I felt rather sorry for her—and pointed out that in Jespersen's *Modern English Grammar,* which is a great English grammar, seven thick volumes in small print and double columns, 75 closely printed, double column pages are devoted to the word *the,* and at the end of this, Jespersen throws in the towel. He says that he knows this treatment is superficial and inadequate, but he has to move on. Three score and ten years is all a man has.

The idiomatic uses of T-H-E—we pronounce it three different ways, depending whether or not it is followed by a stressed vowel or whether it is followed by a comma—the idiomatic uses of T-H-E are beyond bewildering. We go *to college, to the university;* we go *to church,* but *the hospital.* The British don't. They go *to hospital.* We go *to town,* but *to the city.* Americans look *out of the window;* British look *out of window.* We may be found *at home, at the house;* we catch *typhoid,* but *the smallpox;* we catch *a cold,* but *the flu;* we have *diphtheria,* but *the measles.* And this goes on and on and on.

Now, suppose this woman decided, nonetheless, she was going to carry on. Let's assume she becomes deeply paranoid and is determined to teach *the*. Let's suppose she gets a year off with pay in order to understand Jespersen, to codify, to make up rules, and subdivisions, and exceptions, and all the other stuff. With fire in her eye and with Jespersen in her hand, she meets the class the next year and she means this. This is the first grade. She puts the rules down and by God, they shall memorize them. What would she do? She would utterly frustrate the education of those children. Boys would stutter and stammer all the rest of their lives, all of them would be ill at the sight of a book, none of them would ever learn to read. I'm serious about this. She would produce a class of complete and absolute illiterates, with nervous breakdowns.

What's the alternative? The alternative is very simple. Never in my life have I heard a native-born speaker misuse the word *the*. Leave them alone, since they learn it anyway, enormously complicated as it is. No American says "I am going to hospital." And no Englishman says "I'm going to the hospital." And no American says, "I caught the cold." He says *a cold*, if he is a native-born speaker. Since he does all this, amazing as it is, since his ear taught him all this and he will do it anyway and I've never known anyone who didn't, just let him alone. Don't try to teach the use of *the* by rules.

Now writing cannot equal speech. It cannot be the exact reproduction of speech. The language is changing so rapidly. We pick up so many new words. You know the much attacked *Webster's Third New International* had to add 100,000 words to the list they had in 1934. It seems incredible to think that in 1934 people simply didn't have, therefore had no words for, the atom bomb, baby-sitters, coffee breaks, electronic computers, astronauts, nylons, parking meters, antibiotics, and so on and so on. New experiences are bringing floods of new words. And what's more, they are changing old words.

Many of the letters that we got on the show asked us, "Can this word mean that?" Almost anytime anyone asks you that question, the answer is yes. Otherwise, he wouldn't have asked you the question. Nobody asks, "Can *hippopotamus* mean 'pumpkin pie'?" Nobody's ever heard it used that way. You don't ask this question until you have heard the word used and by the time you have heard the word used, and your ear notices it enough so that you don't think it is an idiotic aberration of some kind, then that probably means that, incredible as it may seem, that has become the meaning of that word.

The most common meaning, for instance, of *silo*, that one reads in the papers now is the concrete pit in the ground from which a missile is being launched. The other word, my idea of silo, a thing sticking out of the ground in which you put food for cattle, is still known, is still used, but the word is completely changed. And this is the meaning, which by the way, I see all of the time in the *New York Times.*

The *New York Times* wrote a very silly editorial on the appearance of the Third Webster, in which they stated that they were not going to use it—they were going to stick to the good old Second Webster. If they were, they would be out of business right now. You can't publish a newspaper in '63 or '61 with the language of 1934. Poor Webster, they had very poor public relations, but in their bleating, Webster pointed out that the largest single source they had drawn from was the *New York Times.* Obviously, the editors don't read their own paper.

Incidentally, I happened to be in the hospital at the time this came out, just convalescing. I had a little time on my hands, and I took that issue, the issue of the *Times* in which they made this bold and lunatic announcement, and there were over 170 usages in that issue which were countenanced by the Third Webster which they said they wouldn't use, and were not countenanced by the Second, which they said they would use, and in the very editorial there were two of them.

People often hurl at me the word *permissive.* They say, "You are permissive." What do you mean "permissive"? There are 300 million who speak this language. What am I to do? Club them all on the head? What have I got to do with it? I permit Niagara Falls to go over, too. I don't know what to do about it. I permit the Grand Canyon to remain just where it is. To talk about people being permissive of what 300 million people do every day—back of this is an incredibly arrogant assumption that we who have to do with observing and using speech in some way control it. We don't. The masses control speech. And all we do, ultimately, is follow on.

Now some people believe that words have only one meaning. Of course words have, as we all know, many meanings. And only the context will show you, but the context will show you very clearly. The verb *run* is listed in the *Oxford English Dictionary,* which is now 100 years out of date, as having 265 clearly distinguishable verbal meanings. Now we don't have all those meanings in our vocabulary, but I expect any educated person has maybe 30 meanings of the word *run* in his vocabulary. Well, how do you know which one you mean? You never falter. It's like using *the*. You know. The context almost always tells you.

For instance, what does the word *locks* mean? Well, it means one thing to a locksmith, it means another thing to a delicatessen, it means another thing in a missile base. Anybody who says in a missile base "put some lox in the missile" and finds he's stuffing salmon into it—this isn't likely to happen. Nor is a locksmith likely to shove liquid oxygen through the keyhole.

The words in context almost always define their own meaning. People get unnecessarily agitated about these things. They also get agitated about the use of words. People who believe that words have only one meaning also seem to think they have only one function and they will get very angry and they will say, "You can't use that as a verb, it's a noun." Verbs and nouns are just words which describe what the word is doing at the time you are using it. They don't come first, that is, a verb doesn't mark a species like a dinosaur as against a rabbit.

. . .

Now a more serious charge against the *Post*. I am in a way sorry to single out any paper, because a great many did this, but one has to deal with specific instances. The *Post*, having got its blood pressure up on the matter of usage, ran another editorial. It got very agitated, because it had come across the word *trimester*. Some college was going to go on a trimester system and the editor, huffing and puffing about this, said: "Beginning next fall, state universities will operate on three equal terms each year instead of the present semester system. Incidentally, they are calling the plan a 'trimester system' which implies a miraculous improvement indeed, for *semester* derives from the Latin word *semestris* meaning 'half-yearly'. And trimester, by analogy, must mean 'three halves'. That will be crowding it, even for Florida."

Unfortunately, that isn't what *semester* means at all. Now there is no reason to expect the editor to know Latin, but before he states what Latin means, he ought to look it up. *Semester* is based on *sex mensis,* "six months, a six months period." *Semester* has been in the language very long. *Trimester* has been in the language over a hundred years. All *trimester* means is a "three month period." This is no great crime, except that the indignation is simply unjustified and it is uninformed. And if a man is going to write editorials, scorning the dictionary, and invents facts to his fancy, then he shouldn't get too excited about the incorrect use of words.

Now many words pass in the language simply as errors. We have many established errors. Once an error is fixed by usage, it will stay and you have to use it. For instance, if a child said *gooder, knowed, me am* or *girlses,* he would agitate his parents deeply. Most children do something like this and most parents are agitated. Nonetheless, we all use words like that every day because we don't know that they are corruptions. *Lesser* and *nearer* and even the word *more* are historically exactly the same as *gooder.*

The historical word, which didn't change until Shakespeare's time, is *moe.* When Macbeth says "Send out moe horses, skirr the country round," he is not talking Dixie talk—this is the old English word. The *r* was then added by somebody who didn't perceive that *moe* was an irregular comparative. *Me am* would seem unthinkable to anybody, yet we all say *you are,* which is exactly the same, exactly the use of the accusative for the nominative and fairly recent. *Girlses* sounds awful, but we all say *children,* which is even more awful: *children* is a triplication of a plural.

Let me call your attention to some real changes that are taking place in the language that don't bother these people at all because they simply go on using them. There has been a great increase in empty verbs, that is, where people used to say "Let's drink, Let's swim," they are now inclined to say "Let's have a drink, Let's take a drink, Let's have a swim, Let's take a swim." Where our fathers said "It snowed heavily," we're likely to say "There was a heavy snow." Our fathers "decided," we "reach a decision." Why we put these extra verbs in, I don't know. I have only some theories and won't bother you with them, but this again is a marked change in the language.

There is a great increase in the use of the passive, which probably reflects a civilized or degenerate—the two things are often the same—awareness of the fact that we are being acted on. The barbarian is never aware of this; he is acted on, but he is too aggressive to know it. The barbarian lives in the active present indicative. "I eat," "I steal," "I rob," "I rape," and eventually he drops dead. But the civilized man knows that the forces are working on him. The Greeks had a very elaborate passive, Romans didn't have much of a passive, our language has very little passive.

There is an increased use of the subjunctive in modern American English for some reason. The true subjunctive has now retreated almost entirely. Among illiterate Negroes you will hear the proper use of the subjunctive. "Be he there, see him I will." This would sound very strange, but I heard our laundress the other day, who comes right out of the Delta, say she was going back to see her grandpappy, "Be he still living." This is good, good, fine old historical English.

The new subjunctive you hear in such phrases as "I wouldn't know." In the quiz shows, if someone says "Who was George Washington?" instead of saying "The first president," you'll say "That would be the first president." There seems to be a feeling here that the subjunctive gives a touch of gentility in some way or protects you in some way. I don't know exactly why it's used.

Well now, most people don't know anything about grammar and there's no earthly reason why they should. You don't have to know any more about grammar to speak effectively than you have to know about physics to drive a car. The one is the theory of the other, but you don't have to know the theory. The people who get agitated usually fall back on logic, and there they are on completely false grounds because language isn't logical.

Language knows no logic except itself. You cannot apply mathematics to language. Classical Latin is logical, but classical Latin is a mandarin language; nobody ever spoke it. Spoken Latin was quite different from what Cicero and Virgil wrote. If language were logical, for instance, *unloose* ought to mean "tie up," but it doesn't. If language were logical, an outlaw ought to be the opposite of an inlaw. But it isn't.

One of the commonest charges people make who get logical about languages, for instance, is that you cannot use the plural with *none*. You say, "Well, none of them are coming" and they seem to think you should say "None of them is coming." They base this on the triumphant grounds that none doesn't include one. Well, if it doesn't include one, then you can't use the singular either if you want to be logical. I don't know what to do at that point.

Nonetheless, the simple fact is that people use the plural increasingly. Most people would say "None of them are coming," rather than say "None of them is." When our *Dictionary of Contemporary American Usage* was published, the *Chicago Tribune* did us the honor of ten separate attacks. The thing seemed to agitate them very deeply, and they picked on this. We had said that contemporary usage countenances plural with *none* more often than the singular. This doesn't mean that either one is wrong. They said absolutely no, and I wrote them a letter, pointing out Shakespeare used *none* with the plural, though I didn't expect that to bother them much, but I thought I had a real topper—I pointed out that God uses *none* with the plural in the very first commandment as in Deuteronomy 5:7—but I guess my authority was regarded at the *Tribune* as secondary and they weren't impressed.

We've all heard the business of double negatives—we're all taught in school that you mustn't use two negatives. That's all right if you want to say to a class, "If you use two negatives in a certain way, you will mark yourself as a part of a certain level of education and particularness." "But I was told two negatives make a positive." A more absurd statement in relation to language was never made. Two negatives may make a positive in algebra, but they don't in any Teutonic language. In every Teutonic language, the duplication of the negative simply heightens the negation. When Chaucer says of his Knight that he "hadn't never yet said nothing nasty to no man in all his life," you would be feebleminded to say "well, did he or didn't he?" Chaucer has knocked himself and the language out trying to tell you this man never said anything nasty to people. You ought to know that by that time.

Furthermore, if you want to be logical, if you want to say logic does not countenance a double negative and you say two negatives make a positive, then three negatives make a negative again. So that if it is wrong to say "It doesn't make no difference," then it must be all right to say "It don't never make no difference." This is not true.

No, it isn't all right to say either of these simply because neither is accepted by educated people in either America or England today, though they were in the past. Not because of logic, but simply because custom doesn't countenance them, either one.

Usage is capricious and illogical, but it is tyrannical. Many times the charge has been brought: "Well, then you are saying anything goes." Oh, no, anything does not go at all. There is no activity of human life in which less goes. In speech you are not permitted to deviate one iota from the customs of your group without being severely punished. Consider what was made of Al Smith's pronunciation of what other people call *radio* and he called *raddio*. Maybe his constituents called it *raddio*. I don't know. Actually, *radio* is an artificial word made up of Latin. *Raddio* is nearer what we know of Latin than *radio*. Nonetheless, when I was a boy and the campaign was going on, I heard nothing about his career as governor of New York—all I heard was *raddio*. This man said *raddio*, just as today you hear another man say *Cuber* over and over. If you have any doubt that society will punish you for a deviation, go into a cheap restaurant in Chicago and ask for *tomahto* soup. You will feel public disapproval very quickly. If you can afford the Pump Room, they will furnish you with *tomahto* soup; don't try it in Joe's Beanery. It won't go.

All *idiom* means is something we do in this language which doesn't make any sense, but we do it all the same. And the very people who get so upset about English idioms, because they don't conform to some preconceived theory, are proud of their use of idoms in another language. We say *a couple of dollars,* but we say *a dozen eggs.* Our great grandfathers said *a dozen of eggs* and I suspect in backward rural parts today you would hear *a dozen of eggs.* We say that we *adore* God, but we would be shocked if someone would say that he is *adorable.* But centuries ago, this was said quite seriously in very solemn words. We say *later on.* This sounds all right to us. The English say *early on* and *earlier on* and this baffles us.

Suppose, for instance, you want to be an innovator in language and you just decided that you would say *squoze.* Why *squeezed? Squoze* sounds better. We say *freeze, froze,* and so on—why not say *squoze?* What would happen if you decided on just that one little thing? You are going to change the language. You come down to the office and say "Well, I squoze some oranges for breakfast this morning." The general look would be, "Very funny very early in the morning," and nobody would be vastly amused and they would say, "'He thinks he's a card.'" But suppose you keep up. Day after day you're going to be a "squoze" man. You keep at it. People would begin to say, "Look, this guy has a screw loose. He says *squoze.* What's the matter with him?" And they would be right. That would cost you advancement. I'd be willing to swear that in any organization if you stuck to *squoze,* they wouldn't promote you, and they'd be right. "This guy, there is something wrong with this guy" and there is something wrong with everyone who would deliberately deviate that way.

We have deviations, but usually they are not deliberate. Men have been driven out of public life for deviating one syllable. In our speech, for instance, one of the signs of what we regard as supreme illiteracy is making stops of certain *th* sounds. That is, instead of saying *th-,* saying *dese, dem, dose.* This is supposed to mark you as a person absolutely outside the pale. Yet these sounds don't bother us if we all agree. They don't bother us in the least if we all say *bedlam* instead of *Bethlehem,* which is the proper word. We all say *murder* instead of *murther,* as it used to be. We say *burden* instead of *burthen,* as it used to be, and so on.

Certainly Mr. Kennedy, who is a highly educated man and speaks very effectively, has come in for plenty of criticism for that Boston pronunciation of the last vowel of *Cuba*. I don't know whether he does it deliberately or whether it was necessary in the early parts of his career that he might identify himself with East Boston. I don't know. It comes natural to him. Why shouldn't he speak his own language?

I speak Ohio east overlaid with English where I got my early and later education plus considerable personal idiosyncrasy as a result of adenoids, I guess. At any rate, that's the way you speak. No man ought—I would mistrust a man who changed his speech much more than I would mistrust one who went right ahead.

Truman is a wonderful speaker. Truman's voice is purely American, purely—it's western Missouri.

Well, in conclusion, what are we supposed to do about all this? Are you just to drift? Are you to permit anybody to write the way he wants to? Well, you can't do much about it. You are not going to hire illiterates. You are not likely to hire them as teachers or editorial writers or reporters, though they might make very good ones. That is, there might be a freshness in their speech.

What you have to do is admit that there is a very wide range in this great language we speak. There are many local ways of speaking. There are different ways of speaking at different levels. Everybody has several languages. You couldn't possibly speak at home as you would speak in public. We have highly formal ways of speaking on highly formal occasions, and then we have relaxed ways of speaking with our friends and then you have ways of usually grunting within the family. This conveys your feeling and you shift without any trouble from one level to another.

When you're dealing with the public as with a class or as in a newspaper or an editorial, naturally you conform to whatever the usage of that group is and I mean naturally. And I don't mean naturally in the sense that you make an effort to do it. It doesn't occur to you to do anything else.

Rules, good rules, are those which state as best they can what cultivated, sensitive people who want passionately to express their meaning now say. Bad rules are those which state what such people used to do. Very bad rules are those which state what somebody thinks they ought to do, but don't. And anyway, all rules are simply a means to an end and the end is being understood, expressing ourselves exactly and completely and expressing our emotions as well as our thoughts.

I read, as you probably do also, "Winners and Sinners," put out by Mr. Bernstein of the *New York Times*. I find it very fascinating, and it is high on my list of preferred reading. I often disagree with Mr. Bernstein on questions of grammar, but I don't disagree with him for one moment—indeed I am usually wracked with admiration for the subtlety of his perceptions— that this word in this context is loaded, that you colored this statement by putting this word in there. That is very fine editing indeed. That helps make the *Times* the very great paper it is. What you want to do is express the exact meaning. If you want to color it, fine, but you've got to know that you are coloring. The only sin is not to know this is a loaded word, not to know this word conveys something else to the average reader because you have to know what the average reader means by these words.

All writing is a form of communication and all communication is a form of translation from one man's observation and experience into another's and when you are translating, the important one is the language into which you are translating. You have to know it, of course—reporters do. The advantage of newspaper writing, the reason it is often fascinating reading, is that it has to be written with great haste. You have to meet a deadline. The thing happens, you want to beat another man with the account of it. This compels you to write in contemporary—as close to contemporary as you can, because you haven't time to think of how Shakespeare would have done it, very fortunately. Shakespeare never took time off to think how anyone else would have done it, he just did it his way.

The difficulty seems to be, the reason you get these editorials of the kind I quoted, is that only superannuated reporters become editors. You are far advanced, apparently, into the veil of arteriosclerosis by the time you become an editor. And as you are aware of the change in the language, all you see in it is corruption whereas it isn't corrupt at all, it's very live.

Language isn't made in classrooms, language isn't made in dictionaries, language isn't made in grammar books, language isn't made in editorials. Language is made by the three hundred million people of the English language who are living, who are angry, who are excited, who are greedy, who are passionate about something, and out of this enormous vocabulary that time and fate has given us, put these wonderful words together. I don't believe I've ever heard a remark in a faculty meeting that has suddenly excited me with glory and wonder, at the brilliance, the humor, the aptness of it. You don't hear that sort of thing in faculty meetings, but you do hear it on the street. Suddenly you hear a phrase, you hear something in a bus or somewhere and your heart will leap up and dance with the daffodils.

I remember at a football game once a referee who was introduced as the head of the YMCA league or something. He made a number of decisions which angered one side very much, and when he finally blew the whistle and the whole thing was over, I remember a guy behind me just yelling at the top of his voice:

"Goodbye for good, you Sunday School son of a bitch."

That was good language for that man's purposes at that moment, I thought.

Review Questions

1. Why does Evans claim that in relation to speech, the word "correct" is meaningless? Why does he use the example of the mousologist?
2. Does Evans claim that grammar is descriptive or prescriptive? How does his discussion of the Eskimo grammar support his thesis?
3. What determines what each generation and each locality finds acceptable?
4. How are the "rules of grammar" related to the "great game of oneupmanship"?
5. Why is speech more subtle than writing at conveying meaning?

6. Give two reasons why Evans devotes several paragraphs to a discussion of "like" and "as."
7. Explain Evans' comment, "The great place for learning English in the school system is the schoolyard." What is his attitude toward the memorization of rules?
8. Why does our language constantly change? What indications are there of our being unconscious of these changes?
9. Why does Evans quote from Chaucer and Shakespeare?
10. What are some of the real changes that are taking place in the language? Why are they taking place?
11. Explain why language is illogical but tyrannical.
12. What is the purpose of rules? How does Evans distinguish "good" rules from "bad" ones?
13. Where is language made?

Discussion Questions

1. Evans states, "I want to lay down a few postulates or axioms just to save time." List his postulates and then explain how they are related to the remainder to his speech.
2. Compare the ideas expressed by Evans and those expressed by Lloyd. Consider particularly the ideas about correctness, about the relation between written and spoken English, and about a "scientific" approach to language.
3. Discuss the relation between correctness and social status. Why do people feel it necessary to defend the "purity" of the language? How does "society" dictate the way we speak and write?
4. Evans states, "One sneer in the schoolyard will do more to correct the deviation from the norm of that group than any amount of parental thundering." But suppose there *is* no sneer from the schoolyard. What if the students *all* speak a social dialect that differs markedly from that of a more prestigious social dialect in the larger metropolitan area? If neither parents nor peer group can expose the children to a prestigious dialect, do you think it advisable to teach the students the prestigious dialect? Why? Are the reasons primarily linguistic, or social and economic?
5. Do you think any problems in learning might occur if students begin school not speaking or understanding very well the dialect their teachers use? In such cases, do you think it might be profitable for the teachers to use the predominant dialect of the group for a couple of years (as they do in Switzerland) while the students are concurrently being taught the standard dialect of the area?